To Qer.

CONF

GREAT

~I

Every thing.

CHINN

THE EARLY METHODIST PEOPLE

The Fernley-Hartley Lecture, 1948

By LESLIE F. CHURCH

Dr. Church's work has involved an enormous amount of research amongst the diaries, intimate journals and memoirs of the first two generations of Methodist people. It does not deal with the Wesleys and their preachers so much as with the ordinary men and women who were members of the Methodist Societies. The survey includes their spiritual experiences, personal conduct, family-life and modes of worship. It aims at showing the emergence in the rank and file of a social conscience, and at relating them to Christian and democratic ideals.

The intimate studies of people, rich and poor, educated and uneducated, reveal that they were men and women who, whilst contributing much to the life of the day, yet had their treasure in heaven.

THE EARLY METHODIST PEOPLE

Oglethorpe: A Study of Philanthropy in England and Georgia
If They Had Known: Studies of Everyman at the Cross
Knight of the Burning Heart: A Life of John Wesley
In the Quietness: a Book of Broadcasts
In the Storm: Devotional Essays
And Here a Rainbow: Devotional Essays
Everywhere a Bethlehem: Children of the Middle East
More About the Early Methodist People
etc. etc.

THE EARLY METHODIST PEOPLE

By

LESLIE F. CHURCH
B.A., Ph.D.

1949
PHILOSOPHICAL LIBRARY
NEW YORK

*Published in the United States
by the Philosophical Library
15 East 40 Street, New York, N.Y.*

*Published in Great Britain by
The Epworth Press, London, England*

Made and printed in Great Britain

*To
the Staff of the
Methodist Publishing House
my friends and fellow-workers*

PREFACE

THE work of the Wesleys and the first generation of Methodist preachers has been thoroughly surveyed and assessed by competent writers. Biographies, critical and romantic, have given us full-length portraits of the two brothers and the group of remarkable men who were their 'assistants'. The Journals of John and Charles Wesley and the invaluable diaries of the first travelling preachers provide material which has been so well used that we may see, in close detail, the men who wrote them, and the way they lived. It is natural that such commanding figures should tend to obscure the ordinary people who were the rank and file of early Methodism.

In ecclesiastical, as in secular history, the men in the pew and the men in the street are often forgotten or remembered only in groups, though they each play a part in shaping their world and deciding its tremendous issues. The work of Oliver Cromwell would have been impossible without 'the village Hampdens', and John Wesley and his preachers would have been strangely ineffective without their congregations and especially without the individuals who established the Societies in cottage-rooms and made their separate contributions to the creation of a Church.

This book is part of an attempt to rediscover the first Methodist *people*, and to see them, not only in groups or as followers of John Wesley, but as individuals with definite personalities and lives of their own. The present survey does not cover the whole ground. It looks at these ordinary men and women who, in the first flush of a new experience, were compelled to worship in farm-kitchens and tumble-down sheds. It watches them as they begin to transform the barns and the cottages into temples, and presently, to build their first chapels. It tries to understand the reason for their spiritual agonies and to discover the secret of their triumphs. The spiritual experience, so faithfully recorded in their diaries, reveals the anguish of long struggles and the joy of a real deliverance. They grew in grace *together* and became, in fellowship, part of the family of God. They were not withdrawn from the world, but, being very much part of it, were bound to face problems of personal conduct. How should they use their time and, particularly, their leisure? How far should they conform to the customs and conventions of the communities in which they lived? Most important of all—how did their new experience affect their personal relationships, their family life and their children?

Within these limits very definite personalities begin to emerge, but the picture is not complete.

In a further volume[1] these same people are seen making their first ventures in social service—ventures which laid the foundations of the reform movements in the nineteenth century. A critical examination of the persecution they faced reveals the courage and steadfastness which silenced the mobs and ended the opposition. The 'travelling' preachers were few in number, and a new race of 'local' preachers, men and women, sprang up to meet the emergency. In this second survey, it becomes clear that the first Methodists were not, as has so often been assumed, drawn from one social group. Amongst them were doctors and blacksmiths, philosophers and farm-labourers, soldiers and squires, the cultured and the illiterate. They learned how to live together, and to serve their fellows as they learned to worship God. The second volume ends with an account of their public and private worship, and of the part they played in developing the incarnational and institutional functions of the Society they had helped to found.

To attempt to rediscover one's forefathers and to assess their lives has seemed to the writer an impertinence, yet it has been a labour of love. If, in spite of its many imperfections, this study helps to renew that first Methodist witness he will be thankful.

In acknowledging the kindly interest of many people in the writing of this book, the author would like to express his special gratitude to the Rev. Edgar C. Barton and the Rev. Frank Cumbers, B.A., B.D., for their generous criticism and constant encouragement. He owes much to the patience and loyalty of Mr. R. W. Young, Miss F. Knell, and indeed to the whole staff of The Epworth Press with whom he has worked for so many years with great happiness. The long and painstaking service of the Rev. F. F. Bretherton, B.A., the Rev. Frank Baker, B.A., B.D., and the members of the Wesley Historical Society places every research worker in early Methodist history under a constant debt. To Mr. Cecil Pawson, M.B.E., M.Sc., he is grateful for a memorable journey in the Dales in search of early Methodism. Not least, as always, he is thankful to God for a wife who understands and shares his work, even when it involves correcting proofs or reading almost illegible manuscripts!

May, 1948.

[1] *More About the Early Methodist People*, L. F. Church (Epworth Press: in course of publication, 1948).

CONTENTS

INTRODUCTORY

IN his book, *Adventures of Ideas*,[1] Professor Whitehead says: 'The Methodist preachers aimed at saving men's souls in the next world, but incidentally they gave a new direction to emotions energizing in this world.' The present study is an attempt to gather evidence from which we may measure their success or discover their failure. The lives of the people to whom the preachers went are to be our witnesses. Not only in their expression of new emotions and their acceptance of new values, but also in their thinking, revealed in surprisingly intimate diaries, lie proofs of a transformation which is real and profound. Their subconscious fears were made apparent to them, and in the process hope was born. Deep-rooted despair became triumphant assurance, based on a new conception of spiritual values. They faced life—and death—with confidence. They were no longer afraid of outward circumstance; the only fear that remained was lest by their own lack of faith they might forfeit the salvation which they now knew was offered to them through the love of Christ.

One of the most important features of their experience was that this free grace was universal. God was no respecter of persons, and, believing this, they approached every human problem with the knowledge that each individual was precious to the heavenly Father. No man was hopelessly damned, and they went out, passionate heralds of Good News to all the world. Whether they found their sphere in a little village, in the new-born industrial areas of the north, or west, or far across the sea mattered little. Wherever their lot was cast, they were concerned with the temporal and spiritual well-being of their neighbours. This is abundantly clear, from a wealth of journals and diaries, as well as from the usual first sources of local and more general history.

That they made mistakes, were at times narrow in their application of their faith to conduct, and that they were limited by their lack of educational opportunity no one would deny. Nor was the suddenness of the emotional release without its unfortunate consequences, but in spite of these handicaps the early Methodists became a real force making for righteousness in a disorderly and unhappy world. They were largely responsible for the development of a social conscience, and the revitalizing of personal religion, in an age of *laissez-faire*. The results on the social, political, and economic life of the nineteenth century are only now being appreciated, but their influence in raising the moral level of English life is unquestioned.

Though the impact of this new and vital expression of Christianity was immediately felt by working men and women and small tradesmen, it was not, even in its earliest stages, confined within any narrow class limitations. The yeoman farmer, on the one hand, and a small proportion of the more educated and happier circumstanced population were also directly affected. An appeal was made to the personal experience of each individual, and the response was as remarkable in the case of Lady Maxwell or Samuel Drew, the metaphysician, as it was in the case of 'Foolish Dick', the pilgrim preacher of Illogan. A survey of the early Methodist people shows that they were not contained within boundaries marked out by any mere social or occupational distinctions. 'The world was *their* parish', and this was much more than a geographical term.

To use the language of Mr. W. J. Brown,[2] the first people called Methodists proclaimed a freedom of the spirit as opposed to the bondage of an organization, and they made their appeal convincing because of the reality of their personal emancipation. As the years passed, they preserved their new-found freedom, because they lived near to its divine Source.

Religion became not only a comfort and inspiration, but by creating a new standard of moral values gave to the humblest and most degraded a new confidence in their personal capacity to arrive at right conclusions and, being born again, to experience in themselves the work of divine grace. In the midst of their troubled and hopeless lives they found a new purpose and undreamed-of peace. Convinced that they might expect constant renewal from their resources in Christ Jesus, they set out to battle against the sin and misery and vice which was so manifest in the world in which they lived.

The most profligate of the people were reclaimed from turbulence and crime at a critical time. Their reclamation was sometimes sensational and crude in its processes. 'At Heptonstol (*sic!*) I gave several exhortations,' writes Thomas Mitchell, travelling preacher, in 1746. 'A very tall man who was a butcher, was cut to the heart. But it had a very bad effect upon him for the present. For he went home and beat his wife in a most terrible manner, because he thought she had told me of all his sinful ways. But afterwards he was convinced and converted.'[3] The consequence of such reformations, resulting in the attendance at little gatherings of devout people in primitive 'societies', attracted immediate criticism, which could be, and often was, answered. The answers themselves were a vindication of the whole event. Crudity was forgotten in the victories of the Cross.

'But then you say they neglect their business', wrote Thomas Butts on such an occasion in 1743. 'This charge seems to proceed merely from surmise, on account of their going to hear so often: Whereas, it is evidently known, many Families that used to be sotting and quarrelling at Alehouses in the evenings, so as often to make themselves unfit for work in the mornings, whereby they lived miserable: Now after work, instead of spending part of their day's earnings at the Ale-house, do hear the preaching, and hereby their Hearts are made so glad that they can rise at five to hear the Word, and go cheerfully to work at six, and are better husbands on all accounts. . . . And then they have all Joy and Heaven in their hearts.'[4] There is an air of simple sincerity in this contemporary defence which commends it, and since it was written at once, for distribution locally, guarantees its authenticity. Transformed lives are a complete answer to academic charges, more especially when the living evidence is there for every man to see.

Even where the coming of the Methodists met with only partial success, it was admitted that a change for the better was effected. 'Rudeness and vulgarity are frequently removed; from the principles inculcated, and the doctrines taught, a general respect of man to his fellow is engendered, and thus a platform is raised; the building may follow, but at all events, there is a reformation effected which . . . could have arisen from no other source.'[5]

Here, then, is an indication of the way in which Methodism, in its intense and simple sincerity, attacked the uncompromising individualism which was 'the ulcer of the age'. The new respect of man for his fellow came from his vital personal experience of God's love. 'A governing class, intent only on pleasure or

politics, a Church occupied chiefly with patronage and controversy, were now to feel the force of a great religious wave which
was to bear on every wall of privilege.'[6] The way in which this
affected the ordinary people is our present concern.

It found expression in many types of social service. In his
Journal, John Wesley says, almost casually: 'On July 7th, 1757,
I rode through one of the pleasantest parts of England to Hawnby.
Here the zealous landlord turned all the Methodists out of their
houses. This proved a singular kindness, for they built some
little houses at the end of the town, in which forty or fifty of
them live together.'[7]

Coming to Nottingham in later years, he described the Society
as 'a serious and loving congregation. There is something in the
people of this town which I cannot but much approve of; although
most of our society are of the lower class, chiefly employed in the
stocking manufacture, yet there is generally an uncommon gentleness and sweetness in their temper, and something of elegance in
their behaviour, which, when added to solid, vital religion, make
them an ornament to their profession.'[8]

It was natural enough that the ordinary people should be the
first to respond. Indeed, it would be true to say that most chapters
in the history of Christianity have begun as Christianity itself
began—amongst the nameless folk in the crowd or even the
gutter. In the case of Methodism it was inevitable. Writing of
men whom he himself had heard, Mr. Stephen Tuck, in a small
volume of which only 150 copies were printed, said: 'Like their
great Lord and Master and His disciples, they preached in the
market-places, in lanes, highways, and streets, on a stone, a table,
a chair, or a horse-block; with these for their "pulpit, and the
heavens for their sounding-board", they proclaimed the great
and acceptable day of the Lord.'[9]

In later days the fame of John Wesley and the orderly behaviour
of the first Methodists, who remained within the Church of
England, attracted the notice of the less accessible section of
society which was not accustomed to mingle with the crowd.

'To take the first forty years, that is from 1760 to 1800, it may
be said of the Methodists (in Marshland) that they did not
entirely break away from the tradition of their early life. That is
they regularly attended the service of the Established Church,
when there was service at the Chapel of Ease at Swinfleet, or at

the mother church at Whitgift. . . . The two classes at the "preaching house" were met on Sunday and on Tuesday evening. . . .'[10]

Such conditions survived longer in some isolated parts of the country, where the early Methodist was accepted for a time as a stricter member of the Church of England, and quite distinct from the Dissenter of the period. In the earlier years this was, of course, frequently the situation. In 1751 the Rev. Henry Booker, A.M., then the Vicar of Devlin, wrote to Dr. Maule, Bishop of Meath: 'Last Christmas Day I had at the Sacrament above fifty whose faces I had scarce seen at the church before, and upon enquiry into their characters, found them mostly to have been persons of very profligate lives. About a fortnight ago one of them told me it was a great trouble to the Society that they had not more frequent opportunities of receiving the Communion. . . . Some had come that morning, as I was informed, very near ten miles on foot, though the weather was very severe and had prevented several. I had seventy communicants, true piety and charity sat smiling on their face; and I must say I never saw Divine service heard with so much reverence and attention. I was told there were but three in the congregation that did not profess themselves of that Society. . . .' In a second letter he continued: 'I must declare that my church, at least its Communion table, owes almost nine in ten of its company to their labours, and I can affirm the same of one or two neighbouring parishes.'[11]

Such behaviour, and the increasing respect in which Wesley himself was held, did something to win approval from the more educated and to attract the interest both of the notorious and the distinguished. At the same time it was true of those early years that Methodism did not touch very deeply what were invidiously called 'the higher walks of social life'. Looking back over the years, the Rev. J. B. Dyson said, a little wistfully: 'If there is but little of it in the nation's senate-house, there is much of it scattered amongst the spindles and looms of our manufacturing population. If in some cases the country squire still curls the lip of pride and turns from it with scorn, many of his humble neighbours rejoice in it as a richer patrimony than he can leave to his first-born.'[12]

There was no logical reason for the prejudice either on account of the personal character of the people or their particular beliefs.

'The Methodists of Bingley fifty or sixty years ago', wrote John Ward in 1863, 'appear to have been a plain and earnest-minded people, in their business transactions and social habits as well as their religion.'[13] He was basing his estimate on people whom he had known personally and on their private journals which he had been privileged to read.

'Methodism had no novelty to present to the world', said Agnes Bulmer in her biography of Elizabeth Ritchie. 'The doctrines it propounded, were the great and leading principles of evangelical truth, laid down in the Scriptures, and contained, not only in the formularies of the universal church, but also in those of the Church of England. . . . It was in spirit, rather than in substance, that it differed from that established form of Christianity from which it took its rise.'[14]

It was exactly because of this that so much opposition arose. 'I heard various accounts of a Clergyman . . . who was said to be a Methodist', said Hester Ann Rogers, referring to her childhood in 1773. Because of the 'false stories' she had heard she believed, 'their teachers were the false prophets spoken of in Scripture; that they deceived the illiterate, and were little better than common pick-pockets; that they filled some of their hearers with presumption, and drove others to despair; that with respect to their doctrines they enforced chiefly, that whosoever embraced their tenets, which they called faith, might live as they pleased in all sin, and be sure of salvation, and that all the world must be damned without remedy; that they had dark meetings, and pretended to cast out devils; with many other things equally false and absurd, but all of which I believed. I heard also that the new Clergyman preached against all my favourite diversions, such as going to plays, reading novels, attending balls, assemblies, card-tables, etc. But I resolved he should not make a convert of me.'[15]

It is certain that a noisy assertion of what were described as narrow views produced a wrong impression, but the background of 'high life' in the eighteenth century was notorious for its profligacy and it was little wonder that the reaction of earnest Christian people was likely to go to extremes. There is, however, in the quotation from Mrs. Rogers's letter an indication of the unreasoning prejudice which did not scruple to rake up assertions of 'dark meetings' which are reminiscent of the charges made against the Christians of the first century. The testimony of Darcy, Lady Maxwell, is sufficient answer: 'They are a highly favoured body of Christians, both Ministers and people. I meet with none who enjoy so much of the comforts of religion, of communion and fellowship with the Father and the Son, as they do; nor with any that have such clear views of the blessings of the new and everlasting covenant.'[16]

It was inevitable that this vital Christianity should eventually spread to all kinds of people, for its message knew no distinction of class or circumstance. It was brought to those in dire need. The peril of all sinful souls was the fact which made every Methodist an evangelist, convinced he had good news for all!

In some districts Methodism spread slowly. In particular the southern counties, as a whole, were late in accepting it. Smugglers, poachers, and highwaymen, were openly tolerated in this area, and poverty was accepted as inevitable. It was described as 'the Methodist wilderness!'[17] This may have been due, in part, to the routes taken by the Wesleys and the early itinerants. In the west the position was very different. Bristol had been the first Methodist centre after London. When Frances Pawson, the wife of the Rev. John Pawson, arrived in 1803, she wrote, somewhat timidly, in her journal: 'A preacher here is very differently circumstanced from one at Birstal: everything here among the families has an appearance of affluence, in some sort, surpassing London. What need, then, to watch, to tremble, to live by rule, always endeavouring to be useful.'[18] It was such reaction, uncompromising in its loyalty to personal conviction and determined to achieve a regulated life, which gives to us an impression of narrowness, but which brought to the moral and spiritual lassitude of the age the quickening of the Spirit of the Living God.

In attempting a more detailed study of the people who came to these critical years, so splendid in material achievement, so dull in spiritual adventure, one cannot do better than read by way of preface part of the letter written by Dr. Adam Clarke to Mr. Humphrey Sandwith of Bridlington in 1829. 'Our Societies were formed from those, who were *wandering upon the dark mountains*, that belonged to no Christian Church; but were awakened by the preaching of the Methodists, who had pursued them through the wilderness of this world to the Highways and the

B

Hedges—to the Markets and the Fairs—to the Hills and Dales—
who set up the Standard of the Cross in the *Streets* and *Lanes* of
the *Cities*, in the *villages*, in *Barns* and *Farmers' Kitchens*, etc. And
all this in such a way, and to such an extent, as never had been
done before, since the Apostolic Age. They threw their drag-net
into the troubled ocean of irreligious Society, and brought it to
shore both bad and good: and the very best of them needed the
Salvation of God.'[19]

It is these people who, by the grace of God, accomplished this
great service to their fellows, that we long to rediscover. They
have been overshadowed by the majestic figure of John Wesley
without whom their work would never have been commenced.
His incomparable Journal and the illuminating diaries of the
early Methodist preachers have been brilliantly analysed and
assessed, but there remain for us those homely human documents
which the rank and file of the early Methodists provide in their
many letters and often lengthy accounts of spiritual experience.
From these documents, and from such official records of the
earliest Societies as survive we must strive to make our picture.

NOTES

1. *Adventures of Ideas*, A. N. Whitehead. (Cambridge University Press.)

2. 'Impersonal Ideas,' W. J. Brown. *The Spectator*. (Sept. 19, 1947.)

3. *A Short Account of the Life of Thomas Mitchell*. (London, 1781.)

4. *A letter from a Private Person to his Pastor*, T. B. (W. Strahan, Moorfields, 1743. Quoted, *Wesley Historical Society Proceedings*. VI, 48.)

5. *Methodism in Halifax*, J. U. Walker, p. 8. (Halifax, 1836.)

6. *The Age of Walpole and the Pelhams*, H. W. V. Temperley, M.A., p. 80. (*Camb. Meth. Hist.*, VI, 1909.)

7. *Journal of John Wesley*, III. 223. (Standard Edition, London, 1909.)

8. ibid., VI. 156.

9. *Brief Annals of the Frome Society*, p.v. Stephen Tuck. (Vardy, Westminster, 1814.)

10. *Methodism in Marshland*, George West. (Wesleyan Conference Office, London, 1886.)

11. Letter dated 27th April 1751, quoted in *History of Methodism in Ireland*, C. H. Crookshank, M.A., I. 80–1. (Allen, Belfast, 1885.)

12. *Wesleyan Methodism in Congleton*, J. B. Dyson, pp. 178–9. (Mason, London, 1856.)

13. *Methodism in Bingley*, John Ward, p. 52. (Harrison, Bingley, 1859.)

14. *Memoirs of Mrs. Mortimer*, Agnes Bulmer, pp. 16–17. (Mason, London, 4th edition, 1859.)

15. *Life of Mrs. Rogers*. Letters, with Introduction by Dr. Coke. (Mason, London, 1840.)

16. *Darcy, Lady Maxwell*, pp. 307–8, *Life and Diary*. (Mason, London, 5th edition, 1863.)

17. *Wesleyan Methodism in some of the Southern Counties of England*, W. W. Pocock. Introduction by Dr. J. H. Rigg. (Wesleyan Methodist Book Room, London, 1885.)

18. *The Experience of Frances Pawson*, Joseph Sutcliffe, A.M. (Mason, London, 1834.)

19. Letter of Adam Clarke to Humphrey Sandwith. Quoted in full, *W.H.S.*, XVIII. 26.

CHAPTER I

WESLEY'S IDEAL METHODIST AND THE REALITY

AT the Conference in 1744 John Wesley drew up his *Twelve Rules of a Helper*, a code of conduct which became famous and which still sets the ideal standard for a Methodist preacher. They first appeared in the *Minutes* of 1744, under the title *Rules of an Assistant*, and though some alterations were made in the six subsequent editions of the *Large Minutes*, the final amended form (as contained in the *Minutes* of 1862) does not show any fundamental differences. It is clear that the Conference, in 1797, had decided to accept the omission of some phrases which were felt to be restrictive and narrow. For example, Rule II, 'Be serious', had contained the sentence: 'Avoid all lightness as you would avoid hell-fire; and laughing as you would cursing and swearing.' This was deleted, but the fact that it was originally given as a definite instruction to the first travelling preachers makes it easy to understand why some of the members of their congregations impress us as unnaturally sombre and depressing. The preachers obviously passed on their instructions as a rule of general conduct and their hearers, in some cases, accepted them without question. The situation, like many others, must be seen against the background of the age. It was certainly not the intention of Wesley to rob life of its joy and buoyancy, but it was his conviction that the people must be shaken out of their moral lassitude, and perhaps even frightened out of their brutish a-morality. The obscene guffaws at a bawdy play or in a sottish carouse were very different from the laughter and joy which comes naturally to a purposeful uplifted life. 'Mirth' was a word to be recovered and recognized by people to whom there had come a new and revolutionary experience.

This change was not effected in a moment, and the first fifty years of Methodism produced characters that may easily at first be condemned as hard, or without any real comprehension of the fullness of life. By 1797 there was the suggestion of a more mature and broader outlook. 'Tell everyone what you think wrong in him, and that plainly,' said the original Rule VII, but the Conference of 1797 added the words 'and lovingly'. Amongst other alterations was a deletion from Rule VIII. 'Do not affect the gentleman. You have no more to do with this character than with that of a dancing master.' In the final edition the second sentence was omitted.[1]

It might be argued that these changes came about because of the death of Wesley, and the consequent lessening of discipline, but one would rather conclude that the first stage of the new movement was ended and that the time had come to correct extremist views and behaviour.

In 1742 John Wesley had written a more general explanation of the kind of person he conceived a Methodist should be. *The Character of a Methodist*[2] was translated into French in 1743,[3] and John de Koker offered to translate it into Dutch in 1749.[4] As Wesley, himself, explained in a letter to the Editor of *Lloyd's Evening Post* on 5th March 1767[5] he had written the pamphlet because of his admiration for the character of a perfect Christian, drawn by Clement of Alexandria. Probably he was influenced, also, by his reading of Dr. Cave's *Primitive Christianity*, which volume had impressed him even in the Georgia days.[6] His own portrayal was more spiritual in conception and in language. He certainly never intended it to be 'a panegyric either on himself or his friends'. It was a picture of the ideal Methodist rather than a description of any actual person or persons. At the same time we may take it as a pattern of the kind of people he hoped the Methodist movement would produce.

As is his custom, he begins with a series of negatives: 'The distinguishing marks of a Methodist are not his opinions of any sort. His assenting to this or that scheme of religion, his embracing any particular set of notions, his espousing the judgment of one man or another, are all quite wide of the point. . . . We believe, indeed, that "all Scripture is given by the inspiration of God". . . . We believe the written word of God to be the only and sufficient rule both of Christian faith and practice. . . . We believe Christ to be the eternal, supreme God. . . . But as to all opinions which do not strike at the root of Christianity we think and let think.'[7] Here, then, in his opening sentence is an insistence on a spirit of tolerance, within certain limits. Neither Wesley nor his more intelligent followers were guilty of having a closed mind towards the theological views of others. In spite of controversial bitterness, on occasion, it is generally true to say that the early Methodists were by no means intolerant.

In Lowestoft, for example, one of the most useful class-leaders was Thomas Mallit. He was described as one whose 'cheerful conversation was sought after and valued by persons of various religious denominations. The curate of the parish frequently paid him a visit, to enjoy his friendly and profitable converse, and always spoke highly of him.' This is very different from the average picture of the persecuting or indifferent clergyman and the narrow or aggressive Methodist. In point of fact, Thomas Mallit (*b.* 1748, *d.* 1813) was a well-informed and intelligent man. He read Latin, Greek, and Hebrew, and had developed his natural talent in the study of sacred literature. It is pleasant to picture him, with the youthful Adam Clarke—that great scholar of later years—sitting at his feet.[8] The young Methodist preacher whose name was to become famous, was certainly, in 1783–4, a willing pupil of this early Methodist class-leader. At the height of his fame he remembered him as one of his kindest friends who 'lent him some valuable papers on various passages of Scripture which were of very great use'. He was entertained at his house as 'at the house of a parent'.

His books, which included 'the original edition of Mr. Wesley's works and his Christian Library', Thomas Mallit bequeathed for the use of the Methodist preachers resident in Lowestoft. It is clear that the broad humanity of such a man realized something of the ideal that was not only in Wesley's mind, but at the heart of Christianity. Humbly he went week by week to lead his class and share with simple wayfaring men truth not only as he had discovered it in his books, but as he had experienced it in his deeper life. A recent writer,[9] referring to the oldest register of the Great Yarmouth Circuit, says: 'One would scarcely have thought such a circuit a likely nursery for a scholar such as Dr. Adam Clarke. . . .' The superintendent in 1794–5 was the Rev. Thomas Bartholomew, 'a Biblical scholar of no mean attainments'. The fact that Thomas Mallit was a member and class-leader rather explains the situation, and may even suggest a little judicious 'stationing' in the case of Mr. Bartholomew. Perhaps Adam Clarke had spoken to him of his own experience.

'Neither are words or phrases of any sort,' amongst the distinguishing marks of a Methodist, says John Wesley. 'We do not place our religion or any part of it, in being attached to any peculiar mode of speaking, any quaint or uncommon set of expressions. The most obvious, easy, common words, wherein our meaning can be conveyed, we prefer before others, both on ordinary occasions, and when we speak of the things of God.'

How he abhorred outlandish phraseology! The man who would study the English language might well take as one of his text-books the *Standard Sermons of John Wesley.* 'We never, therefore, willingly or designedly, deviate from the most usual way of speaking; unless when we express scripture truths in scripture words, which, we presume, no Christian will condemn.' His ideal Methodist must speak plain English so that Betty the dairymaid might be as much at home in hearing the word as were the dons of Oxford. More important still, on such terms she could come to her class, and give her experience with no shame for her rustic speech, and no embarrassment if the squire's lady joined the little Society.

It was not by pedantic language nor strange customs nor by the practice of celibacy or any other form of asceticism that Wesley felt the Methodist should be known. Simplicity of dress and even fasting might help to further true Christianity, but these things were not of first importance, and should certainly not become occasions for fanaticism or vain posturing. In word and deed, as in many other things, the keynote was to be simplicity. The Methodist was to be neither childish nor shallow, but simple, teachable and sane.

In 1767 Sarah Bentley was born in the parish of Pannal, near Harrogate.[10] To quote her own words, she 'got a little schooling, learnt to knit, sew, write and read', but this was all she had by way of education. From fifteen years of age she was employed as housemaid, for the most part serving in inns and similar places. For some years her life was dreary enough in spite of an occasional 'mazy dance' and the allurements of a village inn. What concern could she have with Clement of Alexandria and the schoolmen's theories of eternal life? How could she enter into the speculations of Aquinas—or Adam Clarke—unless these things were interpreted in simple speech by the grace of God?

It happened that she was devoted to her father, and when he died his death was 'surrounded with a gloomy uncertainty'. Sarah Bentley paused in her monotonous round to think. The mystery of life and death did not remain a mystery to her—it became, for the first time, a real problem. Her sister Ellen was 'religious', but this had meant nothing to Sarah. Even when their mother lay desperately ill all she could do was to offer to look after the house while Ellen prayed. Then the dying woman said, 'I should like to see Mr. Dawson of York'. Sarah literally leaped to action. She tried hard to borrow a horse, but in vain. 'If the parson won't do for her, she can have nobody,' was the answer. Desperate but determined, Sarah set out to run and walk the seven miles to York. Something was stirring in her mind and heart, and presently she reached the house of the famous old 'local' preacher. He mounted his horse and rode hard over the Yorkshire roads, leaving the footsore Sarah to trudge back, mystified but conscious that she had done something that mattered more than drawing ale. Day after day old William Dawson rode in from York to pray until it seemed to Sarah that her mother had triumphed over the very thought of death. 'She died,' they said, 'in the faith of Jesus', and her daughter knew this strange thing for truth.

Lonely in her orphanhood, Sarah went to live at the *George Inn* at York, with her brother and sister, the genial but quite secular hosts. Once again she must fill the pint-pots and satisfy the customers. But *she* was not satisfied, for in her heart was a great yearning to understand what Mr. Dawson had meant—'in the faith of Jesus'. At night she read her Bible in the attic of *The George*, and at last fell on her knees, asking her Maker to help her to love Him as much as she had loved her parents. In that little room she fought her battle till at last she came in her reading to the eighth chapter of Romans. 'There is therefore now no condemnation to them which are in Christ Jesus, who walk not after the flesh, but after the Spirit.' How could she believe this concerned a barmaid in *The George*? 'Our Sally's going daft,' her friends said. 'Get her out a bit. Let's take her to a dance.' She was no prude, and she agreed to go, spending a hardly-saved £10 on her dress. Neither the gay companionship nor the rhythm held the answer she was seeking. It is important to notice she did not spend herself in futile denunciation of *their* way of 'escape'. She was too completely concerned, at the moment, to find what she, herself, was seeking.

On Christmas Eve she climbed up four stories to a 'large upper room' where Richard Burdsall, 'old chapter-and-verse' men called him, was preaching. She listened eagerly, and presently came back to her little attic to 'wrestle' in prayer. 'No room in the inn'—that had been the word. She opened her heart to the Eternal Love. In utter simplicity she welcomed Him as surely as Teresa or the Blessed Angela of Foligno. Down the rickety stairs she came to tell her friends, round the card-table, the 'Good News'. They saw her only as a madwoman, who must not be left alone—so hard is it for the world to recognize simple piety when they see it! This is no place in which to record the story of her growth in grace and understanding. Unlike Thomas Mallit, she knew nothing of Hebrew lexicons or Syriac versions, but like him she learnt to know the Saviour of mankind! Wondering at first whether she should leave the inn, she decided, with astonishing courage, to stay there. Gradually, her conception of spiritual life widened and deepened. As her biographer says:[11] 'When sin was discovered it was mourned and forsaken; when duty was plain, it was diligently attempted. So the light of heaven waxed brighter. . . . It was grace that saved, but *grace improved*.'

Presently she joined the 'Society' and went to live with her widowed sister in the country, though later she removed to York, managing on her small savings, and giving her whole time to the service of God and her neighbours.

Proposals of marriage came, but she refused them, not without thought and prayer, and maybe a pang or two. More than one distinguished preacher of the next generation owed his early religious training to Sally Bentley.

When Lady Johnstone's guest, a well-known Countess, was in spiritual distress, she sent for her. The interview, which lasted about five hours, and terminated only with the 'noon of night', was honoured with the divine blessing. One can imagine Sarah simply dressed, 'with no unnecessary trimmings . . . adorned as a woman professing godliness', talking and praying with the lady of fashion until 'she obtained that which her soul desired, the assurance of God's forgiving love; and they parted in the hope of meeting again at the right hand of God'.

There is nothing smug or self-satisfied about the homely record, but there is a profound experience which was reached in the simplicity of faith, childlike but never childish. Sarah was dour and practical, perhaps, at first a little forbidding. She went her way, visiting for the Benevolent Society, teaching in a primitive Sunday school, nursing the dying when the cholera swept through

York, growing more mellow and more sure with the years. 'It seemed as if the lamp only burned brighter as the oil was wasting.' Her humble heart was filled with the love of God and of her fellows. Neither John Wesley nor Adam Clarke would have said: 'Noo, luv, hoo are ye? Hoo's yer mother?' but they would have understood her, even as her Lord understood a woman of Syro-Phoenicia striving with Him for her daughter's life.

Having made it plain that Methodists were not to be distinguished by eccentricity of speech or conduct, John Wesley agreed that they said, 'We are saved by faith alone', and went on to explain just what this implied. By faith they meant holiness of heart and life. And this he affirmed 'springs from true faith alone'. To say this was not to deny the law, which he and all other Methodists accepted, but it did mean that they did not base man's salvation on mere legal obedience. 'We do not place the whole of religion either in doing harm, or in doing good, or in using the ordinances of God.'

This statement brings him to a positive definition. 'A Methodist is one who has "the love of God shed abroad in his heart by the Holy Ghost given unto him": one who "loves the Lord his God with all his heart, and with all his soul, and with all his mind, and with all his strength". God is the joy of his heart, and the desire of his soul. . . . He is therefore happy in God.' The reason of this happiness is his assurance of forgiveness. 'He cannot but rejoice, whenever he looks on the state wherein he now is; "being justified freely, and having peace with God through our Lord Jesus Christ".'

This was the point at which so many hesitated and even grew angry or satirical. That a motley company of people, for the most part uneducated, should assert that they *knew* their sins forgiven, outraged the intelligence. No doubt there were some people whose 'assurance' was asserted in an unpleasant way. Their speech betrayed their forgiveness! But it is clear, from a mass of evidence, that the true Methodist in the second half of the eighteenth century entered into an experience so vivid and revolutionary that no one who examined it could doubt either its significance or its completeness. The assurance of forgiveness was no superficial slogan.

Here is a passage from the journal of James Field,[12] a veteran of the Low Countries and the Peninsula War: 'See the great advantage of unshaken confidence in God! Never reasoning *against*, but always *for*, ourselves. Are there not enemies enough without us? Why should we have them within or be our own enemies? If the French Emperor could have persuaded all the English army at Waterloo to turn their swords and bayonets against their own breasts, he would have easily gained the day.'

After long years of active service, James Field settled down and became a devoted class-leader. This is how he wrote to a member whose faith was evidently weak:[13] 'You have as good reason to believe as any one I know. Notwithstanding you have the truth of grace, there is a grand flaw in your experience. God intends we should have two heavens,—one here, as well as hereafter: you have not the former, because you are still subject to bondage occasioned by unbelief, by looking too much at defective self, and too little at Jesus. . . . Mind not yourself farther than to see and feel you are all unclean. As Fletcher says, "He will receive you with a mountain of sin; and the smallest particle of faith in the dust at His feet will remove it".'

One feels in these words of an old soldier, tried on the bloodiest battlefields of the Napoleonic wars, a certainty about his own spiritual experience that will not be denied. He is as sure that God has forgiven him his sins, as he is that the wounds of his body have been healed, and that he has passed through the agonies of earthly war to peace. Nor is the experience irrational or isolated. Writing much later, as an old man, to Robert Huston in Dublin, he says: 'There is only one thing I hate more than error; that is, sin. If my friends mean that my own faith is peculiarly strong, I admit it, and *praise the Giver for it*; but, if they mean that there is anything peculiarly erroneous in my views respecting faith, I deny it. My views of it are the same as those of Messrs. Wesley, Fletcher, Coke, Benson, Watson, Bramwell, Smith and Carvosso. I praise the Lord, I am willing to be taught by a child; but this great truth I cannot give up. . . .'[14] It is an interesting array of names he quotes, as he checks his own experience. There are scholars like Wesley, Fletcher, Coke and Benson, but there are also men who had few educational advantages—Bramwell, the great and saintly evangelist and Carvosso the Cornish farmer who walked with God. Whatever else may be implied by the doctrine of Assurance, the early Methodists insisted that it was an experience possible for all, and conditioned by faith. Such evidence might be multiplied many times and, indeed, more of it will be cited in the detailed consideration of the Methodist experience.[15]

As Wesley develops the positive side he becomes surprisingly broad in his explanation of prayer as he understood it. The Methodist 'prays without ceasing. . . . Not that he is always in the house of prayer; though he neglects no opportunity of being there. Neither is he always on his knees, though he often is. . . . Nor yet is he always crying aloud to God, or calling upon Him in words. . . . But his heart is ever lifted up to God, at all times and in all places.'

There were, it is true, some few Methodists whose idea of *sursum corda* was too often concentrated, in their journals, on death-beds, and whose assurance of sins forgiven could be sometimes mistaken for offensive self-confidence.

The majority strove to reach the ideal, and to enter the privacy of their prayer-life is a humbling experience, but no one has a right to pass judgement on the reality of their communion unless he is prepared to enter this holy of holies, and be still.

Meade Leahy, who became a member of the Society at Kinsale in 1783, and remained faithful till his death fifty years later, was accustomed to go to the preaching-house an hour before the service. There, in solitude, he poured out his soul to God.[16]

In Trelabe in Cornwall John Body wore a hole in the ground by an old tree, in a quiet copse, through kneeling so often and so long in prayer and adoration.[17]

May we be forgiven if, even in thought, we have clattered into the old preaching-house at Kinsale or trodden carelessly where John Body knelt! Are not these places as sacred as El Carceri where Francis prayed, and the footprints of John Body walking to the old plantation as significant as the Italian saint's on Monte Subasio?

When George Eliot wrote *Adam Bede* she took legitimate liberties with her characters. In actual fact it was Seth Evans, not Adam, who married Dinah. She became a preacher, and though her sermons are, for the most part, forgotten, one of her prayers remains. One can almost hear her voice raised in that preaching-house in a Derbyshire dale as the miners bowed their heads and their hearts at the throne of the heavenly grace. 'Saviour of sinners! when a poor woman laden with sins, went out to the well to draw water, she found Thee sitting at the well; she knew Thee not; she had not sought Thee; her mind was dark; her life was unholy. But Thou didst show her that her life lay open before Thee, and yet Thou wast ready to give her that blessing which she had never sought. Jesus Thou art in the midst of us, and Thou knowest all men; if there are any here like that poor woman, if their minds are dark, their lives unholy, if they had come out not seeking Thee, not desiring to be taught, to deal with them according to the free mercy which Thou didst show to her, speak to them Lord; open their ears to my message; bring their sins to their minds, and make them thirst for that salvation which Thou art ready to give. Lord, Thou art with Thy people still; they see Thee in the night watches, and their hearts burn within them as Thou talkest with them by the way, and Thou art near to those that have not known Thee. Open their eyes that they may see Thee weeping over them, and saying, Ye will not come unto me, that ye might have life; see Thee hanging on the cross, and saying, Father forgive them, for they know not what they do. See Thee as Thou wilt come again in Thy glory to judge them at the last. Amen.'[18]

That was the prayer Dinah prayed. It is not the careful creation of the novelist, nor the cool and balanced petition of the priest, but it has a certain torrential appeal and passionate sincerity which survives the years. Dinah is sure of her message for she is convinced it has been given to her by God Himself. Her plea is for those to whom she speaks—lest they might miss the gift she has been commissioned to offer. That was how they prayed, these first Methodists, with a sense of tremendous urgency, conscious of man's need and twice-conscious of God's sufficiency. To have heard them must have been a moving experience. It is a pleasant thing to read George Eliot's book; it must have been a benediction to hear Dinah Evans pray.

Continuing his definition Wesley says: 'He is, therefore, happy in God', being sure of his forgiveness, forbearing and forgiving, and joyfully accepting the commandments of God. 'Whatever God has forbidden, he avoids; whatever God hath enjoined, he doeth; and that whether it be little or great, hard or easy, joyous or grievous to the flesh.'[19]

So, in spite of what seemed an early condemnation of laughter[20] —at any rate for his preachers—John Wesley expects his

Methodists to be 'happy' and 'joyful'. It is unfortunate that he and probably the first generation of preachers, frowned upon a smile! Certainly it made it more difficult for the non-Methodist to believe in their joy. Perhaps there was in the mind of the contemporary observer something which linked them to the traditional Puritan, stern in countenance and generally inclined to be reproachful. It would be a mistake to suppose, however, that the Methodists in general were sour-faced and smugly critical of their fellows.

No one could question the native wit of 'Billy' Dawson, 'Sammy' Hick or 'Dicky' Burdsall. Their personalities were radiant with good humour, and their natural sallies in pulpit or by the fireside were appreciated, not condemned. From their diaries one can judge that an evening spent in their company would have been as rare and memorable an occasion as one spent with Dr. Johnson or Peter McKenzie. The biographer of Samuel Hick, the blacksmith of Aberford speaks of 'the sunshine of the human spirit' as he describes the tall, fair-haired man with his 'soft, quick, blue-grey twinkling eyes' twinkling in thought and 'sending out occasional and inexpressible natural beauties, like streaks of sunshine between dark, rolling clouds'.[21] His Yorkshire common sense forces him to give hard knocks, at times, but we can see the humanity behind his smile as he says: 'In every thing give thanks.' What! For a bad debt, or a dinner of herbs? For a thatched cottage? 'Aye, praise God for all things. . . . We have more than we deserve. . . . If we were more thankful for our mercies, God would give us more.'

A streak of sunshine would have penetrated the severest lecture-room if 'Sammy' Hick had ventured his theological valuations there. As it was, his tremendous congregations guarantee his acceptability and we believe that Wesley, himself, chuckled occasionally at the wit of men whom he knew to be 'good Methodists'. Who could resist the logic of the blacksmith's assessment of what used to be called 'the blessings of salvation'? 'I sometimes compare religion to the best coin of the realm,' said Mr. Hick, whose financial resources were always limited. 'First, there is repentance, this may be compared to a seven-shilling piece; though there is but little of it, still it is good. Then comes pardon; this is like half-a-guinea. Next comes sanctification; this is like a guinea. Now, who would be content with seven shillings, or even with half-a-guinea, when he might just as well have a whole guinea by applying for it?' Translate such words into broad Yorkshire dialect, and let them be said spontaneously by a happy man with irresistible convictions and it is not much wonder that the Conference of 1797 altered the rule which had put laughter on a par with cursing and swearing![21]

The joy of the true Methodist was too deep-seated for him to become a 'misery'. It might be that, at times, his conscience forbade him this or that, things which seemed in themselves harmless enough, but it is certain that his living experience was too radiant to be permanently blacked-out! If there were those who were so entirely introspective that they had neither time nor patience for ordinary social life, and the beauty and humour of God's good world, it was not because they were good Methodists, but rather that they were elementary and even ego-centric in their Christianity.

As we come towards the conclusion of Wesley's sketch of what we have dared to call his ideal Methodist we are struck by his stress of a quality which we would describe as Neighbourliness. 'And while he thus always exercises his love to God, by praying without ceasing, rejoicing evermore, and in everything giving thanks, this commandment is written in his heart, "That he who loveth God, love his brother also". And he accordingly loves his neighbour as himself. . . . That a man is not personally known to him, is no bar to his love; no, nor that he is known to be such as he approves not, that he repays hatred for his goodwill. For he "loves his enemies"; yea, and the enemies of God, "the evil and the unthankful".'[22]

This is the strong meat which sent the early Methodists to the felons of Newgate and the negroes of Antigua, to the wretched children of Cock Hill, Bristol, and to the usurers and the lechers of fashionable Bath and London. It recruited them for the work of healing the sick and wounded, but it enlisted them in a warfare against a slavery that was more terrible and widespread than the black cargoes that were shipped from Africa to the West Indies or the cotton plantations in Georgia. The outcome of this gospel of neighbourliness will be seen in closer detail when we consider social service, as the early Methodists understood it.[23] At the same time it cannot be too strongly emphasized that as they conceived man's spiritual condition to be most grievous, so they conceived his spiritual need to be, in the language of today, priority number one. Nothing was so urgent as the salvation of the human soul. If it might be that bodily needs could be met or social injustice redressed *en route*, well and good, but at all times and in all places, the Methodist must minister the grace of God to the tormented souls of men. 'As he has time he does good unto all men, unto neighbours and strangers, friends and enemies; not only unto their bodies . . . but much more does he labour to do good to their souls.'[24]

In his conclusion, John Wesley meets the obvious objection that these are 'only the common, fundamental principles of Christianity!' He answers tersely: 'Thou hast said: so I mean.' That had been and remained his standpoint. Methodism was no new-fangled notion to save or captivate the world. It was simply an attempt to put into practice the principles of primitive Christianity or—better still—the teaching of Jesus Christ.

Long before the days of Charles Sheldon, the simple Methodist asked himself the question, 'What would Jesus do?' Sometimes he came to conclusions that appear grotesque and stupid. Sometimes he addressed the question too directly to himself or even to the man John Wesley. For the most part, in prayer and in conversation with his fellows in class-meeting or in band, he got an answer. However crude or narrow the decisions may have been, the consequence in his life bore favourable comparison with the conduct of his contemporaries. His witness cleansed and redirected no small part of our own national life, and helped to shape the future of the great American people.

Throughout their lives both John and Charles Wesley strove by an amazing flow of correspondence to keep in touch with a great number of their people. The letters reveal constant 'consultations' as to the 'state of grace' in which the writers found themselves. This correspondence was carefully analysed by Dr. W. F. Howard in the Wesley Historical Society Lecture for 1943.[25] It is sufficient to say that whether the enquiry concerned physical aches and pains, or spiritual perplexities, the letters were usually answered and personal contacts maintained. In some small measure the real Methodist was gradually shaped to the ideal, by the men who were never unmindful that the matrix was to be found only in the Gospels.

In taking this voluminous correspondence into account it should be remembered that John Wesley once wrote to Miss Elizabeth Ritchie[26] stating a principle which guided him in these matters: 'It is not common for me to write to any one first; I only answer those that write to me. But I willingly make an exception with regard to you; for it is not a common concern that I feel for you. You are just rising into life; and I would fain have you not almost, but altogether, a Christian.' Here surely, in spite of breaking rules which he always regretted, is an instance of the very essence of the Methodism he described. The privileged Miss Ritchie abundantly justified his exception, for she, it was, who at last closed his eyes when he reached the end of his earthly pilgrimage, and remained until her death a faithful and experienced leader.

It must not be forgotten that this man who described the character of a Methodist, formulated Rules for the guidance of the members of the first Methodist Societies. Since they affect the formation and development of the Class-meeting, they will be more conveniently considered later.[27] It should, however, be noticed that many of the early Methodists drew up their own rules of personal conduct which were supplementary to these more general regulations.

In a memorandum written by Mary Lyth, of York, there is the record of a code she had personally devised, and by which she tried to live.[28] They are very simple rules, but for that reason the more typical of the people who were struggling, in a brittle and materialistic age, towards a new and living experience. Her son comments on them: 'Those who knew her will be able to recognize in them the key of her life.' She wrote:

1. Let me rise early.
2. Never let me trifle with a book with which I have no present concern; in applying myself to any book, let me endeavour to recollect what I may learn by it, and then beg suitable assistance from God.
3. Never let me lose one minute of time, nor incur any unnecessary expense, that I may have the more to spend for God. When I am abroad let me be desirous of doing good; let me have in readiness some subject of contemplation and endeavour to improve my time as I go along.
4. Let me endeavour to render myself agreeable and useful to all around me; by a tender compassionate friendly

c

behaviour; avoiding all trifling and impertinent stories; remembering that impudence is sin.

5. Never let me delay anything, unless I can prove that another time will be more fit than the present; or that some more important duty requires my immediate attention.

6. O may I never enter into any long schemes about future events, but in general refer myself to God's care.

7. O that I may be delivered from the least inclination to judge my neighbours; and that henceforth I may find fault with none so much as myself.

There is a certain naïveté about this code which, otherwise, would repel one by its dour and remorseless demands. The simple but sincere goodwill in Rules 4 and 7 reveals a neighbourliness in the midst of what seems severity. It would have been pleasant to live near Mrs. Lyth in days of anxiety or stress.

Her journal is written in a stiff and formal style but her personality conquers the conventional phrases and convinces us of her winsome saintliness. The girl who wrote at thirteen, 'O that I had a voice that would reach to all the world, I would tell them how happy I am', retained her joy yet shared it with all who came her way.

The early Methodist was only an imperfect copy of Wesley's ideal, as Wesley's ideal was, in itself, but an imperfect copy of 'the pattern showed him in the mount'. In the last analysis it was not John Wesley they struggled to imitate but the Lord and Master of them all. Their psychological reactions were often complicated and the somewhat scornful age in which they lived was quick to ridicule their agonies, but the ordinary man was gradually impressed by their neighbourly behaviour and their uncommon honesty.

When James Field was discharged from the army, he obtained a situation in Cork.[29] He remained there for twenty-six years, and served his employer 'with the most exemplary fidelity'. Growing old, he asked that his salary might be reduced, because he felt his services were no longer worth what he was being paid. It was an attitude which would be described today as at least unusual! In spite of the protest of his employer, who realized his ability, he refused to receive more than an amount which he thought was fair remuneration. It is a simple enough example, but it is a slight indication of the way in which the spiritual struggle affected the practical issues of daily life.

All human relations and all values were readjusted by these men and women who were struggling, not merely to keep a set of rules, but to scale the higher heights and to bring their neighbours with them.

They were often far removed even from Wesley's ideal but they won their way, step by step, and as they climbed, they sang.

NOTES

1. *W.H.S.*, article by George Latham, VII. 82–4.

2. 'The Character of a Methodist', *Works of John Wesley*, VIII. 340–72. (1830 edition.)

3. *Le Caractère d'un Methodiste*, John Wesley. (Strahan, London, 1743.)

4. *Journal of John Wesley*, III. 447–8.

5. ibid., V. 197.

6. *W.H.S.*, XV. 113–17.

7. *Works of John Wesley*, VIII. 340.

8. *Wesleyan Methodism in Lowestoft*, pp. 52–4. (Mason, London, 1843.)

9. The Rev. J. Conder Nattrass, *W.H.S.*, III. 77.

10. *The Living Sacrifice*, John Lyth. (Mason, London, 1859.)

11. ibid., pp. 33–4.

12. *Memoirs of James Field*, Robert Huston, p. 62. (Mason, London, 1851.)

13. ibid., p. 156.

14. ibid., p. 60.

15. See Chapter III, *infra*.

16. *Primitive Wesleyan Methodist Magazine* (Ireland), 1883, p. 411.

17. *Truly Rural*, Herbert Bolitho, p. 33. (Whitehead, Leeds, 1947.)

18. *Seth Bede*, written by himself, pp. 7, 17–18. (Tallant, London, 1859.)

19. 'Character of a Methodist', *Works of John Wesley*, VIII. 344.

20. 'Twelve Rules of a Helper' (1744), *W.H.S.*, VII. 82–4.

21. *The Village Blacksmith*, James Everett, pp. 173, 181. (Newton, London, 1st ed., 1830.)

22. 'Character of a Methodist', *Wesley's Works*, VIII. 343.

23. *More About the Early Methodist People*, L. F. Church, Chapter I. (Epworth Press.)

24. 'Character of a Methodist', *Wesley's Works*, VIII. 346.

25. To be published shortly.

26. *Memoir of Mrs. Elizabeth Mortimer*, p. 45. See also letter dated 8th May 1774, *Standard Letters of John Wesley*, VI. 84.

27. See Chapter IV.

28. *Religion in Earnest, a Memorial of Mrs. Mary Lyth*, John Lyth, pp. 30–1. (The Book Society, London, 1861.)

29. *Memoirs of James Field* (of Cork), R. Huston, p. 172. (Mason, London, 1851.)

CHAPTER II

THE HOMELESS AND THEIR CHAPEL-BUILDING

IT is a simple fact that people who heard John Wesley preach wanted to hear him again. It is equally true that the majority of his travelling preachers found eager audiences everywhere, in spite of organized opposition or spasmodic outbursts of mob-law.

The churches were presently, for the most part, closed against him. Was he to cease to preach altogether, or change his message and his manner to meet the conventions? 'Not daring to be silent,' he writes, 'after a short struggle between honour and conscience, I made a virtue of necessity, and preached in the middle of Moorfields. Here were thousands upon thousands, abundantly more than any church could contain; and numbers among them, who never went to any church or place of public worship at all. More and more of them were cut to the heart, and came to me all in tears, inquiring with the utmost eagerness, what they must do to be saved.'[1]

There could be little doubt as to his answer when Whitfield requested him to go to preach to the miners in the fields at Bristol. The discussion as to who was first 'in the field' is of purely academic interest. Actually Charles Wesley 'spoke a few suitable words to the crowd' at Tyburn while his brother was absent in Germany,[2] and it is highly probable that both spoke together on a similar occasion on 8th November 1738.[3] It has been pointed out that the Rev. Mr. Morgan preached to the colliers in the Kingswood fields that same year,[4] and Howell Harris— a law to himself—had already been preaching for some time, in Wales, 'generally in a field; but at other times in a house, from a wall, a table, or anything else.'[5]

The most important fact is that these men were possessed by a desperate and increasing sense of urgency. Men were dying in spiritual darkness, and they had begun to see the light that 'could lighten every man'. The news must be brought to them in spite of all questions of convention and propriety. Even legal barriers must yield, and John Wesley was wise enough to realize the danger of infringing canon law. The Conventicle Act forbade the holding of a religious service in a field if it were conducted 'in other manner than according to the liturgy and practice of the Church of England'. Remembering this one must recognize, as Dr. J. S. Simon has pointed out, that 'field-preaching meant much more than preaching in the open air'.

So the Methodists, and at this stage one might substitute the name of John Wesley, realized that far-reaching decisions must be taken. The people must be evangelized, but they must be shepherded. As soon as the Societies were formed, they must be housed, however primitive and temporary the arrangements might be. Even where the parish church welcomed them to Holy Communion, it did not afford accommodation for their preaching or rooms for their Societies to meet. It is doubtful whether the problem in all its complications was apparent at first. The preachers went to the fields, and formed the primitive Societies, and gradually the people set to work to build what were to become known as their 'spiritual homes'—though at first they were called preaching-houses and conventicles!

None the less, field-preaching had its advantages. It had begun partly because the majority of churches were closed against the preachers, and partly because no church could have held the enormous crowds that gathered. It would not suffice as a permanent means of spreading the Gospel because the Societies could not 'grow' in the fields. Concentrated study of the Word and the intimacies of Christian fellowship were obviously impossible in haphazard gatherings in Moorfields or Kingswood.

It was not that open-air worship meant inevitably irreverence. 'I wonder at those, who still talk so loud of the indecency of field-preaching', says Wesley in 1748.[6] 'The highest indecency is in St. Paul's Church, when a considerable part of the congregation are asleep, or talking, or looking about, not minding a word the preacher says. On the other hand there is the highest decency in a churchyard or field, when the whole congregation behave and look as if they saw the Judge of all, and heard Him speaking from heaven.'

Nor was it less than providential that the beginnings of Methodism were in the fields. It is interesting to hear the judgement of so unlikely a person as Lord Byron on this point. 'Were the early and rapid progress of what is called Methodism to be attributed to any cause beyond the enthusiasm excited by its vehement faith and doctrines (the truth or error of which I presume neither to canvass nor question), I should venture to ascribe it to the practice of preaching in the fields, and the unstudied and extemporaneous effusions of its preachers.'[7]

Notwithstanding these advantages it is paradoxically true to say that the churches were not big enough, so the preacher must go to the fields, and the fields were too big, so he must build him a church!

The spread of Methodism was so rapid, and the manner of its growth so conditioned by local circumstance, that it is impossible to attempt more than a general survey. A few examples must suffice to indicate the trend.

When John Nelson came back from London in 1740 to his home at Birstal, he returned, not only as a stonemason who had finished a job, but as a man who had been transformed. The preaching of John Wesley had given him a new outlook on life itself. He was so sure of the forgiveness of his sins, that he was bound to speak about it to everyone he met. When they pressed him for evidence, he opened his Bible, and in humility, but with confidence, read and expounded the Gospel. 'This he did at first sitting in his house, till the company increased so that the house could not contain them. Then he stood at the door, which he was commonly obliged to do in the evening, as soon as he came from work.'[8] He was encouraged to go farther afield, not only by Benjamin Ingham, but by the clamour of the people who wanted to hear him.

Amongst other places, he went to Armley, and though the date of his first visit is uncertain, it is evident that he had preached there before John Wesley came in May 1742. The little group of people whose names are forgotten grew strong in the faith so that when William Shent, a barber, and Matthew Chippendale, a basket-maker, with others who had been stirred by Wesley's visit formed a nucleus, their neighbours were already strong enough to help them. 'Now Armley Society became a nursing mother to the new born souls at Leeds, for there were steady souls at Armley who had stood from the beginning without wavering, and I trust we shall meet together in heaven.'[9]

Such small groups, with little, yet, in the way of organization,

were held together by the reality of a common experience. The
visits of preachers were few and far between and in the early years
quite irregular. Much depended on close association and mutual
intercourse. For the most part they lived in cottages, ill-designed
for large meetings, but they made the best of them. No hardship
or inconvenience could hinder them in their eager desire for
more truth and deeper understanding. In Leeds they gathered
in Matthew Chippendale's house in Boggart Close, though on
special occasions 'Brother Shent provided a large empty house
to preach in'.[10]

To Nottingham the Wesleys and their preachers came and
usually elected to preach at Malt Cross, which stood in the
market-place. 'Its base was four feet high, upon which rested
six pillars, covered with a tiled roof, and the whole surmounted
with six sun-dials and a vane. Within this Cross, and around it,
sat those on market-days, who sold china and earthenware; and
it was from this structure that all proclamations or declarations
of war or peace were read in the face of a full market: it was also
the usual resort of labourers waiting for employment.'[11] The
people who gathered, there, on market-day, formed 'the immense
multitude' to which Wesley preached.[12] Many of them were
moved to tears or blasphemy on such occasions, but some few,
more deeply affected, gathered their neighbours together to go
further into this great matter of their eternal destiny. In Nottingham the first meetings were held in the large house of Mr. James,
near the top of Girdlesmith Gate, later called Pelham Street.
For some reason 'the preaching was afterwards removed to
Matthew Bagshaw's, who resided in Narrow Marsh, opposite the
bottom of Long Stairs, on the right hand side of Crossland
Yard'.[13] Even the direction is complicated, but no more so than
the actual arrangements. However, Matthew was 'an ardent
Methodist' and he determined to adapt his premises! He broke
a hole through the floor of the second story and made a large
opening into the room below. In the upper room he placed the
men, in the lower room the women; the preacher being enabled
by this arrangement to preach to a crowded audience in both
rooms at the same time. What did it matter to Matthew that
the amenities of his house were disturbed! The meetings went
on. What did it matter that the Mayor committed him to the
'House of Correction' because he was said to be encouraging

conventicles! When he got to gaol he turned it into a 'conventicle' and probably found the accommodation somewhat better.

In 1744 John Maden heard a rumour that a 'new kind of preacher' had come into the neighbourhood of Todmorden.[14] Next day he trudged five or six miles to Gawksholme and there heard William Darney (Scotch Will, as Wesley called him) preaching in a barn. The sermon impressed him deeply and, when the people had left, he stole back to the barn to pray. Finding peace at last he gathered his neighbours together from the bleak moor-side, and they met at his house for prayer and fellowship. Once a week he walked to Walsden where there was a more regular Society class, but meanwhile he held together the little company of seekers, in his own cottage. Presently more regular preaching services were held in various houses in rotation. Dissension came, but John Maden and his devoted wife stood firm. The future of Methodism in Rossendale depended not on a building but on two faithful souls. Keeping in touch with wandering preachers like Darney, Larwood, Colbeck and Maskew, he did what he could to communicate the blessing he knew to his neighbours. By trade he was a stone-mason, but when times were hard he eked out a living by clock-mending and shuttle-fettling, till he was able to take a small farm at Top-o' the'-Bank, half a mile above Stacksteads, near Bacup. At once his house became 'the centre of Methodist operations in the valley'. He carved a pulpit in the biggest room, and there a little congregation gathered regularly to worship God.

In such simple fashion the work began, long before any question of building a chapel arose. In the Rossendale areas little groups of people at Todmorden, Shore, Mellor Barn, Cross Stone, Stoneseygate, and Crimsworth Dean were visited not only by Will Darney but by Parson Grimshaw of Haworth, John Bennet and, more rarely, of necessity, by John Wesley himself. The part played by the people themselves cannot be over-emphasized, for the preacher's visitations were few and far between. Consider the following passage from a local history: 'It appears that at a very early period a class-meeting was held at Th' Back o' th' Lowe, situated above Lench, and at the edge of Scaut Moor. An old warper, named Lord, opened his cottage for the meeting, and the preaching-services were held at the house of Edmund Leach, a shopkeeper, who was accustomed to entertain the preachers.'[15]

Any question of convenience was completely answered by the sense of urgency. Sunday after Sunday, after milking his cows, John Rishton set out from his moorland farm, near Musbury Tor, to tramp over mountain-paths to Flaxmoss. He carried one child on his back, led another by the hand, while his wife carried the third child in her arms. It was not because they were going to a quiet and stately building, that they strode on bravely; they were going to join other simple souls in keeping a tryst with God.

After the visit of John Nelson to Lower Darwen, in 1755,[16] little groups of 'converted men and women' gathered together regularly until a Society was formed and later a chapel was built. It was this intervening period which proved their mettle and incidentally gives the cynical critic a problem to ponder. That these people were affected by something much deeper than a passing emotional disturbance is obvious. In 1758 as a development of the effect of Nelson's visit three years earlier, a farmer named Haworth and his three brothers joined with James Oddie and eight others, meeting regularly at a house called 'Th' top o' th' Coal Pits'.[17] The very name makes one pause, yet there are accounts of similar people in places as strangely chosen in the Lincolnshire fens and the Cornish fishing-villages. Whatever it was that was working in the hearts of the people of Lancashire and Yorkshire was working in the same way all over the country. It would be as easy to take our evidence from north or south, from east or west, for the winds of God blow where they list.

A little-known letter of John Nelson describes his urge to preach, long before he had any kind of human commission, and one passage gives us an insight into the conditions. Feeling, as he says, 'like an owl in the desert' he nevertheless continued, because 'a few were bruised by the hand of God . . . and received the doctrine of *Conscious* Pardon.' In spite of warnings that he must preach less boldly, the young stone-mason persisted. It was inevitable to such a man, with such an experience of the grace of God. 'The people of the neighbouring towns', he says, 'have frequently sent for me, to hear of this new doctrine; for they were quite sure that no man could know his sins forgiven in this world. But I proved it from the written word of God, and from the doctrine of the Church of England. In a little time many cried out, "Lord, grant this thing unto me!" Our number of believers soon increased to thirty; then I found I must speak publicly among them, for the people thronged and filled my house.'[18]

That evidently was the mood of the people, in an England which has so often been described in terms that apply only to a small percentage of its population. Deep down in the hearts of the majority was a spiritual unrest and a hunger which craved satisfaction.

When once the spark was struck the flame spread rapidly even amongst what might have been thought to be non-inflammable material. In 1741 a Quaker's daughter found herself drawn to the house of William Shent where John Nelson was preaching. So moved was she by his words that on her return from Leeds to Skircoat Green she could talk of nothing but this 'new religion'. Her father, Abraham Kershaw, and his friend Blakey Spencer, were somewhat intrigued, and the latter went to Birstal to hear him for himself. He was completely convinced and desired, at once, that his friends and neighbours might know what had so strangely stirred him. When Nelson arrived the news of his coming had spread. 'The house of Blakey Spencer was found too strait to contain the people, they therefore adjourned to Abraham Kershaw's, but before the service commenced the people had augmented, insomuch as to render an out-of-door service necessary, accordingly the congregation stood in front of the house. A washing-tub, mouth downwards, served for a standing-place; and here, amid huge and tremendous rocks (with which the habitation was surrounded), far from din and tumult, in the most solitary spot imaginable, the Calder silently murmuring along the valley, and the distant hills echoing with the hymning chorus, Nelson preached the first Methodist sermon in the neighbourhood. The people were deeply affected; the old grey-headed man (he was near eighty years of age), the owner of the house, listened with deep concern, while the tears trickled down his furrowed cheek.'[19] The passage speaks for itself. No one could doubt its sincerity nor be surprised that Blakey Spencer and Abraham Kershaw threw open their houses to accommodate their neighbours who, with them, longed greatly to go on to know.

It was from this little group that Methodism spread, so that Skircoat Green has been called 'the mother church of Halifax'. In order to ensure that the travelling preachers might be fed and sheltered, when they rode across the hills to pay the little Society a welcome visit, they agreed that each should contribute a small sum to provide necessities. It is difficult for a modern world to realize what such visitation meant to the handful of people in a small isolated village, but it certainly helped to clarify their own findings and to lead them to realize they were part of a larger fellowship—the whole Christian Church in heaven and on earth.

It may be noticed in passing that the position in the three centres, London, Bristol, and Newcastle, was somewhat different. The frequent presence of John Wesley himself, and the acquiring of the Foundery, the Old Room, and the Orphan House meant that at an early date, he had his headquarters established. Though the part of the laity there was no less essential and distinguished, it was not so obvious in the early stages. When people who had been trained and guided at such centres went to settle in new towns the result was immediate. In 1749 Sarah Crosby joined the Society at the Foundery, London, and soon became a Class-Leader. Ten years later, a young woman became a member of her class, and removed in 1761 with her husband, Mr. Dobinson, to Derby. Sarah, now an intimate friend, went with her, and at once began to gather a class in the town. Very soon she had two hundred members—far too great a number, of course, to be contained within one class. It was, in short, a Society and a potential congregation. At first Mrs. Crosby was outfaced by her problem. A building and a preacher was an obvious necessity. To meet the immediate need she found herself conducting a service! 'I was not sure', she says, 'whether it was right for me to exhort in so public a manner, and yet I saw it impracticable to meet all these people by way of speaking to each individual. I therefore gave out an hymn, and prayed, and told them part of what the Lord had done for myself, persuading them to flee from all sin.'[20] How the two-fold problem of the woman preacher and the building of the chapel was solved is a separate consideration, but the incident shows the probable influence of a close association with John Wesley in the work at the Foundery.

The immediate problem was to provide even limited accommodation for those of the Methodist preachers' hearers whose lives were so radically changed that they described themselves in scriptural terms as 'born again' or 'new born'. The time soon came when opposition, organized or spasmodic, made the offering of a room in a house a dangerous procedure. However willing the person concerned may have been, it was soon obvious that he exposed himself to the risk of persecution and maltreatment by the mob or to prosecution for infringing the law as contained in the iniquitous Conventicle Act. Such dangers were not confined to the town-dweller, though for years certain parts of the countryside remained remote and undisturbed.

In some of these isolated places Methodism survived longer without separate buildings, and the members met together in humble surroundings without outward interference. The village of Tetney, for example, was particularly dear to the heart of John Wesley. Its little Society was grouped round the personality of Micah Elmoor, a shepherd. Having a brother living in Grimsby he asked him to persuade a Methodist preacher to visit the hamlet, and John Nelson came in 1743. In his journal he gives the following account: 'Some friends from Tetney and Cleathorpe prevailed with me to go to a shepherd's house near the sea-coast. There was a large company gathered together in that desert, and I opened my book at Galatians i. 3:—"Grace be unto you and peace from God the Father, and from our Lord Jesus Christ, who gave Himself for our sins, that He might deliver us from this present evil world, according to the will of God and our Father." I felt much of the Lord's presence, and the power of God was so great among us, that the people fell flat on their faces, or kneel'd down upon their knees, so that there was not one left standing; and their cry was so great that my voice could not be heard: then I fell upon my knees and called upon the Lord to heal the bones that were broken, and I believe many will praise God for that meeting to all eternity.'[21]

The strong personality of John Nelson, like the amazing figure of John Wesley, has often, quite unintentionally, overshadowed those who, living more circumscribed lives, were yet responsible for the tending of the lambs so long without a fold. It is well that they should have a proper place in local history.[22] When Wesley visited Tetney one might well expect that the shepherd would greet him with some trepidation, but this was not so. He had no cause to be ashamed of his stewardship: 'At noon I examined the little Society at Tetney', writes John Wesley recording his visit on 24th February 1747. 'I have not seen such another in England. In the class-paper (which gives an account of the contribution for the poor), I observed one gave eight pence, often ten pence a week; another thirteen, fifteen or eighteen pence; another, sometimes one, sometimes two shillings. I asked Micah Elmoor the leader (an Israelite indeed, who now rests from his labours), "How is this? are you the richest society in England?" He answered, "I suppose not, but all of us who are single persons have agreed together, to give both ourselves, and all we have to God: and we do it gladly; whereby we are able from time to time to entertain all the strangers that come to Tetney, who often have no food to eat, nor any friend to give them a lodging." '[23]

That was the spirit which sustained these little Societies though they were homeless so many years. In 1748 Micah Elmoor died, and the preaching was 'moved' from Coat Garth to the cottage of Thomas Ludlam, a labourer. For some years the walls of his humble little house sheltered the faithful few. Afterwards they met in Christopher Parker's until, at last, their numbers having increased, they went into a barn lent to them by George Lamming. This exodus occurred in 1783 and they used the barn for the next two years, until they were able to build a tiny chapel. That these simple but faithful and earnest people could have survived for forty years as a distinct entity, under such conditions, is a fact which no historian could avoid in an honest assessment of early Methodism, or indeed, of the Christian Church.

When the cottage-room was no longer adequate to house the increasing numbers, or when the threat of mob-violence or magisterial hostility became too strong, the little company searched high and low for some convenient place. Generally speaking they had little money and not much influence. The only thing of which they had an ample supply was the determination to continue. To them this new and vital experience was by far the most important thing in their lives.

Frequently the only shelter they could get was an old barn or laith, and such rough housing was not criticized but welcomed. In Ewood, John Sutcliffe had heard Mr. Wesley preach.[24] In 1774 he joined the class which had been formed. Removing to Pilling in 1779 he started a prayer-meeting in his own house. The prayer-meeting became a class, and the class grew so that John was driven to seek a place big enough to hold them all. He found it at Luddenden, not very far away. It happened that a dying man had sent to ask him to come and pray with him. He went, and on his way back, he noticed an old disused barn. He paced its floor; it was only twelve yards by seven, but the walls were good! It was the very thing—but it was not at Pilling or Midgley and the distance might be an objection to some—but not to John Sutcliffe! He moved to Luddenden. There was no house available, but he dug rooms under the barn, and there he lived, and moved within limits, yet had his being in a spacious world of spiritual adventuring, where God walked and talked with men.

There were countless stories as simple and as downright. They are not the annals of a vague and vanishing sect, but of a form of primitive Christianity which had its roots too deep to be destroyed by hardship or intolerance. In Warrington an old malt-kiln was rented as the first home for the Methodist Society.[25] In Ireland the first meeting-place was sometimes a corn-kiln, and at Donaghadee such shelter served until the luxury of a barn was possible.[26] In Bingley a blacksmith's shop was the only accommodation[27] until a room was secured over 'a big block of buildings', though the renting of this was a serious venture for it involved raising the sum of thirty shillings a year! In Harden a room over a stable was secured, and in Cullingworth, Mally Northrop told her husband she had set her heart on an old barn, near their house, for a chapel! He doubted the willingness of John Ellison the landlord, but Mally was not to be put off. To the astonishment of her neighbours, she succeeded, and John Ellison gave her the barn and the materials on condition that they should 'fettle it up' and that he should have the front pew in the gallery for his use 'for ever'! The incident is prophetic of the chapel-building period which was to follow, but it is typical of the character of the people who were, humanly speaking, the founders of the Methodist Church. In the first buildings they erected, they often changed the whole character of a locality by their action. The village of Denholme, for example, had become notorious for its cock-fighting and 'other brutal games', but in 1793 the Methodist Society bought the cock-pit, in order to build their first chapel.

In Belfast it was difficult to get a foothold. 'Where to preach in Belfast I did not know', wrote John Wesley on 21st April 1762. 'It was too wet to preach abroad, and a dancing-master was busily employed in the upper part of the market house till at 12 the Sovereign put him out, by holding his court there. While he was above I began below to a very serious and attentive audience.'[28] The problem was solved on a later occasion by the generous loan of the First Presbyterian Church in Rosemary Street.

At Dalkeith the Methodists worshipped for a time in the ex-Episcopalian chapel, though it 'was in a ruinous condition and completely out of repair'.[29] Over the room where they met there was a dove-cote, and underneath a stable!

In Grantham the conditions in those first years were difficult, and the fact that they were overcome is a testimony to the toughness of the men and women who conquered them. An iron-monger, Mr. Newcome, living in a house next to the Angel Inn, 'opened a place for the Methodists at the bottom end of the yard, next to the Back-lane, in which they continued to assemble for the space of sixteen years. . . . The preaching-place was a chamber over the smithy, and that not a very large one. The ascent was a movable step ladder, in a narrow passage, leading from the yard into the lane, at the end of the building.'[30] Apparently it was necessary during the service to set a watch, lest the ladder were pulled away, and the congregation left marooned. Rather pathetically, Thomas Cocking, in his description comments: 'The value of religion, however, was not diminished by the homeliness of the situation thus occupied; nor were the presence of the Saviour and His benefits withholden on that account.' One cannot but admire the choice of the word 'homeliness' when one discovers that the brazier and whitesmith at times decided to make the devotions in the upper room as difficult as possible. 'His mode of annoyance was to blow the bellows and hammer away on his steady [sic], during their occasional meetings for prayer and preaching on week nights.' The final remedy, when the strength of the Society permitted, was to take over the whole building and so eventually 'all the noisy Vulcanian implements were removed to a situation where their inharmonious sounds became less offensive'.

As a result of the preaching of the Wesleys in the Newcastle district in 1742, many farmers took back the 'Good News' to the surrounding villages, and amongst them was John Brown of Tanfield Lea, who became the pioneer preacher of the Derwent Valley. One of the places to which he came was Blanchland, a village that has been described as one of the most beautiful in

Northern England. Here Methodism was established, before the
coming of Wesley himself, and the services were maintained in
various farms at Allenshields, Newbiggin House, and Ropebarn.
On special occasions, such as Quarterly Meetings and Missionary
Meetings, the company gathered in a more spacious room at the
Craven Arms. It was long and narrow, and tradition says that at
such times it was crowded to excess, but it would appear, as in
many other cases in the eighteenth century, that 'mine host' the
innkeeper was not always hostile to the Methodists.[31]

In Manchester which was to become so great a stronghold of
later Methodism, the first meeting-place was in a desperately poor
quarter. As nearly as can be decided the house was on 'a rock on
the bank of the Irwell, exactly over the main sewer . . . on the
north side of Blackfriar's Bridge, immediately adjoining it'.[32]
There were, according to the evidence of Thomas Berry,
two public-houses, the *Rose and Crown*, and the *Ring of Bells*
in the yard, and 'a number of wood-built cottages, partly
thatched, on each side . . . but the house in which the room was
occupied for preaching, was built of brick, three stories high,
slated on the roof, and had a cellar in the back part of it. . . .
The ground floor was occupied as a joiner's shop; the two rooms
in the middle story, by my father and mother, who had not long
been married; and the garret by the person who allowed the use
of it for preaching. . . . The garret was generally well filled,
when there was preaching; and I have heard my mother say,
that she was often afraid of the roof falling through, for one of
the main beams was very much cracked.'[33] The interior of the
room, which had been taken by some 'young men' whom Charles
Wesley met in 1747[34] was a grim place. 'A person lived in the
room, where she had her spinning-wheel, her coals, her bed,
chairs and table.'[35] In his subsequent recollection of the
times when he had preached there Christopher Hopper said:
'I preached in an old garret that overhung the river, in the
neighbourhood of the old bridge. The coals were in one corner
of the room—the looms in another—and I was in danger of
breaking my neck in getting up to it. When the congregation
was collected the first evening, it did not consist of more than
twenty to thirty persons.'[36] It was certainly not a Gothic cathedral,
but it sheltered a few honest folk who were seeking to know the
will of God, and presently went out down the rickety steps to

D

do it to the best of their knowledge, and by the grace that had been given to them in that strange place.

Amongst the more unusual of these first Methodists was a little company at Maldon in Essex. The small coasters bringing coal from the north discharged their cargoes on the wharves along the Blackwater, and in a cottage on the quayside some of the seamen met with the villagers in Christian fellowship.[37] By 1753 they had so increased in numbers that they were compelled to seek bigger premises. A quaint old house stood empty. Rumour said that it had been built by the Romans, and apparently its rough walls were made of Roman bricks. Its door, Gothic in style, swung on hinges set in stone. The natives called it the Cats' Castle, because its last occupant had kept cats, twenty or more, in residence! It was a strange place with an uncertain history, but for three years the Methodists met there, and amongst them Mary Denny was outstanding. She was described as 'a woman possessed of much general information on religious subjects and of true piety'.[38] Her aunt had introduced Methodism to Maldon and entertained John Wesley.

The choice of these early meeting-places was neither a matter of taste nor convenience, but only of sheer necessity. Barns or blacksmiths' shops, garrets or the Cats' Castle—no place was rejected on the ground of its past history or its present state of dilapidation. It is not surprising, therefore, to discover that more than one theatre was 'taken over' by the Methodists. In Exeter the experiment was not a success. There is an account in Curwen's *History of Booksellers* which says: 'When the play-actors (of Exeter) were purchased out of the theatre by the Methodists who converted it into a chapel, and indicted them as vagrants, Brice, a bookseller, published a Poem, *The Playhouse Church; or New Actors of Devotion*, which so stirred up popular feeling that the Methodists were fain to restore it to its former possessors, who, under Brice's patronage, opened their house for some time gratis to all comers.'[39] Not much seems to be known of this incident, and the account of the financially-involved Mr. Brice cannot be taken too seriously.

The position in Birmingham was quite different. In a satirical mood, Hutton has described the occupation by the Methodists of various Birmingham theatres in the latter half of the eighteenth century.[40] In somewhat cavalier fashion he dismisses the question of origins, in a few words: 'After the institution of this sect by George Whitfield [*sic*], in 1738 they were first covered by the heavens, equally exposed to the rain and the rabble; and afterwards they occupied for many years a place in Steelhouse Lane, where the wags of the age observed "they were eat out by the bugs". They therefore procured a cast-off theatre in Moor Street, where they continued to exhibit till 1782; when, quitting the stage, they erected a superb meeting-house in Cherry Street, at the expense of £1200. . . .' Later, he gives an account of the theatre in Moor Street, which when it was built in 1740 'gave a spring to the amusement; in the day-time the comedian beat up the volunteers for the night' and did his best to entice the passers-by. Its popularity declined when a larger theatre was erected in King Street, and it was realized that the town could not support two London companies. 'It was afterwards found that the two theatres were more than the town chose to support (i.e. in 1752) therefore that in Moor Street was set for a Methodist meeting, where it was said, though it changed its audience, it kept its primitive use, continuing the theatre of farce.' Let the gibe pass for the moment, as Mr. Hutton tells us of the decline of the theatre in King Street, and the erection of another 'richly ornamented with paintings and scenery' in New Street. With all his sarcastic asides he tries to be an historian, and so is bound to conclude: 'Methodism still trod upon the heels of the player, for in 1786, the spirit of the stage drooping, the itinerant preacher took possession of the vacant theatre in King Street, erected his pulpit upon the stage, and converted pit, box and gallery into pews for the reception of such as chose to weep, smile or sleep.'

But what of those who chose in that strange place to begin to live! There were many such. That is why Miss Hutton is a good, if unconscious, commentator on her father's criticism when she writes later, of an exhibition she thinks cannot succeed. It may even fail before the building is erected to receive it— 'but if afterwards, it is no matter; it will serve for a Methodist meeting-house. That Society is flourishing enough to take possession of all public edifices whatever.'[41]

Perhaps the best answer to Hutton's sneering description of Methodism as a theatrical farce is to confront him with a little company of very poor people in Belfast. In 1764 since they had no chapel and were eager to worship God together, they took possession of an old, disused slaughter-house—not the modern hygienic *abattoir*, but a grim and nauseating place, hidden in a back street. Its very walls reeked, and unless it were strangely at variance with its contemporaries, its history would be coarse and brutal. It is possible to go in imagination to one of its services, for a record survives.[42] (If only Mr. Hutton could be there too!) Two soldiers are taking the service, and amongst the mixed crowd is a youth of eighteen who had come 'for sport!' Something beyond the reach of psychological analysis happened to the boy. The Methodists would have told you the heavens were opened to him, and he saw himself in the light of divine love. On his way home his companions jeered at the place and the service. To their astonishment he turned on them, asking if they were not ashamed to mock as they came out of that holy place! 'It's only an old slaughter-house', they said. 'Maybe', he said, 'but it was the house of God to me.'

The provision of cottage-rooms was not merely a question of the willingness of the owners to open them for meetings, nor was the acquisition of barns or other places just a matter of securing the rent. A set of complicated legal problems sprang up, to the dismay of the simple worshippers, and the surprise of John Wesley.

The attempt to secure uniformity in public worship, even by compulsion involving civil penalties, persisted from Elizabethan days till the Act of 1812 which repealed the Five Mile Act and the Conventicle Act.[43] During the first fifty years of Methodist development the chief difficulty lay in the interpretation of the Conventicle Acts of 1664 and 1670, and the Toleration Act of 1689. In the latter half of the seventeenth century there were many religious people who did not belong to the Church of England. Besides Roman Catholics, the Presbyterians, Brownists, Quakers, Baptists, and many other semi-religious semi-political sects formed a considerable portion of the population. The government was not unreasonably perturbed at the possible subversive activities of some of the more irregular and independent bodies. Having passed the Act of Uniformity (1662) which has been described as 'a powerful lethal weapon' and which had a cruel incidence on many ministers and preachers of irreproachable lives, it struck at their congregations through the Conventicle Act in 1664. This was designed to prevent the attendance of people 'at any unlawful assembly, conventicle or meeting, under colour or pretence of any exercise of religion in other manner than is allowed by the liturgy or practice of the Church of England, in any place within the Kingdom, dominion of Wales, and town of Berwick-upon-Tweed, at which conventicle, meeting or assembly, there shall be five persons or more assembled together, over and above those of the same household'. Severe penalties, including imprisonment, fines, and transportation could be imposed by any two justices of the peace or the chief magistrate of the place where the offence was committed. The details of this earlier Act only concern us in so far as they define the meaning of a 'conventicle' and the range of responsibility. This definition was retained and was operative during the whole of John Wesley's lifetime. The wording of the Act (sect. XI) was as follows: 'Every person who shall wittingly and willingly suffer any such conventicle, unlawful assembly or meeting aforesaid to be held in his or her house, outhouse, barn or room, yard or backside, woods or grounds, shall incur the same penalties and forfeitures as any other offender against this Act ought to incur, and be proceeded against, in all points, in such manner as any other offender against this Act ought to be proceeded against.' It is evident from the passage that the ban included meeting in the open air.

This first Conventicle Act was a temporary measure, but when the time-limit had ended, the 'Nonconformists' remained as determined, even as sturdy as ever. A new Act was therefore passed in 1670 which was, in general, the natural successor of those which had gone before. It added, however, to the definition, a few words which were to impose a heavy burden on the first Methodists. Not only did it repeat the description of inhabited houses with their yards and grounds, but it continued: 'or if it be in a house, field or place where there is no family inhabiting'.

The new Act was less severe in its penalties but much wider in its scope. Though the general punishment was to lie in the levying of fines, it was now possible for a little group of poor people, meeting to worship in a farm kitchen, to be deemed 'an unlawful assembly'. One doubts very much whether Micah Elmoor, the shepherd of Tetney, had any idea about this when he gathered his little band into the shepherd's hut at Coat Garth. Nor did the full significance of it dawn immediately on the keen mind of John Wesley. It will be found, later, that this legislation was the alleged justification for part of the persecution which the first Methodists suffered[44] but at present our concern is to see, as clearly as may be, the position with which they were faced in their earliest years.

The Act of 1670 was outrageous in that it placed almost unlimited power in the hands of a single justice. When he received what was described as 'notorious evidence and circumstance of the fact' he was able, without further consultation or trial, to convict and punish. Even if he made a mistake he was completely protected.[45] It was also permissible for him to issue a warrant to the constables or tithing-men to enter and, if need be, break open a house suspected of being a conventicle and arrest the people gathered in it. Even troops could be called in, as a final expedient.

In 1689 some relief was granted by the passing of the Toleration Act which exempted Protestant Dissenters who so called themselves. The title makes its purpose plain. 'An Act for Exempting their Majesties' Protestant Subjects, Dissenting from the Church of England, from the penalties of certain laws.' The Conventicle Act was specified as one to which this new measure referred. The tragedy was that, whilst it provided alleviation for those who professed themselves 'Protestant Dissenters', *it excluded such as still insisted they were members of the Church of England*. After 1689 meetings of Protestant Dissenters even in the so-called 'Conventicles' could be legalized, but the position of Methodists was unprotected.

The conditions under which such legalization could be obtained were clearly set out, and Sections XVI and XIX are therefore reproduced in order that they may be compared with some of the early licences which were obtained by the Methodist people who were anxious to keep the law, but determined to worship God in the fullness of their new and transforming spiritual experience.[46]

The Toleration Act of 1689 sanctioned if it did not bless the meetings of Dissenters, as is obvious from the following provisions:[47]

XVI. 'Provided always, and it is the true intent and meaning of the Act, that all the laws made and provided for the frequenting of divine service on the Lord's day, commonly called Sunday, shall be still in force, and executed against all persons that offend

against the said laws, except such persons come to some congregation, or assembly of religious worship, allowed or permitted
by this Act.

XIX. 'Provided always, that no congregations or assembly for
religious worship shall be permitted or allowed by this Act until
the place of such meeting shall be certified to the bishop of the
diocese, or to the archdeacon of that archdeaconry, or to the
justices of the peace at the general quarter sessions of the peace
for the county, city or place in which such meetings shall be
held, and registered in the said bishop's or archdeacon's court
respectively, or recorded at the said general or quarter sessions;
the register or clerk of the peace whereof respectively, is hereby
required to register the same, and to give certificate thereof to
such person as shall demand the same, for which there shall be
no greater fee nor reward taken, than the sum of sixpence.'

This seemed to clear the way for bona-fide 'Protestant Dissenters' who took the required precautions by licensing their
assemblies, but it is not true to say that the Conventicle Act was
now dead. In 1712 a further 'Act for preserving the Protestant
Religion, by better securing the Church of England, as by Law
Established', was sufficient proof. It deliberately forbade the
merely 'occasional conformity' of mayors, aldermen, recorders,
bailiffs, town clerks, common council men and other persons bearing any office of magistracy or place of trust' and penalized such
as attended conventicles or similar assemblies. The Dissenters
were thus excluded from the service of the State.[48]

The effect of all this legislation on early Methodism has been
summarized by Dr. J. S. Simon: 'From 1739 to 1791 Wesley lived
under the shadow of the Conventicle Act. At first he stoutly
denied that the Act applied to his meetings. Then he began to
yield, and some of his Preaching-houses, and private houses in
which the Methodists worshipped and met for "the exercises of
religion" were registered under the Toleration Act. At last he
had to abandon his position.'[49]

If the condition of the people in the little Societies, without any
constant or adequate supervision, is to be appreciated one must
consider some points in closer detail. Neither the people themselves, nor in many cases, the local magistrates were competent
to interpret the Acts. The nicety of the distinction between
Methodists still in association with the Church of England and

'Protestant Dissenters' was not at first appreciated. Presently there was the further question of the licensing of Methodist preachers. This does not come within our consideration except, in so far, as it raised a further distinction between the 'local' preacher, and the 'travelling' though not ordained preacher.[50] Even then a further discrimination had to be made between the 'local' preacher who decided to wander far afield on self-determined tours, and the man who was definitely appointed by John Wesley himself. During the formative years of what was to become a definite and distinct communion of the Christian Church, it was inevitable that such problems should remain for years undetermined, and that the usage and circumstance should vary widely.

On 15th January 1750, for example, a long and careful inden-ture with reference to the purchase of ground at Allendale refers to 'the Christian Society or Congregation of protestants . . . commonly called or known by the name of Methodists', and authorizes them to 'build a Meeting House or place of Worship for the use of the said Society in the Exercise of their Religious Worship'.[51] The document, which is carefully drawn up, evi-dently by a competent solicitor, raises no question at all of the legality of such a meeting-place.

On 19th June 1750 John Wesley wrote from Dublin to Mrs. Gallatin, the wife of Colonel Gallatin, then stationed in Man-chester: 'The reason why we refused for several years to license any of the places, wherein we preached was this. We supposed it could not be done without styling ourselves Dissenters. But the Recorder of Chester showed us this was a mistake, and procured a licence for Thomas Sidebotham's house in that county, although he (then as well as at other times) professes himself a member of the Established Church. Since then we have licensed the house at Leeds and some others.'[52]

A considerable number of these early licences survive[53] and comparison shows that they differed in the style adopted. Gener-ally the situation was accepted and the term 'Protestant Dissenters' used, but at other times it was avoided and licence granted, perhaps through ignorance or oversight.

A noteworthy case which shows how a group of humble people were involved, occurred at Rolvenden, Kent, in 1760.[54] In Layne farm-house sixteen Methodists had gathered to worship.

One of the 'travelling preachers', John Morley, was present and with him were Thomas Osborne the farmer and Jane his wife; Philip Norris, yeoman; Thomas Reeve the elder, shoemaker; Thomas Reeve the younger, shoemaker; Henry Bigg, thatcher; Joseph Bigg; John Bigg, labourer; George Pike, servant; Betty Vine; Mary and Elizabeth Bigg and Hannah Young, all spinsters; and Ambrose and Hannah Buckland, who had walked in from Benenden. Information was laid against them to the magistrate, Robert Monypenny of Maytham Hall. The informant was a yeoman farmer named Thomas Witherden. The defendants were charged under the Conventicle Act, 1670, and according to the records were fined a total amount of £43 10s. od. which included the crippling sum of £20 for the poor preacher, £20 for Thomas Osborne the owner of the house and five shillings each for the remaining fourteen. The right to appeal to the Quarter Sessions was exercised, but Charles Whitworth, M.P., and the bench of magistrates at Maidstone confirmed the convictions, and some-what savagely, ordered in addition 'the payment of £8 treble costs in each case'. The three appellants, Thomas Osborne, Philip Norris and Thomas Reeve pluckily decided to take the case to the Court of the King's Bench and there the convictions, to the astonishment of Mr. Monypenny and Mr. Whitworth, were quashed. The case attracted considerable attention.[55] Naturally John Wesley was gratified by the result and wrote to Brother Charles, stressing the importance of the verdict. 'It is of more consequence than our people seem to apprehend. If we do not exert ourselves, it may drive us to that bad dilemma—Leave preaching, or leave the Church. We have reason to thank God it is not come to this yet. Perhaps it never may.'[56]

Such were his sentiments on 23rd June, three weeks after the case had been heard in the Court of the King's Bench, but it does not require much imagination to picture the struggle of the little communities scattered all over the country. Many of them had passed through times of severe persecution and had no knowledge of higher courts of justice nor any hope save to gather their broken chattels, lick their wounds, and begin all over again, to practise the faith which refused to surrender.

Another *cause célèbre* came to the King's Bench in 1766.[57] The Derbyshire Justices had refused to license a Methodist Meeting-House, and application was made to the Court of the King's

Bench for a Writ of Mandamus to order the Justices to make the registration. The complete report of the case is available,[58] but the arguments against granting the writ were based on the fact that the parties had not specified their denomination as Protestant Dissenters—'Methodists do not dissent from the Church of England', it was asserted, 'but only pretend to observe her doctrine and discipline with greater purity than their neighbours', further that the parties were not of the neighbourhood, and that they 'do not appear to have complied with the terms of the Toleration Act by taking the oaths and making the Declaration'. The Court, in spite of these objections, granted the writ, but protected the Justices by stressing the fact that, in spite of the registration, the persons resorting to the meeting-house would be liable if they did not bring themselves within the Act of Toleration.

The idea of these legal intricacies coming to the notice of the simple but sincere people who only wanted to worship God in their own way, would be ludicrous, if it had not been sometimes tragic in its consequences.

It is clear that Wesley himself was often perplexed but quite determined to resist any easy acceptance of the description 'Protestant Dissenter'. By this attitude, of course, he put himself outside the benefits of the Toleration Act, but he remained still in communion with the Church of England. As the years passed it became more and more obvious that this relationship was becoming strained. In some cases, it appeared altogether theoretical, if not, indeed, artificial.

He is by no means clear in his instruction to his preachers. Writing to Samuel Wells, on 28th January 1779, he says: 'According to the Act of Toleration—1. You are required to certify to the Registrar of the Bishop's Court or the Justices the place of your meeting for divine worship. This is all you have to do. You ask nothing at all of the Bishops or Justices. 2. The Registrar or Clerk of the Court is "*required* to register the same, and to give a certificate thereof to such persons as shall demand the same; for which there shall be no greater fee or reward taken than sixpence". I advise you to go once more to the Sessions, and say, "Gentlemen, we have had advice from London: we desire nothing at all of you; but we *demand* of your clerk to register this place and to give a certificate thereof, or to answer the refusal at

his peril." '[59] Here seems, on first sight, to be a confident assertion of rights and privileges, but it should be noticed that there
is no description of the place as being for the use of Protestant
Dissenters or otherwise. Sometimes, we repeat, the licence was
granted without this, but usually either innocently without
knowledge of its implications, or under protest, the applicants
were obliged to accept the classification which Wesley opposed.

In the parallel problem of the licensing of Methodist preachers,
he maintained strongly that several who were licensed were 'not
licensed as Dissenters' and in a letter to the Rev. Thomas Adam,
rector of Wintringham, dated 19th July 1768, he cited several
cases to prove his point. He concludes: 'When others applied
for a licence, the Clerk of Justice said, "I will not license you,
but as Protestant Dissenters." They replied, "We are of the
Church; we are not Dissenters: but if you will call us so we cannot
help it." They did *call* them so in their certificates, but this did
not *make* them so. They still *call themselves* members of the Church
of England; and they believe themselves so to be.'[60] There is no
doubt that this was his own view, and the view he proclaimed,
whether it applied to buildings or to men.

In spite of all these technical difficulties the people went on
building each other up, and emerging with many a struggle from
the cottage to the barn, and from the barn to the independence
and dignity of the first chapels which they built.

Towards the end of his life John Wesley realized that it was
no longer possible to continue the legal contention. On 3rd
November 1788 he consulted Mr. Clulow, the attorney, 'on that
execrable Conventicle Act. . . . We are both clearly convinced
that it was safest to license all our chapels and all our travelling
preachers, not as dissenters, but simply as preachers of the
Gospel.'[61] Evidently Lawyer Clulow had put the case strongly,
and made the old man see that, until the Act was altered, there
was only one way to ensure peaceful progress. He had taken a lot
of convincing. Even in the preceding July, he had written to
Sarah Mallet saying: 'I do not require any of our preachers to
license either themselves or the places where they preach.'[62]
Two years later, on 26th June 1790, he wrote a strong protest to
the Bishop of Lincoln pointing out that 'the Methodists in
general . . . are members of the Church of England. They hold all
her doctrines, attend her service, and partake of her Sacraments.

. . . Do you ask, "Who drives them out of the Church?"
Your Lordship does; and that in the most cruel and disingenuous
manner. They desire a licence to worship God after their own
conscience. Your Lordship refuses it, and then punishes them
for not having a licence!'[63]

The struggle had gone on for more than fifty years, and it
seemed likely to continue, unless the Methodists acknowledged
themselves as a separate communion. Like many of his successors
John Wesley resented the notion of being a member of a 'sect'.
As late as July 1790 the old man heard, with grief, of the sufferings
of his people. In desperation he wrote to William Wilberforce
asking him to speak to Mr. Pitt himself, about the anomaly of a
Toleration Act that aided and abetted intolerance: 'Last month,'
he said, 'a few people met together in Lincolnshire to pray and
praise God in a friend's house. There was no preaching at all.
Two neighbouring Justices fined the man of the house twenty
pounds. I suppose he was not worth twenty shillings. Upon
this his household goods were distrained and sold to pay the fine.
He appealed to the Quarter Sessions; but all the Justices averred
the Methodists could have no relief from the Act of Toleration
because they went to church, and that so long as they did so the
Conventicle Act should be executed upon them.'[64] The letter
cites the case of a preacher whose licence was held by the magistrate to be good for nothing because he was a Churchman.
'Now, Sir,' John Wesley continues, 'what can the Methodists do?
They are liable to be ruined by the Conventicle Act, and they
have no relief from the Act of Toleration!' There were two
obvious courses, either the Methodists must separate from the
Church of England or accept the situation and its limitations.
In the end, but not till after Wesley's death, they were compelled
to sever their slender link with the Church they still loved, and
to press, with increasing urgency, for the amendment of the Act.
The severance came, virtually, in 1795, with the Plan of Pacifica-
tion, and the legal restrictions were lifted by the Earl of Dart-
mouth's Emancipation Act in 1812. In this connexion it should
be recorded that the rejection of a proposed reactionary measure
in the House of Lords in 1811 and the eventual drawing up of
the new Act was largely forwarded by Thomas Allan and his
friend Joseph Butterworth, M.P., who was a staunch Methodist.
As Thomas Jackson far too mildly says: 'It has secured to the

Wesleyan ministry and societies more ample protection than they heretofore enjoyed.'[65] Had he been thinking of those long years, with their terrible periods of persecution, his words must have flamed in celebration of a great deliverance. The agonies of many a little Methodist Society have been too little realized by the historians of the past. It was not the spectacular episodes in the Midlands or Cornwall which were the most serious obstacles to their progress, but rather the long-drawn-out and partially understood sufferings of humble people over whom there loomed the constant threat of punishment. The most tragic feature of their experience lay in the fact that they never fully understood why they should be liable to such heart-breaking penalties when all they asked was to worship God, together, in their own homes, in peace.

How did they survive and why? Only the consideration of their spiritual experience and their passionate conviction of its reality can provide an answer. In the little hamlet of Farnley Tyas in 1780 John Schofield attended a service on Easter Sunday and, suddenly conscious of his sin, 'began there and then pleading the merits of the risen Lord, and presently came to know the power of His resurrection'. He and two neighbours opened their houses for a regular fortnightly preaching service. One of them, Joseph Shaw's, was 'licensed for preaching'. Whether Joseph subscribed to being a 'Protestant Dissenter' no one can say; the thing, obviously, that mattered supremely to these people was that nothing should hinder them from their direct approach to the Source of their new life and, since they had been 'awakened' so recently, and were but new-born babes in the faith, they clung to one another in those first tremendous adventures. The house of Joseph Shaw had been built in 1717 and a 'slab-stone' was built into the wall over the door. It offered, in silence, a message to the passer-by:

> Remember, thou that passeth here,
> Thy naked soul must soon appear
> To give account before thy God
> For all thy actions good and bad.

The verse might have been better, but it warned Joseph's visitors that he was a man whose horizon was not bounded by the hills round Huddersfield. There was an eternal quality in his new

life, and it mattered more than anything else to him—and, he
believed, to them.

It would seem that the inhabitants of Farnley Tyas had
circumvented the Toleration Act and, with Yorkshire thrift,
saved two sixpences, for only one of the three cottages was
licensed.[66] It happened, on one occasion, that the service was
being held in one of the unlicensed houses when a drunken
mob, no doubt egged on by an 'informer', came to storm the
place. The wife of Joseph Shaw came out at the head of the
congregation and led them to the licensed house where the service
was continued. The little congregation, marching in procession,
passed the inn, the headquarters of the opposition, singing
confidently,

> Jesus, the name high over all
> In hell or earth or sky.

On the premises, duly registered, no one could legally molest
them. The mob, subdued and humbled, melted away and the
worshippers, within the circle of the law, remained undisturbed.

The normal progress of Methodism, as has already been seen,
was from the cottage-room or farm-kitchen to some larger
temporary shelter. It was natural that the next stage should be
the building of actual chapels, though it is impossible to suggest
any date as an absolute line of cleavage. The growth of the
Societies varied with the time of the planting of the seed, with
the soil, i.e., the character of the first members, and with the
climate, as represented by the reaction of their neighbours to
the new phenomena.

Sometimes the Wesleys themselves took the first steps to provide
a preaching-house, but usually it was the people who offered or
secured the premises.

In 1747 Charles Wesley found many earnest people in Dublin,
and saw an opportunity of preaching to the weavers if only he
could get some place for regular ministration.[67] In Cork Street
he went to the Weavers' Store, where the looms were kept, and
there preached to more than five hundred. The crowd unable
to get in was so great that he was driven into the fields for his
next meeting. Encouraged by his reception, he decided to buy
Dolphin's Barn, which had been used as a weaver's shop. The
ground floor, forty-two feet by twenty-four, was converted into

a 'preaching-room with two rows of benches and a pulpit at the end'. The upper rooms were used to house the preachers. Incidentally he wrote to his brother[68] and to Ebenezer Blackwell[69] telling him of his intention, and asking their opinion of the venture.

Usually, however, it was the people who acted for themselves. When John Wesley rode to Worcester in March 1769, he confessed to being 'a little tired'. He continues: 'I began preaching about six in the riding-house. Abundance of people were deeply attentive; but towards the close a large number of boys made a great noise. When we came out, men and boys joined together in shouting and pushing to and fro. Many were frightened but none hurt. Hitherto could Satan come, but no further.'[70] It is obvious the local Methodists had secured the place, which though temporary, at least made his service possible. It was, to say the least of it, an unusual choice for a preaching-service. 'The Riding House is an old building in Frog Lane, used for teaching soldiers riding, and for administering to them the discipline of flogging. The building has an open timber roof, and would hold three or four hundred people standing. Mr. Bell, one of the founders of the Bell and Lancaster system of education, lectured in the old house, which is still the property of the Government.'[71]

Much later, in 1785, the *Journal* refers to Copperhouse Chapel, which astonished even John Wesley.[72] The Cornish Methodists at Hayle had secured a circular building with a conical roof, and windows set high in the wall. For more than twenty years they worshipped in this strange 'tabernacle' surrounded by slag-heaps from the copper-works, and sheltered, to some degree, by the hard, brittle, brick-like cubes which had been cast out as dross.[73]

It may be possible now to arrive at a general view of such chapel-building as occurred during the first fifty years.

Though there were no general rules for building the first Methodist chapels, it was gradually understood that Mr. Wesley had his definite views. Indeed he issued directions which, perhaps fortunately, were not always received or obeyed.

The plan he desired the builders to follow had eight main principles: '1. Build all Preaching-houses, where the ground will permit, in the octagon form. It is best for the voice, and on many accounts more commodious than any other. 2. Let every octagon house be built after the model of Yarm; every square house after the model of Bath or Scarborough. 3. Let the roof rise only one-third of its breadth: this is the true proportion. 4. Have doors and windows enough; and let all the windows be sashes, opening downwards. 5. Let there be no Chinese paling, and no tub-pulpit, but a square projection, with a long seat behind. 6. Let there be no pews, and no backs to the seats, which should have aisles on each side, and be parted in the middle, by a rail running all along to divide the men from the women, just as at Bath. 7. Let all Preaching-houses be built plain and decent; but not more expensive than is absolutely necessary. 8 Wherever a Preaching-house is built see that lodgings for the Preachers be built also.'[74]

The plans have certainly the marks of austerity and utility, but it is a mercy that they were not so completely received or obeyed as to result in mass-production or even, at an early stage, in pre-fabrication. As it was, his instructions influenced the next generation very strongly, and it was generally accepted that 21 to 18 should be the proportion of length to breadth in all new chapels.

The early Methodists, however, in spite of their veneration for him, were men and women of strong character, who were inclined at times to draw their own plans. Moreover, they were not in constant touch with any kind of headquarters. At this stage in their development this was not altogether a disadvantage. Indeed, in their earliest attempts, there are marks of courage and personality which are welcome. The people who decided to live their lives according to rule, might have become stereotyped had they not taken liberty to express themselves even in their crude buildings. Nothing could have been more fatal than a mass-produced spiritual experience. This tragedy did not happen, as will be seen presently, but one of the lesser reasons for this may have been that the local Societies developed freely, even in the matter of erecting their first permanent buildings. This, of course, applied only to the early period when technical advice, expensive materials and expert craftsmanship were equally unavailable.

The need of separate buildings was more apparent as the years passed. It is not true to say, as has often been said, that this was because so many parish churches were shut against the Methodists. 'Had all the churches of the land been open to them', Thomas

Jackson wrote, 'the means which they felt it their duty to adopt for the revival and extension of scriptural Christianity, would have rendered other places of worship indispensably necessary.'[75] There were class-meetings and band-meetings, love-feasts, watch-nights, prayer-meetings, week-night preaching, and preaching at five o'clock in the morning. All these fell outside the scope of statutory services and, generally speaking, outside the sympathy or understanding of the contemporary parish priest. As in so many other circumstances, it seems probable that the entire situation might have been dealt with very differently by an adaptable and enlightened clergy. It is certain that it was never the original intention of Wesley or his first followers to break away from the Church they loved and of which, for so long, they felt themselves to be a part.

In 1752 the first Methodist chapel in Halifax was erected. The property was made over to six trustees: Titus Knight, Thomas Dickenson, Richard Booth, Blakey Spencer, Jeremiah Swift and John Hallowell 'who had advanced the money, by way of security'.[76] It was a simple building, fourteen yards by ten, and 'the structure was not underdrawn, the funds not allowing it, which occasionally put the congregation to inconvenience'. John Hallowell lived in a cottage, next door, so that he could 'put up' the travelling preachers when they came. Inspired, no doubt, by the example of Halifax, the Methodists at Stainland, in 1755, decided to build. The feeling of the majority of the people is no doubt rightly interpreted by the local historian: 'It was erected with the probable intention of being a chapel of ease under the establishment. It is vested in trustees, and the deeds require the performance of the Church of England service. A dispute, however, arose among the trustees soon after its erection, when those who strenuously opposed its becoming a chapel of ease gained the ascendancy. Since that time it has been occupied, according to the temporary pre-eminence of each party, both by the ministers of the Wesleyan Methodist body, and by those of the Independent persuasion.'[77]

According to Myles' *Chronological History of Methodism*—which, in spite of minor inaccuracies, is generally reliable—there were one hundred and twenty-six preaching-houses in England by 1771. Ninety-five had been built in eleven years, from 1760 to 1771. In this period two years appear to have been outstanding, for in 1766 nineteen new chapels were opened and in 1770 no less than thirty.[78] By this time two editions of the Chapel Model Deed had appeared,[79] and John Wesley was making a valiant attempt to guide, if not to direct the fervour of the chapel-builders.

In actual fact he would not have admitted the use of that last phrase. He spoke of 'the Foundery' not by accident, but by design. It was, as the Rev. John Telford has pointed out, 'a secular (very secular) building adapted for Methodist worship' whereas 'the West Street building was a consecrated chapel'.[80] Generally he called the first places of worship 'Preaching-place' or 'Preaching-house' and the premises sometimes included buildings used, for example, as a school at Kingswood, an Orphanhouse at Newcastle, or a clinic, a book-shop and a hostel at the Foundery. In the first fifty years the terms were not clearly defined, but in the following half century the use of the term 'chapel' was generally accepted, and was presently to become, in many places 'church'.[81]

The days when William Edington, Benjamin Phillips, Jonas Moore and his wife, John Parkman, Rebecca Roe and Samuel Richardson formed the whole Methodist Society in Frome passed. Facing persecution and abuse they grew strong enough to build a chapel. 'The place behind town for many years was uncomfortably crowded . . . they therefore purchased a piece of ground on an elevated spot at Keyford . . . and erected a place capable of seating 420 persons; and though they were but few, and comparatively poor, yet by their own arduous exertions they built the place, and it was opened in 1779, by Mr. R. Carr Brackenbury.'[82]

The little company that met in the 'Long Baulk', over two cottages at Scarr Hall, Slaithwaite, stood firm.[83] The faith of 'Blind Mary' who had so long 'testified' at their love-feasts was justified, and the congregation needed no longer to climb the flight of stone steps to the first landing and then mount the wooden ladder that led to the 'room'. It was many a year before their dreams were realized in wood and stone, but they did not waver, for whether it were in 'Long Baulk' or in 't'Chapel' their aim was the raising of the city whose builder and architect is God.

The early efforts of the chapel-builders were either pathetically crude and unlovely in appearance, or sometimes florid and much more repellent. Such a statement must not be taken as wholesale condemnation of the people responsible. In a few cases they were to blame, and often they yielded to some strange inhibition that beauty was dangerous, but for the most part they were cramped by their own circumstance.

In 1839 Thomas Jackson, living at a time when he could form his conclusions from the evidence of the people themselves as well as from the chapels they built, said: 'In these buildings of primitive Methodism, elegance of architecture was little studied. They were plain and substantial, intended for use and not for ornament. The most remarkable circumstance connected with them was the amplitude of their accommodation for the poor. The pulpits also were large, and contained a bench of considerable length for the use of the Preachers who might be expected successively to address the congregations at the quarterly watch-nights, and other similar services. The preaching in these sanctuaries was plain, pointed, searching and powerful. The singing was lively. . . .'[84]

Such was the judgement of one whose youth had been lived at the end of the eighteenth century, as the first period of chapel-building came to its close. A closer investigation of some selected cases will help in the understanding and appreciation of the people concerned.

The bases which were established in London, Bristol, and Newcastle must be considered first, although Wesley's personal influence was here paramount.

In London, the Foundery was secured in 1739, and although the Old Room in Bristol was the first Methodist chapel built, it is claimed that the first opened for divine worship was in London.[85] In Windmill Hill, Moorfields, then surrounded by pasture-land, but now in the heart of the City, the Government Foundery stood. The Marlborough campaigns had resulted in the defeat of the French and the subsequent arrival in London of cannon beyond repair, but suitable for recasting. The process was regarded as a public spectacle, and in 1716 before a great crowd, including many distinguished people, the operation was commenced. An explosion occurred, and many lives were lost.[86] For twenty-three years the building lay derelict—'a ruin in the midst of pasture-land'. The description of the locality is too astonishing to the modern Londoner to omit. 'At the north-west corner of the fields in which the building stood, the Lord Mayor's dog-house was situated, in which the city-hounds were kept. . . . Close by stood a toll-gate, called the Dog-Bar. The ground situated southward from the Foundery . . . was (partly) laid out as pleasure-grounds, with walks and promenades, shaded by trees, and in the summer-time decorated with flowers and shrubs.'[87]

It was essential that Wesley should have some place in which he could preach in London, without depending on the consent of a local incumbent. The tremendous change in his own spiritual experience had quickened his whole ministry. It is true as Tyerman observes[88] that from April to December 1739 he preached 'five hundred sermons', but even if the number had been five thousand, the important thing is that every sermon after his 'conversion' had in it a new note of urgency and conviction. Perhaps it was not surprising that so many churches shut their doors against this tempestuous prophet! One wonders whether all the doors, even today, would have swung widely open. Certainly the common people detected the new note, and it brought hope to their despondent hearts. In November 'vast multitudes' gathered to hear him, but he was no itinerant showman. He knew, from bitter experience, that spiritual struggles could be protracted, and he could never be satisfied with 'awakening' a crowd, and leaving its individual units, like new-born babes, untended. Where then could he gather even a few of them, to help them through their growing-pains to spiritual manhood?

'Again and again he was urged to make use of the old ruined Foundery, and at last he consented.'[89] At first, apparently, he preached to great crowds within the battered walls. Then he was persuaded to buy the 'vast, uncouth heap of ruins' for £115 and, although he was not hampered by modern economic restrictions, he had to find a considerable sum for repairs and reconstruction. Friends lent him the purchase-money, and the people poured in their little gifts. In three years these amounted to £480, and the debt remaining was less than £300, a result which is, in itself, a commentary on the goodwill and earnestness of these first Methodists in London.

The old ruin was transformed—not, perhaps, into a cathedral, but certainly into a house of God. They came, these first eager worshippers, along the lanes, lit only by the lanterns they carried, to the early morning service at five o'clock. The building[90] for which they were so thankful, measured forty yards by thirty-three. 'It had two front doors, one leading directly to the chapel, and the other to the preacher's house, the school and band-room. It held fifteen hundred people, but was without pews, though a slight concession was made by putting on the ground floor, immediately before the pulpit, a dozen seats with back rails, appropriated to female worshippers. Under the front gallery were the free seats for women; and under the side galleries, the free seats for men. The front gallery was used exclusively by females, and the side galleries for males.' John Wesley makes it quite clear that he was training the people in what he conceived to be the ways of the early Christians. 'From the beginning the men and women sat apart, as they always did in the primitive church; and none were suffered to call any place their own, but the first comers sat down first. They had no pews; and all the benches for rich and poor were of the same construction.'[91]

Behind the chapel was a band-room, holding three hundred people. It was used almost incessantly for early morning service, the 'charity-school', class-meetings, prayer-meetings, a clinic with its 'electrifying machine' and a bookstall. Above were rooms which sheltered Susanna Wesley till she died, and where Wesley himself usually lived when in London. In addition to all this there were quarters for the assistant preachers, the domestic staff and, beyond, a coach-house and stable, with yard. At the south end, as shown in contemporary engravings, there was 'a walled garden in which were some forest trees, giving the premises the appearance of the country'. In spite of Silas Told's description of it in June 1740[92] it seemed to have been a comprehensive and, at the time, a desirable property for the modest sum of £800. It evidently endeared itself to the homeless Methodist people because, for years after City Road Chapel was built in 1777, they referred to the new and imposing building as 'the New Foundery'.

It has sometimes been a mistake to focus attention on the inspired and commanding though slight figure who often preached at the early morning service, and was riding westward long before London was awake. He remains incomparable in many ways, but it was the fidelity and growth of the people whom he loved and so wisely led, which made what might have been a vanishing congregation into an abiding Church.

In Bristol the details of the beginnings are different, and yet, through the whole story, one can discern the same steadfast purpose. Within two months of his arrival in Bristol in 1739, John Wesley was forced by circumstance to obtain an independent and permanent centre. There were already 'religious societies' meeting in Nicholas Street, Baldwin Street, Weavers' Hall, Castle Street, Gloucester Lane, and Back Lane. They had been affected by the preaching of Whitefield, but were without any real organization. Wesley visited them, conducted love-feasts, and expounded the Sermon on the Mount, the Acts of the Apostles, and the Epistle to the Romans. In these Societies occurred most of the remarkable 'scenes' which have baffled so many investigators, and which certainly did not please Wesley himself. How far they were forms of hysteria, occurring in neurotic subjects, has never been satisfactorily decided.[93] The clergy of Bristol were, generally speaking, opposed to both Whitefield and Wesley, and the exaggerated accounts of what were certainly disturbing circumstances, stiffened the opposition. Most of the churches were closed but, on the other hand, the Religious Societies were crowded out. Wesley sought a site on which he could raise a suitable building, as a centre for his work. One can imagine the relief with which he fixed on the land between the Horsefair and Broadmead, with its garden and 'a little tenement lodge'. His decision to build marks an important point in the religious history of England. It is doubtful whether Wesley realized the full significance of his action, but it was to lead to 'the formation of one of the greatest Protestant churches in the world.'

On Wednesday, 9th May 1739, he writes: 'We took possession of a piece of ground near St. James's churchyard, in the Horsefair, where it was designed to build a room large enough to contain both the societies of Nicholas and Baldwin Streets, and such of their acquaintance as might desire to be present with them, at such times as the Scripture was expounded. And on *Saturday*, the 12th the first stone was laid, with the voice of praise and thanksgiving.'[94] 'At first the intention was that it should be merely a "society-room".'[95]

Unfortunately, he appointed eleven trustees or feoffees, without sufficient definition of their functions. He had to pay the work-men on the building himself, and was soon confronted with a bill of £150 which he had to discharge. His friends urged him to alter the deed, fearing that the men to whom the property had been conveyed would be able to control him 'and', as he bluntly said, 'if I preached not as they liked, be able to turn me out of the room I had built'. Needless to say, the deed was cancelled and he assumed control.

On Sunday, 3rd June 1739, the first meeting was held and Wesley's words are significant of the unrest in the other 'religious societies': 'In the evening, not being permitted to meet in Baldwin Street, we met in the shell of our new society-room.'[96] The accommodation provided in the original building was limited but since much, if not all, was changed by the reconstruction in 1748 it is impossible to describe it in detail. There was most probably, in addition to the 'society-room', some simple pro-vision for the housing of John Wesley and his brother. In 1748 what would today be called a 'scheme' was prepared to enlarge and fortify the existing, hastily-constructed rooms. A sum of £230 was collected, five stewards appointed and a larger insurance policy—for £500—taken out. This New Room held twice as many people and was planned for community life. It has been suggested that Wesley was influenced in his planning by the Moravian settlements at Herrnhut and Herrnhaag.[97]

In these first enterprises at Bristol and London there is something which is prophetic not only of the future development of the Methodist Church as a whole, but also of the quality of the people who were to form it. When Wesley had planned and built the room at Bristol, someone had to pay for it. By 1742 the little Society expressed its sense of mutual responsibility, and from the suggestion of Captain Foy came the idea of a weekly payment by the class-members. The details will be considered later,[98] and it is sufficient at this stage to notice that Christian fellowship was already beginning to mean something more than the exchange of opinions or social intercourse. The members began to bear one another's burdens, to care for other people, and in under-taking mutual responsibility to grow into a closer intimacy.

In the northern centre at Newcastle the position was simpler. On 4th December 1742, Wesley was offered and accepted a piece of ground outside Pilgrim Street Gate. Three days later Mr.

Stephenson, a merchant, offered him a piece of his garden adjoining the site. He accepted this also, not wishing to withdraw from his previous agreement. On 20th December the first stone of the new 'house' was laid.[99] It is significant that in recording the day he ends: 'Three or four times in the evening I was forced to break off preaching that we might pray and give thanks to God.' This suggests the mood of the people. It would never be an easy thing to interrupt John Wesley when he was 'proclaiming the Gospel'. Nothing less than an irresistible wave of thankfulness could have swept his friends into such an action!

The cost of the building was estimated at £700 and Wesley had twenty-six shillings in hand to meet the bills.[100] He was not daunted nor were the Society. Three months after the foundation stone was laid he opened the building, though it had not yet roof, doors, or windows. He preached on the Rich Man and Lazarus, and not only was there 'a great multitude' present to hear him, but most of them stayed on, in spite of the weather, to a watch-night service.[101] In 1746 he established the Orphan House on a trust, the seven members of which were Henry Jackson, weaver, William Mackford, corn-dealer, both of Newcastle; John Haughton, weaver of Chinley End; Thomas Richards, late of Trinity College, Oxford; Jonathan Reeves, baker, late of Bristol, and Henry Thornton, gentleman, of Gray's Inn, London. The deed is recorded in full by Luke Tyerman.[102] Again the nature of this northern centre is as comprehensive as that in London or Bristol. It was at once a place of worship, a school and orphanage, a hospital, a hostel, and in some senses a theological institution!

In leaving the account of these first bases for the pivotal Methodist Societies, it may be noted that the first Methodist chapel in Wales was opened by John Wesley in Cardiff in 1743. In his *Journal* he gives the local Society full credit for the brave enterprise: 'Friday, May 6, 1743.—I preached at eleven in the new room, which the society had just built in the heart of the town; and our souls were sweetly comforted together.'[103] The building survived until 1829, when a new chapel was erected on the same site, in Church Street.[104]

In Ireland it was not till 1748 that a site was secured in Dublin and the first chapel built by the Irish Methodists. It was of considerable size, and a generous contribution was made towards the cost by Mr. Lunell, who afterwards became decidedly Calvinistic in his views. When John Wesley came to preach he described it in his customary terms: 'The house here is nearly the same size, and of the same form, with that of Newcastle; but having deep galleries on three sides, it will contain a larger number of people'.[105] It was built in a favourable position, and had a minister's house on either side. Later, a girls' school, a book-room, and an almshouse were added. It was reputed to be big enough to accommodate a thousand people and included rooms for classes and band-meetings.[106]

In Scotland the first Methodist chapel was at Aberdeen. 'In 1764 the Society acquired a piece of ground near the north-east end of Queen Street, and upon it erected an octagon chapel.'[107] Though it was large enough for ordinary occasions, it could not accommodate the crowds who came to hear Wesley and he usually preached in the College Kirk, and in the open-air, as well as in the 'New Room'.

By 1752, then, it is evident that Methodism had permanent chapels established in three centres in England and also in Wales and Ireland. The English and Irish centres were designed to maintain a community life as well as to provide accommodation for preaching and public worship. It remains, now, to consider the attempts of the more isolated Societies to secure permanent premises, and so to ensure their continuity.

The little group which was responsible for building the first chapel in Armley, for example, is worth studying in some detail.[108] When the first Methodist preachers came to the district there was nowhere for them to preach except on the common. There John Nelson in 1742, and later, Charles Wesley, stood 'with their backs to the gable end of the house of Hannah Close, which stood by itself at the bottom of the moor'. A preaching-house was eventually secured, which was the only place available for services for many years. It was described as 'a large chamber over a house in Mistress Lane'. It seems probable that it was either not open or not convenient for the frequent and more intimate meetings, and in 1776 the house of Samuel Gott was licensed. The following, typical of all such documents, is a copy:

'These are to certify, to whom it may concern, that the house of Samuel Gott, in Westgate, in the town of Armley, in the parish of Leeds, in the County or Diocese of York, was this day registered in the Consistory Court of his Grace the Lord Archbishop of York, as a place of public worship of Almighty God, for Protestant Dissenters.

'As witness my hand this 22nd day of November, 1776

'H. A. Wright
'Deputy Registrar.'

Quite a formidable document for sixpence, which was all it cost—in coin of the realm! But what of the long years of faith and hope which had made that day's achievement possible for Samuel Gott? When John Nelson first came, Samuel was a boy of eight. All his life had been a struggle. Twice he had been forced to sell all his pitifully few possessions to pay what were described as his 'just and honest debts'. Everyone respected Samuel because, at such great cost, he had always paid his way. In his heart he dreamed of building a house of God in Armley, and he lived three years after his dream had become a reality. In the churchyard one may read his epitaph. Its poetic rapture leaves much to be desired from the standpoint of literature for it contains such lines as:

> Our eyes the happy saint pursue,
> Through liquid telescopes of tears.

But though one may criticize the language it is impossible to doubt the sincerity of the tribute in the verses. It seems highly probable that the stone was raised by the little company who helped 'this certain poor man' to build the chapel. It had been a hard task in the face of much opposition. The local clergyman refused them permission to wheel their barrows of bricks through a gate which led to the site. One of the trustees, William Hawkswell, had a right of way to his own ground and so forced the lock! He helped to wheel the bricks and lay them though it cost time, and money, 'but his business came back again and he had greater prosperity than before'.

There were eight other trustees. Among them John Walker, Snr., had saved through the years the sum of thirty pounds, of which he immediately gave ten to help to buy the bricks. Another, William Clarke, a convert of John Nelson, as was his wife, had been a noted sportsman of the district, and became probably the leading spirit in the whole adventure. His changed life was a

challenge to his neighbours, though common report marvelled
even more that the day 'God set his soul at liberty he lost a great
impediment in his speech which had often mortified his pride . . .
and he was ever after free from it.' He stood faithfully by the
new chapel for forty-one years, dying at the age of eighty-five.
The other members of this original trust were John Crossfield,
Edward Walton, a 'listing manufacturer', John Walker, Jnr.,
Joseph Stead, William Pickard, and John Hutchinson, who farmed
the land known as 'Pasture Hills'. The last-named fed the horses
of the preachers in his fields during the sittings of the Conference
in Leeds in 1775. In his house at Redcote prayer-meetings were
held for many years. Such were the men who built the chapel,
and cared for it as a sacred trust,—ordinary men distinguished
for their virile faith. Amongst them all one seems to see the
figure of Samuel Gott, baffled by the common-place problems
of life, but honest in his dealings with his fellows and triumphing
through his faith in God. How he would have rejoiced had he
lived to see the day when John Wesley preached from the pulpit
he had helped to carve, or that other day when Thomas Olivers
gave out his own majestic hymn, 'The God of Abraham
praise'! Simple men but temple-builders these, in an age that
had been forgetting God.

In 1751 there were fourteen members in the Society at Rossendale.[109] They had their meetings in one another's houses except
on some rare occasions when a preacher came and they borrowed
the old school-house. To hear a sermon meant, normally, walking a few miles across the bleak moorland. Coming back from
hearing John Bennet, three of the little Society began to talk
about building a chapel themselves. Their resources were small,
but their faith was great. Nicholas Slater, a poor tailor, had, in
his pocket, a sixpence. It was true it was a crooked sixpence,
but it was current coin. Turning to John Earnshaw and John
Maden, who had a little farm at Top o' th' Bank, he said: 'This
is all I have at present, but when I get more I will give it.' Beginning with the battered sixpence, the three men vowed to find
money for a plot of ground which, eventually, they secured on
the steep Lane Head Lane at Bacup. The chapel was built by
the efforts of seven men and seven women, all unable to give
more than their few pence and their labour. There is something
feudal about the sentence: 'John Maden gave one hundred days

work to the new and arduous undertaking.' The building was completed, and Mary Hargreaves, a widow, had a 'cottage' under the chapel! The sudden death of her husband had left her with the responsibility of a family and no income. She made a small sum by teaching young children, but the Society helped her, for their Christianity did not end with building chapels!

Mary Hargreaves was a personality. One of her functions was to make bread for the Love-feasts, and when told it must be specially good, she used to snap back: 'I'll make it pure', as though that were the final standard of excellence. They called her 'Old Purey' and perhaps they could not have devised a better name. So closely did it fit her that though its origin was forgotten, her great grandson, a hundred years after, was still called by the same name.

The registration of births was a somewhat uncertain procedure, and parish registers were not infallible. Mary had her own system. As each new baby arrived, George, her son, was sent to the brook to bring back a smooth slate stone, shape it into an oval, and inscribe on it the name and date of birth of the new arrival. These stones Mary kept and presented to her children on their twenty-first birthdays.

For many years, in the queer little cottage, she 'entertained' the travelling preachers. In his journal Christopher Hopper wrote in 1780, 'I met with a perfect hurricane at Bacup. I was shut up with mountains of snow with a poor old woman till the 27th, with little fire and small provisions, but God was with us. The same day I set out with James Dawson and John Earnshaw over the hills to Colne, well in body, and in perfect peace of mind.'[110] As Mary remarked about these pastoral visits, 'They had no wants, I took care of that.'[111] Even the scanty records that survive prove, to the most exacting critic, that these people as they built their chapels, were being themselves built into the living Church. Within the circle of their little Societies and within the heart of each individual, God Himself was giving to human spirits an eternal meaning and a new sense of solidarity.

The early efforts were so humble that they caused amusement, in some places, rather than serious opposition. In Kirkgate, Huddersfield, the chimney of the house where the Methodists met was so faulty that the meeting-place was described by neighbours as 'old Reek-em'.[112] Indeed, they seem to have had a genius for nomenclature for after the first chapel at Highfield became overcrowded and a more commodious building, the Bank Chapel, was erected it was promptly dubbed 'Catch-em'. There is an air of friendliness about such namings which is a pleasant relief from the grimmer story of contemporary persecution.[113]

The Mile End Chapel was built at Newchurch in 1761 not without difficulty, but with special care for the preservation of sound doctrine.[114] A manufacturer of flannels, Henry Cunliffe, who carried his goods 'on the backs of galloways, the leading animal having a bell attached to lure on the more dilatory members of the cavalcade', gave the first five pounds towards the new building. What was even more important, he carted all the stones to the site. The seven trustees agreed to pay an annual rent of 8s. 4d. for the ground, and held it on condition that they built 'a Meeting House for Divine worship, for the use of Charles Wesley and Mr. Grimshaw, while they continue to preach agreeably to the doctrines of the said John Wesley'. There was an additional proviso imposed by the landlord, himself a trustee, to the effect that they should permit 'Henry Hargreaves, his heirs and assigns, to erect and fix a seat in the said Meeting House, to contain and hold two persons, to hear Divine service or services therein'.

The work did not proceed without interruption, for John Lord, dyer, showed his objection to the Methodist 'forward movement' by rolling a barrel full of stones amongst the little party. It is worth recording because of its sequel, which is typical of many similar cases. He came, somewhat sheepishly, to hear a soldier preach in the new chapel and returning home, 'said to his wife, "Yon man is right and I am wrong", after which he gave himself to the Lord'.

At Bradshaw the idea of a chapel came through a snowstorm.[115] In the winter of 1772 a blizzard developed. John Atlay had just arrived at James Riley's house, on his 'round'. For four successive nights, in spite of the storm, the house was filled with people who fought their way through the snow to hear him preach. On the fourth night he was so impressed by their enthusiasm that he urged them to build a chapel, and securing a piece of waste ground on Tod-moor-green, they eventually erected the four walls but were so eager to begin the services, that they held them, before they were able to pitch the roof, 'in the roofless shell of the building'.

Sometimes it seemed as though Nature herself conspired to make things more difficult. The little Society which had begun in Whitby in 1750 built a chapel in Henrietta Street in 1764. The site was an unfortunate choice, for twenty years after the chapel was built the whole street was threatened by the sea. A battery had been placed at the end of the hag, or cut in the cliff, and in 1785 part of the cliff broke away, and a deep cleft appeared behind the houses. On Christmas Eve, 1787, came disaster. 'A new-built staith gave way about midnight, and the buildings which it supported fell with a tremendous crash, followed by large masses of earth and stones, and shortly after by several of the adjacent buildings.'[116] The chapel was destroyed, but by 1814 the Methodist Society had not only replaced it, but built an additional 'large and elegant stone building'.[117]

Sometimes material was difficult to obtain locally, but this was probably a less formidable problem than the raising of large sums of money. The young men of Ferriby bought timber in Hull and gladly brought it to the village by water. For forty pounds and their own hard labour they built their chapel.[118]

For the most part the first Methodists were poor, but here and there a 'man of substance' became a member of one of the Societies and made the chapel-building easy. Amongst such was William Sagar who was born at Southfield, near Colne in 1751.[119] His father, a cloth merchant, put him into the business, but was particularly anxious that he should 'cut a figure' amongst the local gentry. To please him William often hunted all day and worked all night. On a business journey in Scotland he was deeply influenced by a sermon he heard, and subsequently, to the chagrin of his father, joined the Methodist Society. Soon after, a hunting party gathered at the house, and there was not enough stabling for all the horses. The older Sagar said casually to his son, 'You shall either build a stable for your own horses or a Methodist Meeting House.' To his astonishment William took him at his word and built a family chapel, where domestic services were regularly held, and where, in days to come, the Methodist Quarterly Meeting met. These earlier events had an inevitable sequel. William decided that a chapel must be built for public worship. He and his friend John Wood of Padiham decided that they must shoulder the financial burden. Unfortunately, William, only then twenty-five years of age, had no large personal income. As he passed down Colne Lane, he noticed the building was only half finished, but the builders had departed because their wages were not forthcoming. He rode on depressed, but presently dismounted and knelt by the roadside to pray. It is worth pausing a moment to think of this young sportsman concerned about a half-built meeting-house! Next day three separate people came spontaneously with gifts of money for the cause so near to his heart. In spite of damage caused by winter storms the building was at last completed, and, because of the confidence John Wesley had in him, he agreed that Alexander Mather should be appointed to the circuit and help him to clear the debt. The correspondence with William Sagar is illuminating.[120]

There is a private manuscript relating an amusing incident in which John Wesley showed himself the diplomat! A horse had been bought for him by William Sagar, but unfortunately he found himself without the money he had intended for its purchase. He had given away all he possessed to various poor people that very day. He examined the horse, and then said coolly: 'It is the very thing, but unfortunately its tail is too long.' The astonishment of Sagar was only dissipated when Mr. Wood, one of the travelling preachers, explained the position privately. Needless to say John Wesley received the horse!

It has seemed worth while considering, in some detail, the case of William Sagar, because so often criticism has been levelled, particularly in the north, at the chapel-builders who happened to be well-to-do men. No doubt some of the criticism is justified, but there were many whose material prosperity blinded the critics to their deep-rooted piety and their commercial integrity which had sprung from it.

The Methodists at Haslingden and Blackburn owed much to William Sagar and a group of his friends, amongst whom were John Wood and John Holden. More than once when the idea of a chapel was little more than a wild dream to some of the small Societies, these men met, at breakfast, before their day's work began, and prayed together about sites and buildings and their bounden duty. No wonder that William turned to his friend on one such day in the home at Southfield and said: 'You and I, John, have built many a chapel in this parlour.'[121]

Nor were such benefactors confined to Lancashire. One might

find examples in most parts of the country. There was a building in Lambeth which was opened by John Wesley on 7th January 1779 and had a similar origin. 'Mr. Edwards built the little old chapel in Lambeth Marsh. . . . The dimensions of this chapel were twenty-three feet wide by twenty-two feet deep. This soon proved too small, and Mr. Edwards enlarged it at his own expense. During his life no rent was charged. After his death only a moderate rent was charged by his widow, who . . . maintained and educated more than twelve preachers' daughters.'[122]

The case of James Hogarth's Chapel at Whitehaven is a romantic story, but the building itself was rather more proprietary than most others.[123] It was built in 1789. Hogarth was a philanthropist, eccentric but benevolent, and was called the King of the Mount. His benefactions included the provision of a Free Charity School for the children of Mount Pleasant, and a Dispensary. The church he built remained unconsecrated and unused till 1791, when he offered it to the Methodists because their own building was becoming unsafe owing to sinkage caused by colliery workings below. The chapel was left, eventually, to the Rev. John Braithwaite, and after many vicissitudes passed into the keeping of the National Children's Home and Orphanage. The details are not within the scope of the present study, and the incident is quoted only because it illustrates one of the many unexpected quarters from which help came in the acquisition of buildings for use as Methodist Chapels in the first fifty years.

In Ireland there were similar cases of liberality on the part of individuals to whom Methodism was personally important, and who believed its people to be divinely-inspired agents in the reviving of religious life in the British Isles. At Athlone John Wesley preached in a chapel which had been built by Mr. S. Simpson, Justice of the Peace.[124] He erected it in his own garden, built a room above for the accommodation of the preachers, and paid all costs himself. In describing his generosity John Wesley links him with two other Irishmen: 'This house was built and given, with the ground on which it stands, by a single gentleman. In Cork one person, Mr. Thomas Jones, gave between three and four hundred pounds toward the preaching-house. Towards that in Dublin Mr. Lunell gave four hundred. I know no such benefactors among the Methodists in England.'[125] Whilst one realizes what Wesley meant, it would be difficult,

looking back over the years, to assess finally the relative liberality
of William Sagar and his friends, this group of Irish gentlemen,
or Nicholas Slater with his crooked sixpence.

This is not the place for a critical or technical description of
early Methodist architecture. Indeed, in the first fifty years it
would be impossible to classify styles. The buildings were generally uninfluenced by any ecclesiastical precedents. They were
the plainest, most economic accommodation that could be provided, and often their shape was governed by the strange sites on
which they were built. It is true that John Wesley had a few
leading principles which he tried to enforce, but the way in
which the groups of generally poor and often isolated people
grew strong enough to build a chapel disarms criticism of style.
It was unfortunate that circumstances led to plainness that was
often ugly, but it is not this first generation of chapel-builders
who can be justly blamed for lack of taste.

It has been seen that Wesley himself preferred an octagonal
shape for a 'preaching-house'. He directed building operations
like many other things, in person, when it was convenient,
though, he was far too busy on his journeyings as a rule. At
Heptonstall a chapel was built, about 1764, 'under the direction
of Mr. Wesley, and erected, of course, in the octagon form of
which he was particularly fond.'[126] When he preached at Colchester, in 1759, he seems to go beyond even the octagonal in
his preference.[127] 'I went to Colchester,' he says in 1759, 'and
on Sunday the 23rd preached in the shell of the new house. It is
twelve-square, and is the best building, of the size, for the voice,
that I know in England.' Apparently Lawrence Coughlan had
gathered a Society of a hundred and twenty within three months.
The chapel was built next year, but whose influence determined
the shape of the polygon, as it was popularly called, it is impossible
to discover. It certainly pleased John Wesley.

In Haworth William Grimshaw, who had arranged for the
Methodist preaching in the kitchen of the parsonage helped 'the
society to build their chapel in 1758'.[128] The site was rented on
a nine hundred and ninety-nine years' lease, at thirteen shillings
and sixpence a year. The building itself was twelve yards by nine,
and a three-storied house for the preachers was built close by.

The chapel at St. Hilary was another evidence of Wesley's
supervision, for Mr. Mildren of Trevean told his surveyor in 1865

that 'the roof was as sound as when put up by Mr. Wesley'
ninety-nine years before.[129]   In Edinburgh the first Methodist
chapel, in the Low Calton, was opened in 1765, and was
octagonal in design, apparently in deference to Wesley's strong
and frequently expressed preference.   However slight his contacts may have been with the chapel-builders at the time of
their operations, he did not hesitate to criticize some of their
attempts, characterizing buildings at Alnwick and Glasgow as
'scarecrows'.[130]

The first Methodist chapel in Nottingham was the Tabernacle,
which was often called the Octagon. Its cost was £128 2s. 7d.
and was paid 'in full' on 8th September 1767—a fact which is
recorded by the local historian with a certain air of triumph, and
is a commentary on the struggle that their financial adventures
involved.[131]

Only occasionally was there a departure from the plain square
or 'octagon' building. Perhaps the extraordinary adaptations
that had, perforce, to be made to provide temporary accommodation had some effect, though more probably it was the reaction
from what was mistakenly held to be 'worldly' even in beauty of
design. It is surprising to discover, therefore, that in the first
chapel in Derby there was a clerestory with square lights set at
intervals. The feature is probably explained by the theory of
John Wills, an architect, who thought it was not originally
intended for lighting or beautifying the chapel, but rather to
make possible rooms above the ceiling, for the caretaker, or as
seems still more probable for the travelling preachers.[132]

Because the assistants of Wesley were itinerant preachers, with
vast 'rounds' to cover, the problem of their board and lodging
was no small anxiety especially in many of the poor hamlets to
which they rode. Though they were usually entertained by
kindly hosts—and no communion in the Christian Church has
earned a better reputation for homely hospitality—there was an
early necessity to assure that they had certain settled quarters.
As in the case of the first Societies, so with the travelling preachers,
the accommodation was opportunist, and it was only when
chapels were built that permanent residences were able to be
provided for them.[133] Until this was done the little Societies
offered such hospitality as they could, in their own homes.
Sometimes it was pathetically meagre but always willingly and

generously offered. When Mrs. Elizabeth Shaw went visiting she recorded in her diary: 'October 17th. Mr. B. and I called to see John and Nanny Bray at Penforder, two old travellers, who are got almost to their journey's end, and have a blessed prospect in view. I went upstairs to see the bed which the preachers sleep in, and found it, as I had been told, decorated with evergreen curtains. The ivy had crept through the wall or window, and was curiously entwined about the bed.'[134]

The first stage in the evolution of the Methodist 'manse' began with the chapel-building. Where possible the earliest chapels included a room or rooms for the preacher, though they were not always in the most desirable place. In recording developments in Halifax this passage occurs: 'The preachers had long laboured under great inconvenience with respect to their place of residence *under the chapel*. . . .'[135] This was confirmed by Frances Pawson when she wrote in her diary: 'Aug. 31.—We have been at Halifax a week. Our house, under the chapel, seems but gloomy; and I was at first discouraged, in seeing no openings to be useful.'[136] Fortunately, as those who are familiar with her fine personality would expect, it took more than an underground manse to discourage her permanently.

The early period of chapel-building shows a necessarily slow development. One is inclined to believe that there was something in the intimacies of those cottage-rooms and farm-house kitchens which it was not easy to surrender. Sometimes the preacher's house prolonged the old conditions. In 1790 John Valton wrote: '31 October. This evg. I preached in my own home. The people seemed better satisfied than myself. I believe that several felt the Word, and some contrite tears were shed. When I returned from the Land's End I found that the preaching was shut out at the Cupola thro' the bad conduct of the people there; however my wife had opened our Room for them, and I hope it will be made useful.'[137] The incident is in the true tradition of the manse, with its open door and its open hearts. A hundred and fifty years later, when many a chapel was destroyed in the madness of war, the Society gathered again in the preacher's house, and 'felt the Word'.

The chapels, of course, varied in size, and tended to be bigger and more costly towards the end of the century. The provision of large houses for travelling preachers, and stabling for the horses became less necessary, though in 1775 a preacher's house, with stable, was built at a cost of £144 at Rochester. Five years before, the chapel, twenty-nine feet by forty feet had been built for £446 3s. 4d. which gives some idea of the comparative outlay involved.[138]

A definite procedure before the undertaking of building schemes was inevitable and it evolved gradually. In 1775 Conference *gave permission* for the erection of another chapel in Halifax, though it was not till 1777 that the building was finished.[139] The cost was £1,230 10s. 4½d. apart from the land. The description of the chapel is worth noting for it was typical of the period. 'The interior was plain and comely, consisting of two sides and one front gallery, the pulpit being affixed to the wall, with the singers' pew beneath, and the communion table in front. There was no school-room or vestry attached.' There was, however, a dwelling-house for one of the preachers and 'a spacious burial-ground'. (The vexed question of the availability of consecrated ground in the parish churchyard led to many of the earlier Societies securing a plot of ground for interments.[140])

A somewhat original feature of the chapel caused dissension! A sounding-board had been placed over the pulpit, but several of the congregation thought it had 'a meagre appearance, and decided to remedy the defect'. A subscription list was opened, and it seems probable that the two principal subscribers were the prime movers in the scheme. An image of an angel blowing a trumpet was duly placed over the sounding-board. The congregation was astonished, and some were deeply perturbed. The preacher, Mr. Murlin, refused, apparently after his first surprise, to preach any more 'under it'. Fortunately John Wesley arrived at the critical juncture.[141] He describes the situation in his own way: 'Thursday, April 15th, 1779, I went to Halifax, where a little thing had lately occasioned great disturbance. An angel blowing a trumpet was placed on the sounding-board over the pulpit. Many were vehemently against this: others as vehemently for it: but a total end was soon put to the contest, for the angel vanished away. The congregations, morning and evening were very large; and the work of God seems to increase in depth as well as extent.'—A meeting was called at which John Wesley put the matter to the vote. The votes were equal until 'John Hatton of Lightcliffe came into the room, and on the nature of

the proceedings being explained to him, gave his vote for the
destruction of the angel'. The preacher, Mr. Murlin, hurried
into the chapel-yard and 'hewed the *dagon* in pieces'—which
pieces were then burnt to ashes! Far-off days, and yet with a
strange charm that defies the power of words to define, as do
the people who walked abroad in them.

Towards the end of the century the needs and the confidence
of the chapel-builders increased, and in some places buildings
were planned to accommodate a thousand people or even more.
The 'old chapel' in Queen Street, Huddersfield, was found to be
too small and was twice enlarged. The extension was certainly
justified by the overcrowding. 'If through unutterable heat,
members of the congregation were overcome by drowsiness, they
rose in the pew and stood until the drowsiness passed off; if per-
chance one fell asleep, he was awoke by the rod of an official
whose duty was to rouse up the sleeping.'[142]

In 1795, Ebenezer Chapel was opened in King Street, Bristol.
It was built to seat twelve hundred people, and was described by
Charles Atmore as 'the best constructed place of worship I ever
saw in which to speak or hear. It is not superb, but elegant and
neat.'[143] The difference in outlook at the end of fifty years is
reflected in this contemporary description; the idea of ever
building—still less needing to build—such a 'meeting-house'
would have astonished John Maden and his friends as they
gathered in the cottage at Top-o' th'-Bank, above Stacksteads.
Nor must these later ventures be regarded as wild experiments
or the result of local egotism. They were the inevitable answer
to a growing need. The 'people called Methodists' had arrived,
and were rapidly becoming a factor to be reckoned with in the
affairs of the nation. Before the chapel at King Street, Bristol,
was opened forty-one leaders were needing rooms for their
classes, and there was a congregation sufficiently large to fill
the new building.

The opening ceremonies had become local 'occasions' and it
was only ignorance or prejudice which sneered at the Methodist
people. The contemporary accounts should be read in the light
of the long struggle which had led to the great day. To recall
the bitter persecution, for example, in Nottingham and the Midlands is to make one hesitate to discount the enthusiasm of those
who had won through. At Hockley a chapel seating a thousand

people was built 'substantially' of brick. Its measurements are given with exactitude—52 feet 9 inches by 51 feet 2 inches! The account was written near enough to the event to be reliable in detail, and to express something of the spirit which local tradition had preserved: '1783. On April 4th, the new Chapel in Hockley was opened for divine worship by the Rev. John Wesley, and the Rev. Dr. Coke, both of them appearing in the usual vestments of the clergymen of the Established Church. In the morning, Dr. Coke read the service from the Book of Common Prayer, and Mr. Wesley preached from the Epistle of the day, Hebrews ix. 11, 12. The Sacrament of the Lord's Supper was afterwards administered. At five o'clock Dr. Coke read the evening service, and Mr. Wesley preached from Isaiah iv. 6, 7. On both occasions the place was excessively crowded.'[144] It was less than forty years since Charles Wesley had been mobbed as he preached in the market-place.[145] Covered with filth and bleeding from his wounds, he had sought shelter in a friendly Quaker's! Brother Sant, one of the little Society, had been 'brought home for dead. The mob had knocked him down, and probably would have murdered him, but for a little child, who, being shut out of doors, alarmed the family by his cries.'[146] Against that background the men of 1783 may be forgiven for being not only thankful, but proud, that by the grace of God the crowds gathered at Hockley in peace and even that John Wesley and Dr. Coke appeared suitably apparelled! That the opening of a new chapel was more than a display or a superficial victory is seen in many an intimate record. When the new building at Trowbridge was dedicated in 1790 by John Valton, Joseph Sutcliffe recorded: 'He opened the new chapel at Trowbridge while I took his place in Bristol. On my return I found the most grateful sentiment, that so blessed a man had been sent amongst them. In the chamber at Mr. Knapp's where the preacher lodged, was a Bible placed for his use. On the blank leaf between the old and the new Testament, I found in Mr. Valton's own hand three texts: Jeremiah xlviii. 10 (quoted); Jeremiah vi. 8 (quoted); Genesis vi. 3 (quoted).'[147]

These later days of growing strength did not come first through numerical increases, but as the result of a new respect for the persecuted and a belief in the faith for which they were ready to die. The sight of small village congregations going quietly across the fields to worship God and continuing to go whether blessed or cursed or stoned by their neighbours, impressed the more reasonable part of the community. As through the years they watched them out-living and out-dying the godless, many were drawn to join with them in their spiritual pilgrimage.

There was a little chapel at Swinefleet, in 1784, which stood in the south corner of the field near the Foulsy Drain, over-shadowed by tall elms. 'It is a plain and unpretending edifice,' says the chronicler.[148] 'There is a good footpath of flagstone, leading from the quiet back street of the village to the place of worship.' The two entrance doors are a reminder that males must go in on the right and females on the left. Near the entrance are a few pews but the rest of the seating consists of forms without back rests. Only the pews are painted, but the forms have been scrubbed till they are spotlessly clean. On the white-washed walls are 'hat-pins' for the use of the men. From the ceiling hangs 'a branch of six lights . . . with the figure of a dove on it', the only evidence of ornamentation. A few extra candlesticks are fixed here and there, but there is no stove or heating apparatus of any kind. If the weather is cold, extra clothes are worn and a splash of colour is added to a wintry day by the all-enveloping red cloaks worn by the older women.[149] At night their steps are lighted by a tallow dip in the household lantern. So they gather, Abigail Duckles, serving-maid at Reedness farm; Daniel Hodgson, the village shoemaker; Sally Foster, growing old and taking longer now to cross the fields, but walking with determination to arrive. Their worship together meant everything to these people, and their neighbours knew it. That was why they came presently to see for themselves and often to be transformed by the Spirit who hovered like the Shekinah over the humble but holy place.

Curious sidelights are thrown on the personalities and eccen-tricities of some of the chapel-builders. There were some doubts as to the propriety of any form of ornamentation at all, so that what was later described as 'chapelicity' might be preserved, but this was an attitude of mind that developed in the earlier part of the nineteenth century[150] and was less often found amongst the first Methodists. At this later date the local historians occasionally broke out into exultant verse to describe their buildings as, for example, at Grantham:[151]

Magnificent indeed it is,
And stately it doth stand.

.   .   .   .   .

It stands in FINKIN STREET,
The centre of the town.
The *Philosophic Institute*
stands rather lower down.

Whether the intention was to convey merely a geographical situation in the last two lines must remain undecided. There are seventy stanzas which might help in forming an opinion!

In Frome, membership on the committee appointed to build the new chapel in 1810 was confined to those who contributed £10 or upwards—a decision which was regrettable and not in line with the generally established principle of democratic representation.[152]

Amongst the eccentrics must be named James Lackington, a man who became a famous and wealthy bookseller, but had a strange personal history.[153] He was born in Wellington, Somerset, in 1746, and received little education, his father being a shoemaker whose children suffered because he was an inveterate drunkard. After James had earned a few pence by selling 'halfpenny apple-pies' for a kindly baker, he was apprenticed at fourteen years of age to a shoemaker in Taunton. There he worked from six in the morning till ten at night, except on Sundays, when he went with his master to the Baptist chapel. Two years later he joined the Methodists, read his Bible and Wesley's hymns and became quite zealous. 'Frequently in frost and snow', he writes, 'I have risen a little after midnight . . . and have wandered about the town till five o'clock when the preaching began; where I often heard a sermon preached to not more than ten or a dozen people. But such of us as did attend at this early hour used afterwards to congratulate each other on the great privilege we enjoyed; then off we went to our work, shivering with cold.' His apprenticeship ended, he went to Bristol, and after a period of lax living, heard Wesley in the New Room, and renewed his faith. In 1770 he married, and after the ceremony he and his bride faced life with a halfpenny as their capital. Coming eventually to London he was helped by John Wesley who advanced him £5 from his Lending Society. With this he rented a small shop, deciding to combine shoemaking with the selling of books! During the next two years his business prospered but he, reading voraciously and indiscriminately, again lost his faith. Meanwhile he built up a very large business, selling more than a hundred thousand volumes a year. In 1798 he retired, a wealthy man, and immediately set himself to write his auto-biography, in which he attacked Methodism viciously, basing his criticism on what was palpably false evidence.[154] Within five years of retirement he had changed his opinion once more and wrote a sequel in which he made a handsome apology for all his mis-statements. 'If I had never heard the Methodists preach,' he said, 'I should have been at this time a poor, ragged, dirty cobbler.'[155] He certainly appeared to be a reformed character when he settled at Thornbury, in Gloucestershire, built a chapel and became a local preacher. In spite of the caustic criticism of T. P. Bunting it must be recorded that on removing to Taunton he built a chapel in 1806 which he called 'The Temple', on which he had an inscription placed: 'This Temple is erected as a monu-ment of God's mercy in convincing an infidel of the important truths of Christianity. Man, consult thy whole existence, and be safe.' In Budleigh Salterton where he died in 1815, he built another chapel and put aside a sum of money so that a Travelling Preacher should preach twice on Sundays, once on weekdays, and meet a class there, and that a preacher to whom he was partial, Captain Hawtry, should be accepted as a fully-accredited itinerant. These conditions suggest that he was a dominating personality, and an individualist, but it is not just to condemn him as a worthless character. His spiritual pilgrimage was erratic and his chapel-building eccentric, but at least his career is evi-dence of the influence of early Methodism as being far wider than the casual historian or romantic writer has so far admitted.

The story of the first London chapels has been well told by J. H. Martin and only such features as reveal the personality of the people immediately concerned in the building of them need be considered.[156]

A centre for Methodists was necessary farther west than Moor-fields, and the Foundery. An old Huguenot chapel which had become the property of St. Clement Danes was acquired by the goodwill of the rector, the Rev. Thomas Blackwell, in 1743. For many years it served as a chapel, and, being a consecrated building, John Wesley felt free in those early days to celebrate Holy Communion there. The Sunday after he opened it as a Methodist Chapel, no less than eighteen hundred communicants presented themselves.

In 1798 it was given up because a new and much bigger chapel had been built in Great Queen Street.[157] This was largely the achievement of John Arthur, an Edinburgh lad who escaped from his apprenticeship to a cruel master, and found his way to London. Here he became a cabinetmaker and a good Methodist, winning a real place in the affection and confidence of John Wesley. Prospering in business, he moved to a house in Great Queen Street in 1790. By the earnest efforts of John Arthur an old Episcopal Proprietary Chapel on the estate was bought, and in 1798 was opened as the new centre for Methodism in that area.[158] The old chapel in Snowsfields, used by the famous Madame Ginn, was secured by Wesley in 1740, and served for twenty years until Long Lane Chapel was built, again largely through the efforts of a successful business man, Samuel Butcher, leather merchant. In Spitalfields and Wapping the Methodists occupied disused Huguenot chapels for short periods, and in Deptford a preaching-house was built in 1757 and another in Poplar in 1772. These places were under the immediate eye of John Wesley, and their structure does not afford much evidence of the personalities in the original societies.

The case of Wesley's Chapel is, of course, very different. Its records have filled a large volume,[159] and there is abundant material for a further development of the subject. It is only necessary to indicate here some of the main features of its origin. It was obvious that the Foundery was no more than a temporary expedient. In 1764 it had been repaired and enlarged, but at the end of forty years it was again neither safe nor convenient, and certainly not fit to meet the needs of the population that was shortly to come to the new houses being rapidly built in the district. John Wesley had his dream of the new chapel that was to become the 'Cathedral' of Methodism. One can imagine him, after such a moment, sitting down in the library at Ramsbury Park to write to his brother: 'A lovely spot and a lovely family. On Friday I hope to be in London and to talk with the committee about building a new Foundery.'[160]

What kind of people could one expect to be available to form a 'committee' for such a responsible task? The Society at the Foundery was no longer a weak and insignificant body. As early as 1763, during a hard winter, a London journal[161] referred to the relief work being done by them. 'Great numbers of poor people had pease-pottage and barley-broth given to them at the Foundery at the expense of Mr. Wesley; and a collection was made at the same place of worship for further supplying the necessities of the destitute, at which upwards of a hundred pounds was contributed.' In 1778 when the 'New Chapel' was opened, John Wesley reviews the situation, and finds the members growing stronger and more independent: 'This week I visited the society, and found a surprising difference in their worldly circumstances. Five or six years ago one in three among the lower ranks of people was out of employment, and the case was supposed to be nearly the same through all London and Westminster. I did not now, after all the tragical outcries of want of trade, that fill the nation, find one in ten out of business;—nay, scarce one in twenty, even in Spitalfields.'[162] It was therefore not a poverty-stricken community which had undertaken the work.

The circular which he sent out to the whole 'Connexion' asking for subscriptions was signed by him and he pointed out that the 'Society at London' had assisted their brethren in all parts of the country for the past thirty years. To the first appeal for 'the general debt' they had responded with a gift of nine hundred pounds and had given an average of three hundred pounds every year since. Now they needed six thousand pounds themselves to complete their scheme. The idea of mutual responsibility had already become a fundamental principle of the great Methodist family. This did not, of course, mean that the London Methodists were idle. At the first three meetings in 1776 they had themselves given a thousand pounds.

The site was secured—part of some fields used as tenter-grounds, i.e. for cloth-stretching. It was only two hundred yards north-west of the Foundery, but had a frontage on the main road. The City Fathers were evidently mistrustful of the local Methodists' conception of architectural beauty—and one can hardly blame them! They insisted that a row of houses should be built in front of the chapel, allowing only an entrance way between. Fortunately they needed a piece of ground in the rear for the construction of a new road, and this was given up on condition

that they waived the matter of the houses. The subsequent
frontage, with the short avenue of trees approaching it, was no
disgrace to the local amenities.

The foundation stone was laid on 21st April 1777, and Wesley
felt the rain to be a blessing, since it kept away 'thousands who pur-
posed to be there; but there were still such multitudes that it was
with great difficulty I got through them to lay the first stone.'[163]

The actual building was undertaken by Samuel Tooth, a
leader and local preacher, and a builder of considerable experience, who had been for one year an 'itinerant'. The years have
proved the honesty and efficiency of his work, and the excellent
quality of the materials he used. It was no small undertaking for
the plan included a roof, which, at that time, was 'the widest in
England unsupported by pillars'.[164] However, 'Sammy' as Wesley
addressed him in correspondence[165] was undaunted. He did his
work well and, in spite of some harmless eccentricities was, with
his family, of great help to the London Societies at West Street
and City Road.

The building was not completed for several years, and this
may explain the absence of contemporary records of its opening,
but operations were sufficiently advanced for John Wesley to
preach dedicatory sermons on 1st November 1778, when, in spite
of the crowds 'all was quietness, decency and order'. His own
description of the chapel was restrained: 'It is perfectly neat but
not fine; and contains far more people than the Foundery.'[166] It
was *not* octagonal! One is a little curious to know whether this
was due to the shape of the site or the strength of the committee!

Actually there were two rows of seats in the gallery, the space
behind being used as a standing-room. The sexes were still
separated, in deference to Wesley's wish, but there was a strong
element of opposition amongst the trustees and the people. In
spite of pew-rents no one was allowed to claim a particular seat
as his own, which was another concession to Mr. Wesley. Two
wicket-gates guarded the galleries, one at the foot and the other
on the first landing of the stairs. At the gates were hatch-keepers
who received £4 per annum for being on duty at the services.

The Trustees of the New Chapel were appointed on 9th August
1779, and formed a group of interesting and reliable people. They
were of varying trades and circumstances as will be seen from
the following list: 'John Wesley, parish of St. Luke's, clerk;

Charles Greenwood, Rood Lane, upholder; John Duplex, parish
of Christ Church, weaver; John Folgham, Fleet Street, cabinet-
case maker; William Cowland, St. John Clerkenwell, brazier;
Charles Wheeler, parish of St. Luke, sailcloth maker; Rev. Charles
Wesley, St. Marylebone, clerk; Ebenezer Blackwell, Lombard
Street, banker; John Horton, Lawrence Pountney Lane, mer-
chant; Richard Kemp, St. Leonard, Shoreditch, framework
knitter; George Wolff, St. Mary, Whitechapel, merchant; John
Cheesement, parish of St. George, merchant; George Urling,
Leadenhall Market, butcher; Luke Houlton, parish of St. Luke,
weaver; John Butcher, Dog Lane, Bermondsey, currier; Joseph
Woolley, parish of St. John, Clerkenwell, scalemaker; Thomas
Forfitt, parish of St. Luke, gentleman; James Dewey, Artillery
Lane, weaver; James King, St. Leonard, Shoreditch, weaver;
James Hammond, Gould Street, weaver; Samuel Petty, Billiter
Lane, City, silk broker; John Hallam, St. George, Southwark,
grocer; Thomas Day, St. Saviour's, Southwark, master carman;
Thomas Simons, St. Leonard, Shoreditch, dyer; James Smith,
Fish Street Hill, brushmaker.' Of these twenty-five men five were
weavers, three are described as merchants and one as a banker.
The whole group formed a reasonable cross-section of society and
Methodism could no longer be described truly as a coterie of
fanatics. Some record of the lives of most of these trustees remains,
and interesting details are to be found in George J. Stevenson's
volume on City Road Chapel.

Amongst these Trustees Ebenezer Blackwell and George Wolff
were men of outstanding ability, who enjoyed a constant intimacy
with John Wesley, and were always his steadfast friends.[167]
Captain John Cheesement was a different type—an old sea-
captain who had retired but suffered a succession of financial
disasters which brought him from wealth to sudden poverty.
His friends made it possible for him to begin again, and he very
quickly amassed a second fortune. For four years he was a
faithful trustee, and at his death, the following inscription was
carved on his tomb in City Road graveyard: 'He was a native of
Seaton, near Sunderland, and came to an anchor in a place of
rivers and broad streams within the veil of Fair Havens on the
20th February 1783, in the fifty-second year of his voyage.'[168]

Another trustee, Thomas Day, is a more complex personality.
He had joined the Methodist Society, because he was in revolt

from what H. J. Foster has described as 'debased Calvinism'. He was evidently something of an amateur theologian and had the temerity to challenge John Wesley on his Notes on the New Testament.[169] This fact is the more remarkable because he was by trade a carter and horse owner. His father had been Master of the Carters' Company and, with whip and smock, had proudly led the Carters in the Coronation Procession of King George II. Living in Southwark Thomas Day had been a member of the Foundery before he became a Trustee of the New Chapel in City Road. His son Isaac succeeded his father in the office.

It happened that Captain Cheesement and Charles Greenwood died in the same fortnight as two other members of the Society, Sarah Clay and George Hufflet. The comment of John Wesley helps one to understand the standard of values which was maintained: 'So within a few days we lost two of our richest and two of our holiest members—Sarah Clay and good old George Hufflet, who had been a burning and a shining light. He lay fourteen weeks praising God continually, and had then a triumphant entrance into His Kingdom.'[170] Reading the sources cognate it is certain that the entry implies no reflection on Captain Cheesement or Charles Greenwood, but is an inevitable corrective to Wesley's own mind, in case he were tempted to forget those whose lives had been obscure. The attitude is not peculiar to him, but is typical of the judgement of those early Societies. They were not financial corporations; they were rather families of the household of God.

The story of the Society at City Road is an inspiring record of astonishing success in face of great odds. It was not without royal recognition, for King George III presented John Wesley with the masts of dismantled ships of the line to serve as pillars to support the gallery of the New Chapel.[171]

In 1779 the income amounted to £811 10s. 6d. but in 1782 this had risen to £1,046 14s. 6d. in addition to subscriptions towards the debt on the building which totalled £1,377 3s. 1d. and was, of course, exclusive of money raised for various benevolent activities. In 1803 the income had risen to over £2,000, which was half of the total of the London Circuit. The membership of the Society in London was 2,950 at the death of Wesley in 1791, and by 1803 had risen to 3,680.[172] Remarkable as are these figures it will be seen that their greatest importance lay, in London as in the rest of the country, in the quality of life which was guaranteed by searching tests and intimate contacts. It has often been remarked that the early Methodists seemed to live to 'a good old age'. Casual as the phrase may be it is accurate. Of the five thousand four hundred people whose burials are recorded at City Road Chapel, two hundred and seventy-nine were over eighty when they died—a very high percentage in comparison with other contemporary records. The comment of G. J. Stevenson is in striking contrast to some superficial judgements on the Methodists of the period. He says: 'The threefold blessings which resulted to these people were, they lived happy lives, they lived long lives, and they died well. . . .'[173] These three things are closely related and the basis of the happiness depended on the reality of their spiritual experience.

Statistics have only a secondary value in this survey, but it is well to remember the numerical growth of Methodism during the first fifty years, in so far as larger numbers affected local circumstance and the possibilities of personal witness. Whilst it would be unwise to rely on Myles' *Chronological History* for close details, such as the exact dates of the building of a chapel where he sometimes confuses chapel-opening with chapel-registration[174] he may be trusted for more general figures and approximate calculations. Remembering the primitive apparatus with which he worked, his results are extremely good. Basing calculations on his records and on local histories the probable number of Methodist chapels at the time of Wesley's death in 1791 was 626,[175] in 1800 it was 915, though an allowance must be made for some of the buildings included in this figure being little more than adapted 'preaching-houses'. It does not, of course, include houses 'which are not wholly appropriated to the worship of God'—in other words it excluded literally thousands of cottage-rooms and farm-kitchens which were so used. In Scotland, Ireland, and 'the British Isles' the number of chapels in 1812 was 1,540.[176] Local statistics are available and reveal the sometimes sudden increases caused by revivals and decreases caused by the Kilhamite secession at the end of the century. In a centre like Huddersfield, more immediately affected, the Circuit returns fell from 1714 members in 1797, to 949 two years later.[177] In Hockley, Nottingham, 19 leaders and 320 members retained the chapel, leaving 8 leaders and 280 members 'homeless'. A new chapel was soon

built, in spite of the difficulties, for the dispossessed Wesleyans.[178]
In some places the Kilhamites appropriated the local chapel, in
others they built a new one for the Church that was to become
the 'Methodist New Connexion'. Whilst the secession was tragic,
the fact that it occurred without destroying Methodism shows
clearly its strength in 1795.

The growth in numbers had been phenomenal. The first
complete connexional returns in 1767 showed 25,911 in full
membership. In 1776 the number was 39,000 and this figure
had increased to 62,000 ten years later. In 1791 the membership
was 72,000 in Britain, but reached a total of 136,000 in Britain
and America.

The position of Methodism was stabilized. Its properties were
vested for the most part in reliable trustees, and its theological
position was clarified and established. There were a few amongst
the trustees who assumed an attitude of proprietorship. In the
manuscript accounts of King Street Chapel Trust, Bath, the first
trustees called themselves 'proprietors' and each held £100 share
in the property.[179] 'Profits and emoluments' were legally transferred when occasion arose, and the shares were even sold at a
figure below par. The Annual Trustees' Meeting was duly cele-
brated, and the whole affair had some elements of a financial
corporation about it. This is by no means typical of any large
number of Methodist trustees, but it is cited because it is one
more proof that Methodists were not oddities isolated from the
main stream of eighteenth-century life. It was a normal procedure for proprietary trusts to be established in connexion with
a great variety of undertakings, including the founding of an
important British colony.[180] It was perhaps Wesley's earlier
association with the Georgia Trust that led him to accept the
conditions at Bath, and indeed become one of the 'Proprietors'.

That there were occasional disputes about the settlement of
trusts was natural during the evolution of Methodist ecclesiastical
polity. Such technical questions must be left for consideration by
legal experts; they only have relevance to this study when they
reveal the personalities of the people concerned. It is, however,
amusing to discover that the sense of proprietorship extended not
only to the chapels but also to the pews in them.[181] The early
'account books' of St. Just reveal payments in 1791 for 'the front
seat in the gallery'. On 1st January Jane Thomas, Mary Hicks,

and Mary Harvey each paid 1*s*. 6*d*. and evidently established their right to this prominent position. Less privileged persons, Margaret Thomas, Margery Thomas, and Constance Williams, paying only 1*s*. each, were proprietors—if we may use the word—of second seats, which at any rate was an improvement on the standing-space provided behind.

The ultimate fate of these first chapels is astonishingly varied. Their stones were literally mortared at times with blood and tears, but some survived only a few years and were sold to help pay for the building of larger and more suitable places. The building which served the early Methodists at Warrington became the booking-office of the town's first railway station. This was not looked upon as a desecration or the abandonment of a position but, apparently, as the means to move forward towards the real objective. They were advancing, not surrendering, and any sentimental regrets were overwhelmed by this fact. ·

Other places were none too well built and Nature had her way with them. It was not till 1796 that the Methodist preachers came to Wellingore in Lincolnshire, and they were received at first with 'bitter hatred and resentment'. A small class, however, was formed in 1799 as a branch of the Navenby Society. The only building they were able to secure was bought from 'the Ranters' who had abandoned their own efforts in the village.[182] On 29th February 1827, a tremendous hurricane struck Wellingore. Many houses were destroyed and the chapel was wrecked. The contemporary account of its rebuilding in the summer gives an excellent picture of the kind of people produced by village Methodism, and certainly leaves one in no doubt as to their loyalties. The little Society in Wellingore was desperately poor, but cheerful and determined. Tornadoes passed, but God remained in their midst. 'As the days were long, most of the Society, both men and women, volunteered to labour gratuitously towards the re-building of the house of their God, after the labours of the day . . . were brought to an end. Their services were accepted, and they engaged in clearing away from the ground the ruins of the former house, in digging the foundations for the new one, in cleansing the old bricks and materials from the lime and plaster which adhered to them, and so making them fit to be used again; they dug all the sand to be used in the building, and conveyed it to the proper place, levelling the field again . . .

G

and as the water for the lime had to be procured from a distance, it being a dry season, they fetched that also up the cliff, as it was needed for the work. Thus were they all very laudably animated by the same spirit of zeal for the honour and glory of God . . . and, in due time, the work was happily brought to an end. . . . Soon a pleasing revival of the word of God took place, as if to reward their recent labours. . . . The power of God came down upon them. . . . In about five or six weeks the Wellingore Society experienced an increase of upwards of thirty souls, many of whom were made happy in God. . . . Now, where no place could be obtained, on any terms whatever, in which so much as a prayer-meeting could be held . . . there is scarcely a house in the whole of that village in which a prayer-meeting might not be held at any time, if it were required.' That is the account written and published within a few months of the happenings. It records the answer of a simple but passionately sincere people to the 'bludgeonings of chance'.

Besides the buildings that were superseded or battered and rebuilt, there were those which stood the test of time and whose people established a tradition which the years have had no power to destroy. Amongst these none has claim to a more honoured place than Portland Chapel, Bristol, and its people. To some it is the most sacred shrine of Methodism, and it is certainly one of the most historic.[183] It was built in the critical period immediately after the death of John Wesley. He had often wondered how far his policy would be continued when he was no longer there to expound, if not to enforce it. In old Portland Chapel a most critical part of the problem was focused for Bristol Methodists.

Largely through the aid of Captain Thomas Webb, late of the 48th Regiment of Foot, and a veteran of the French war in Canada, the chapel was built in 1792, in Clifton, a 'genteel suburb' of Bristol. It is a beautiful building of its kind, and was described by Charles Atmore as 'one of the most elegant chapels in the Methodist Connexion, if not in the Kingdom'. The local Press in 1797 pronounced it 'spacious and handsome with a large gallery and painted altar-piece, a turret with a bell, and the service of the Church of England read by preachers in Mr. Wesley's Connexion'. The original building was not quite so long as it is at present, and 'the two entrances were on opposite sides and exactly in the centre, with an aisle right across from door to door, and three longitudinal aisles—one down the centre and one down each side'.[184]   There were inner staircases to the gallery and two stoves in the side aisles.   The pulpit, a double-decker, stood some distance from the Communion rail.   The bell was bought from St. Ewen's Church for £4 10s. 6d.   It bears the date 1698 and has on it the inscription, 'Come away; make no delay'.   It has hung in its modest little belfry since 1792 calling the neighbours to worship every Sunday, save during the years of the late war, when its plaintive appeal was silenced to be sounded only as a signal of enemy invasion.   A long description of this hallowed place could be written, but there is something more than its stones which cry out—something which sounds even above its beautiful music maintained so lovingly still by Arnold Barter.   There are voices which whisper in old Portland, and when a man kneels at Holy Communion early on Easter morning, he can hear them in the silence of his heart.   They are not the raucous sounds of ancient controversy, but the songs of adoration and the cadence of a worshipping throng, unseen but very near.

The part old Portland played in the defeat of the 'Old Planners' and the advance of the new Methodism may be considered later. For the moment it shall suffice to find in that quiet, hallowed place the focus of the efforts of the men and women who, for these first fifty years, gave themselves in building houses made with hands, because there had been given to them the where-withal to build anew the fallen temples of the spirit.   To the present writer there is no place where their struggles have seemed more real or more triumphant than the chapel, with its ancient bell, high up on the hill, that looks down on the city of Bristol.

NOTES

1. *Works of John Wesley*, VII. 422–3.
2. *Journal of Charles Wesley*, I. 122–3.
3. *W.H.S.*, XI. 55–6.
4. ibid., VI. 102.
5. Tyerman's *Life of Whitefield*, I. 170–1, 189. Letter of George Whitefield to Howell Harris, 20th December 1738.
6. *Journal of John Wesley*, III. 373.
7. *Byron*, app., p. 768. (Murray.) (Note F, by Byron, to *Childe Harold*, Canto III.) 1837.
8. *Journal of John Wesley*, III. 12.
9. 'Journal of John Nelson', *Early Methodist Preachers*, I. p. 65.
10. *Methodism in Armley*, T. Hardcastle, p. 7. (Hamilton, Adams, London, 1871.)
11. J. F. Sutton's *Date Book*. Quoted in *History of Wesleyan Methodism in Nottingham*, p. 13. G. H. Harwood. (Ellis, Nottingham, 1872.)
12. *Journal of John Wesley*, II. 466.
13. *History of Wesleyan Methodism in Nottingham*, pp. 10–11.
14. *Methodism in Rossendale*, W. Jessop, pp. 40, 54, 67, 85, 148, 195, 227.
15. ibid., p. 191.
16. *Lives of Early Methodist Preachers*, I. p. 65.
17. *Methodism in Rossendale*, p. 139.
18. *Collection of Letters on Sacred Subjects* (letter from J. Nelson to an unknown). (Sheffield, 1761.)
19. *Methodism in Halifax*, J. U. Walker, pp. 26–7. (Hartley and Walker, Halifax, 1836.)
20. *W.H.S.*, XV. 109.
21. 'Journal of John Nelson', *Lives of Early Methodist Preachers*.
22. *Grimsby Methodism*, George Lester. (Wesleyan Methodist Book Room, London, 1890.)
23. *Journal of John Wesley*, III. 281.
24. *Methodism in Halifax*, J. U. Walker, pp. 152, 174. (Hartly and Walker, Halifax. 1836.)
25. *W.H.S.*, VIII. 81.
26. *History of Methodism in Ireland*, C. H. Crookshank, II. 46–7. (Woolmer, London, 1886.)
27. *Methodism in Bingley*, John Ward, pp. 26–7, 105, 90, 82. (Harrison, Bingley, 1863.)
28. *Journal of John Wesley*, IV. 499. See also *W.H.S.*, XVII. 57–63, for a full account.
29. *W.H.S.*, XVII. 127.
30. *Methodism in Grantham*, Thomas Cocking, pp. 235–6. (Simpkin, Marshall, London, 1836.)
31. MS. based on oral tradition, and written by Mr. Coleman of Allenshields, Blanchland, to whom the author was introduced by his friend, Cecil Pawson, M.B.E., M.Sc., of Newcastle. See also *W.H.S.* (for John Brown).
32. *Methodism in Manchester*, James Everett, pp. 57–9. (S. Russell, Deansgate, 1827.)
33. ibid. Quotation of evidence by Thomas Berry, referring to 1747.

34. Letter of John Bennet to Charles Wesley, from Chinley, 7th March 1747.

35. *Methodist Magazine*, 1819, p. 695.

36. ibid., 1781, p. 90.

37. *W.H.S.*, XVIII. 14–17.

38. *Wesleyan Magazine*, 1843, p. 1053.

39. Quoted from a MS. by the Rev. R. Butterworth. Ref. in *W.H.S.*, XII. 141–2.

40. *History of Birmingham*, Hutton, pp. 188ff. (3rd edition, 1806.) See also *W.H.S.*, III. 96–8.

41. *Reminiscences of a Gentleman in the Last Century;* Letters of Miss Hutton, daughter of the historian of Birmingham, Wm. Beale, pp. 156f., *W.H.S.*, III. 98.

42. *History of Methodism in Ireland*, C. H. Crookshank, M.A., I. 177–8. (Allen, Belfast, 1885.)

43. A comprehensive and critical study by Dr. John S. Simon is in *W.H.S.*, XI. 82, 93, 103–8, 130–7. See also *Minutes of Conference* (1812), III. 316–22, *Myles' Chronological History*, pp. 406–11, Act of 52 Geo. III, c. 155 (28th July 1812).

44. *More About the Early Methodist People*, Chapter II.

45. *W.H.S.*, XI. 89–90.

46. See Chapter III.

47. Toleration Act (24th May 1689), William III and Mary.

48. *Abridgement of Mr. Baxter's History of his Life and Times*, Calamy. (2nd edition.)

49. *W.H.S.*, XI. 93.

50. *More About the Early Methodist People*, Chapter III.

51. Complete record in *W.H.S.*, XV. 93–100.

52. *Letters of Rev. John Wesley, A.M.*, III. 42. (Standard Edition, 1931.) See also *Journal of John Wesley*, III. 39, *Large Minutes*, 1770, *Works of John Wesley*, VIII. 331.

53. *Inter alia, W.H.S.*, I. 126; XX. 140; IV. 196 (date of licence, 1787). *Methodism in Armley*, p. 22 (date of licence, 1776). *Methodism in Marshland*, p. 23 (date of licence, 1772). *Methodism in Huddersfield*, p. 35 (date of licence, 1770).

54. *W.H.S.*, XVIII. 113–20.

55. *London Magazine*, 1760.

56. *Letters of the Rev. John Wesley, A.M.*, IV. 99–100.

57. *Burrow's Reports*, IV. 1991.

58. *Reports of Cases Determined in the Several Courts of Westminster Hall from 1746 to 1779*, Sir Wm. Blackstone, I. 605ff. (2nd edition.)

59. *Letters of John Wesley*, VI. 336. (Standard Edition, 1931.)

60. ibid., V. 98.

61. *Journal of John Wesley*, VII. 339.

62. *Letters of John Wesley*, VIII. 78.

63. ibid., 224.

64. ibid., 230.

65. *Centenary of Wesleyan Methodism*, Thomas Jackson, p. 229. (Mason, London, 1839.)

66. *Methodism in Huddersfield*, Joel Mallinson. (Kelly, London, 1898.)

67. *History of Methodism in Ireland*, C. H. Crookshank, I. 21. (Allen, Belfast, 1885.)

68. Letter of C. Wesley to J. Wesley (9th October 1747).

69. Letter of C. Wesley to E. Blackwell (10th October 1747).

70. *Journal of John Wesley*, V. 305.

71. *Worcester Sects* (1861). Quoted *W.H.S.*, III. 179.

72. *Journal of John Wesley*, VII. 110, 325.

73. *W.H.S.*, IV. 195.

74. *Chronological History of the People called Methodists*, William Myles, p. 426. (London, 1813.)

75. *Centenary of Wesleyan Methodism*, Thomas Jackson. (Mason, London, 1839.)

76. *Methodism in Halifax*, J. U. Walker, p. 87. (Hartly and Walker, Halifax, 1836.)

77. ibid., p. 103.

78. Comment in *W.H.S.*, IX. 42.

79. *Large Minutes*, 1763, and *Minutes*, 1770.

80. *W.H.S.*, I. 64.

81. ibid., II. 24.

82. *The Annals of Frome Methodist Society*, S. Tuck, pp. 32ff. (Tuck, Frome, 1814.)

83. *Methodism in Huddersfield*, J. Mallinson, pp. 76–8. (Kelly, London, 1898.)

84. *Centenary of Wesleyan Methodism*, Thomas Jackson, p. 111. (Mason, London, 1839.)

85. ibid., p. 109.

86. Contemporary account recorded in *City Road Chapel*, G. J. Stevenson, p. 13. (Stevenson, London, 1872.)

87. ibid., p. 15.

88. *Life and Times of Wesley*, L. Tyerman, I. 234. (Hodder and Stoughton, London, 1890, 6th Edition.)

89. *City Road Chapel*, G. J. Stevenson, p. 20.

90. *Life and Times of Wesley*, L. Tyerman, I. 272. *Centenary of Wesleyan Methodism*, p. 109. *City Road Chapel*, pp. 20ff.

91. *Wesley's Works*, XII. 245.

92. *Life of Silas Told*, p. 74.

93. *John Wesley and the Religious Societies*, John S. Simon, pp. 282–8. (Sharp, London, 1921.)

94. *Journal of John Wesley*, II. 194–7. See also *W.H.S.*, XIX. 135.

95. ibid., p. 194, footnote.

96. ibid., p. 208.

97. *W.H.S.*, XIX. 135. *John Wesley and the Advance of Methodism*, John S. Simon, pp. 54–60. (Sharp, London.) *Journal of John Wesley*, II. 225, footnote.

98. See Chapter IV.

99. *Journal of John Wesley*, III. 54–5. See also *Orphan House of Wesley*, Stamp, pp. 13–14.

100. *Life of Wesley*, Henry Moore, I. 551.

101. *Journal of John Wesley*, III. 72.

102. *Life and Times of Wesley*, I. 520.

103. *Journal of John Wesley*, III. 76.

104. *W.H.S.*, III. 176.

105. *Journal of John Wesley*, IV. 38.

106. *History of Methodism in Ireland*, C. H. Crookshank, I. 89. (Allen, Belfast, 1885.)

107. *Methodism in Scotland*, Wesley F. Swift, p. 44, W.H.S. Lecture No. 13. (Epworth Press, London, 1947.)

108. *Methodism in Armley*, T. Hardcastle, pp. 22–6. (Hamilton, Adams, London, 1871.)

109. *Methodism in Rossendale*, pp. 85–8.

110. *Lives of Early Methodist Preachers*, I. 43.

111. *Methodism in Rossendale*, p. 87.

112. *Methodism in Huddersfield*, pp. 23–4.

113. *More About the Early Methodist People*, Chapter III.

114. *Methodism in Rossendale*, pp. 90–1.

115. *Methodism in Halifax*, pp. 123–4.

116. *History of Whitby*, Dr. Young, II. 621. (Whitby, 1817.)

117. *W.H.S.*, V. 95.

118. ibid., III. 135.

119. *Methodism in Rossendale*, pp. 114–18.

120. *The Letters of John Wesley*, VI. 384, VII. 136, 319, 321, 376.

121. Private MS. and also *Tyerman's Wesley*, III. 345.

122. *Lambeth Wesleyan Chapel* (anonymous pamphlet, 1885). *Journal of John Wesley*, VI. 218.

123. *W.H.S.*, XVIII. 142–9. *Cumberland Pacquet*, 26th March 1786; 11th June 1788; 11th November 1789; 22nd March 1791.

124. *History of Methodism in Ireland*, I. 208.

125. *Journal of John Wesley*, V. 407. *W.H.S.*, II. 34.

126. *Methodism in Halifax*, J. U. Walker, p. 109.

127. *Journal of John Wesley*, V. 362. *W.H.S.*, XX. 97.

128. *W.H.S.*, X. 166.

129. *Wesley's Itineraries in Cornwall*, Symons, p. 95. *Journal of John Wesley*, V. 186. *W.H.S.*, IV. 193.

130. *Journal of John Wesley*, VII. 391–2. *Wesleyan Methodist Magazine*, 1828, p. 803.

131. *Wesleyan Methodism in Nottingham*, p. 38.

132. *W.H.S.*, XV. 111.

133. This, of course, occurred at an earlier date in London, Bristol, and Newcastle.

134. *Memorials of Mrs. E. Shaw*, Robert C. Barratt, p. 24. (Wesleyan Conference Office, London, 1875.)

135. *Methodism in Halifax*, J. U. Walker, p. 251.

136. *The Experience of Mrs. Frances Pawson*, Joseph Sutcliffe, A.M., p. 113. (Mason, London, 1834.)

137. 'John Valton's MS. Journal', quoted in *W.H.S.*, VIII. 193.

138. *W.H.S.*, II. 214.

139. *Methodism in Halifax*, pp. 141–4, 149–51.

140. ibid., pp. 252.

141. *Journal of John Wesley*, VI. 229.

142. *Methodism in Huddersfield*, p. 57.

143. *Centenary History of Ebenezer Chapel, King St., Bristol*, R. Burroughs, p. 39. (Hemmons, Bristol, 1895.)

144. *Methodism in Nottingham*, H. G. Harwood, pp. 55–6.

145. See Chapter V.

146. *Journal of Charles Wesley*, I. 350.

147. *Early Methodist Preachers*, VI. 130–1.

148. *Methodism in Marshland*, pp. 97–8.

149. See Chapter V.

150. *Religious Methodism at Radcliffe Bridge*, Frank Merriday, p. 25. (Hayhurst, Radcliffe.)

151. *Origin and Erection of the New Wesleyan Chapel, Grantham*, John Rogers, Junr. (J. Rogers, Grantham, 1840.) Quoted by J. D. Crossland, *W.H.S.*, XIX. 74–5.

152. *Brief Annals of Frome Methodist Society*, p. 48.

153. *Methodism in North Devon*, pp. 51–3. *W.H.S.*, XVIII. 85–92.

154. *Memoirs of Forty Five Years of the Life of James Lackington, written by himself in Forty Seven Letters to a Friend.*

155. *The Confessions of J. Lackington, late bookseller at the Temple of the Muses, in a series of Letters to a Friend.*

156. *John Wesley's London Chapels*, Rev. J. Henry Martin. (W.H.S. Lecture, 1946; Epworth Press, 1946.)

157. *City Road Chapel*, George J. Stevenson, pp. 562–3.

158. ibid.

159. ibid.

160. *Letters of John Wesley*, VI. 179.

161. *Lloyd's Evening Post*, 26th January 1763.

162. *Journal of John Wesley*, VI. 180.

163. ibid., VI. 144.

164. *City Road Chapel*, p. 478.

165. *Letters of John Wesley*, VI. 321.

166. *Journal of John Wesley*, VI. 215.

167. See Chapter   .

168. *City Road Chapel*, pp. 81–2, 522–3.

169. MS. Letters of Thomas Day. Quoted in *W.H.S.*, VII. 106.

170. *Journal of John Wesley*, VI. 395–6.

171. *W.H.S.*, XV. 139.

172. Account Books. Quoted *W.H.S.*, XVI. 8.

173. *City Road Chapel*, p. 607.

174. *W.H.S.*, VI. 58.

175. *Methodism in Bingley*, pp. 27–8. *Chronological History of People called Methodists*, Myles. (3rd Ed., 1803.)

176. *Chronological History of People called Methodists*, Myles. (1812 Edition.)

177. *Methodism in Huddersfield*, pp. 47–8.

178. *Methodism in Nottingham*, pp. 85–6.

179. *W.H.S.*, I. 127. Quotation from MS. source.

180. *Oglethorpe: A Study in Philanthropy in England and Georgia*, L. F. Church. (Epworth Press, 1932.)

181. 'Account Books of St. Just, 1761–96.' Quoted from MS. by *W.H.S.*, XVIII. 71–3.

182. *History of Methodism in the Neighbourhood and City of Lincoln*, A. Watmough, pp. 90–3. (Mason, London, 1829.)

183. *The Chapel on the Hill*, A. J. Lambert. (Bristol, 1929.) *W.H.S.*, XVII. 136–45.

184. ibid., p. 40.

CHAPTER III

THEIR SPIRITUAL EXPERIENCE

IT has often been said that Methodism contained nothing 'new' and this is perfectly true though it may disappoint the modern Athenians. Neither did it make any noteworthy and original contribution to the theological opinion of the eighteenth century. This does not mean that Wesley was out of date in his philosophical approach to Truth. His appeal to the phenomena of experience was not discredited then, still less is it outmoded by the thought of our modern scientists and philosophers. As Dr. Workman has pointed out in his brilliant epitome of Methodism in the Cambridge Manuals: 'In his appeal Wesley was one, however unconsciously, with the English philosophers, with one all-important difference. The philosophers had confined themselves, almost exclusively to the intellectual factors. Wesley urged . . . an enlargement so as to embrace spiritual phenomena of the contents of the mind to which the philosophers applied their methods of introspection.'[1] The spiritual experience was as real as the intellectual and could not be neglected or ignored by scientific or psychological investigators. At the same time Wesley 'did not set out to discover buried truth, but to live out a forgotten life. . . . Unlike Wyclif, his object was not to overthrow existing dogmas, but to galvanize them into life.' That was what so many of the contemporary clergy and dissenting ministers found so difficult to understand. He was passionately loyal to his Church, but anxious, above everything else, that it should be apostolic and pentecostal in its ministrations.

It was impossible for him to contain his spiritual experience within his own soul or a smaller parish than the world. It was expansive and creative, in its very nature. He must communicate it to everyone; it was 'Good News'—the Gospel—for the whole of mankind. Such men, says Rufus Jones, 'live more dynamic lives because of these experiences which rise within them'.[2]

The eighteenth century has been described as a Golden Age, but all is not gold that glitters, and brocade in high places hid rags in the dens of London and the hovels on the countryside. There was an undertone of sadness which Wesley heard more plainly than most, and hard facts prove that the message of free grace for all men brought new hope and a glowing experience to many thousands.

He was a born leader, and inspired his first race of preachers so that their plain words burnt their way into the hearts of men. A layman, J. R., who wrote an interesting account of early Methodism,[3] remarking on their differing education and quali-fications, says: 'They all preached the same doctrines, and the invariable characteristics of their preaching were sincerity, sim-plicity and fervour. They believed, and therefore they spoke as they did. They were themselves affected with the truths they uttered, and their hearers could not long remain unaffected.' That was the secret of their success. They had not been *taught* a theological system; they had *caught* a spiritual experience. It had not been an easy spiritual pilgrimage for Wesley nor was it for his preachers. Though some of them entered quickly into a great joy, it is only necessary to read their journals[4] to discover something of the travail of their souls before they found peace. Once this was a reality they were able, by the grace of God, to direct other 'poor travellers' towards the same triumphant experi-ence. They offered the fullness of God's grace to all men and gave them an intelligible interpretation of Arminian theology which 'marked one of the great advances in the liberation of the human spirit'.[5] If this gospel of spiritual opportunity was not new, it was because it was based on the timeless teaching of Jesus.

The message beginning with Wesley was transmitted through his preachers to the common people. It did not remain a message with them, any more than with the messengers. It became a living and joyous experience. The Minutes of a meet-ing held in the Leaders' Room in Cork record an appreciation of the life of James Field to whom reference has already been made. He had served his church for fifty years after his 'honour-able discharge' from the army, and the eloquent tribute paid to him contains this passage: 'He was a Wesleyan Methodist in the truest sense; for he *loved* as well as believed the doctrines taught by Wesley. . . . He delighted to urge all believers to the attain-ment of "perfect love", the possession and exemplification of which was the secret of his own uniform character and success.'[6]

A man of entirely different temperament and circumstance, George Osborn of Rochester, records his father's rather quaint attempt to describe his new and vital experience. Whilst believing the doctrines and observing the ordinances of the Church, he confessed that he had no other apologia for his membership of the local Methodist Society than that he believed: 'Methodism is Church of Englandism *felt*.'[7]

In attempting even a limited analysis of this spiritual experience the difficulty is not to collect evidence, but to select a few typical instances from the wealth of material available. The early Methodists had a liking for recording their spiritual struggles, and the study of many of these journals, written quite independently, by people who had little or no contact at all with each other, shows an astonishing similarity. The language is different, the grammar, syntax, and spelling varying with the very different educational standards of the writers, but the experience itself, in its several stages and its climax, is the same whether it is recorded by Darcy, Lady Maxwell or Seth Evans and 'Sammy' Hick.

The Doctrine of Assurance was criticized and scornfully condemned by some who thought it an impertinence to claim that one knew one's sins were forgiven. It was unfortunate that at times the fact was announced in an 'extreme and uncharitable form'. Even John Wesley in his earlier days might have been so criticized, but the doctrine was an inevitable result of the appeal to experience. What was really claimed was that the ordinary man or woman might be conscious of a personal relationship to God in Christ Jesus. Instead of thinking of God as 'an unrelated and irresponsible being' a man might think of Him as Father and know that he, even he, was received by God Himself as a son.

What the ignorant and pagan Englishman would never have understood through the logic of Butler or Berkeley he began to realize through the sermons of John Wesley and the songs of his brother Charles. The fact became still more obvious in the changed outlook of his neighbours.

> My chains fell off, my heart was free,
> I rose, went forth and followed Thee.

That was what they were singing, and it was the song of free men whose bondage was ended, and ended so plainly that doubt was silenced. There was a new confidence in their approach to life, but it was based on faith in God, not on themselves.

The daughter of a sincere and indeed, a narrow clergyman of Macclesfield, Hester Ann Roe, was distressed about her spiritual condition.[8] In spite of a religious background, her life had been unsatisfactory in that she had experienced no personal relationship to God. Her journal records in close detail the struggles she experienced in her efforts to arrive at reality. At Holy Communion, for a moment, the Comfortable Words: 'If any man sin, we have an Advocate with the Father, Jesus Christ the righteous, and He is the propitiation for our sins', seemed to offer her peace, 'but it was only for a short season'. Again, stealing away to hear Samuel Bardsley, the Methodist, preach, she was deeply moved: 'I thought every word was for me. He spoke to my heart as if he had known all the secret workings there; and pointed all such sinners, as I felt myself to be, to Jesus crucified. I was much comforted.' Again the respite was short and incomplete. Perhaps it was influenced by the opposition of her mother who confined her to her room, and by the threatened withdrawal of her godmother's material gifts, but most of all by an inward restlessness that had not yet found its rest in God. Self-denial, the reading of some of Wesley's sermons and constant prayer still left her unassured. Some of her phrases, in the description of her spiritual struggle, sound, today, extravagant, but they are certainly sincere. At last she comes to her crisis. She had been reading a pamphlet given to her by Cousin Charles Roe: *The Great Duty of Believing on the Son of God*. 'I was much encouraged in reading this, and would gladly have spent the night in prayer, but my mother (with whom I slept) would not suffer it. I therefore went to bed, but could not sleep; and at four in the morning rose again, that I might wrestle with the Lord. I prayed but it seemed in vain. I walked to and fro, groaning for mercy; then fell again on my knees; but the heavens appeared as brass, and hope seemed almost sunk into despair; when suddenly the Lord spake that promise to my heart, "Believe on the Lord Jesus Christ, and thou shalt be saved". I revived, and cried, "Lord, I know this is Thy word, and I can depend on it. But what is faith?" '

Her journal continues, at length, to describe her effort to understand how to believe. Like St. Teresa she agonizes in 'dryness of soul'. Then comes the deliverance, and it is so true an emancipation that it must not be paraphrased: 'Again it came, "Only believe". "Lord Jesus," said I, "I will, I do believe: I now venture my whole salvation upon Thee as God; I put my guilty soul into Thy hands, Thy blood is sufficient. I cast my soul upon Thee for time and eternity." Then did he appear to my salvation. In that moment my fetters were broken, my bands were loosed, and my soul set at liberty. The love of God was shed abroad in my heart, and I rejoiced with joy unspeakable. Now, if I had possessed ten thousand souls, I would have ventured them all with my Jesus. I would have given them all to Him! I felt a thousand promises all my own: more than a thousand scriptures to confirm my evidence; such as, "He that believeth shall be saved,—shall not perish,—is not condemned, —hath everlasting life,—is passed from death into life,—shall never die;—there is no condemnation to them that are in Christ Jesus," etc. etc. I could now call Jesus Lord, by the Holy Ghost; and the Father, my Father. My sins were gone; my soul was happy; and I longed to depart and be with Jesus. I was truly a new creature; and seemed to be in a new world.'

So the rapture continued, not only in her journal but in her life. In reading the account it must be remembered that it was not written by a neurotic or, as the candid critic of today might say, 'a sex-starved woman'. She was a perfectly normal, well-educated person, who later married and became the mother of several happy children. (She is better known as Mrs. Hester Ann Rogers and is one of the figures in the historic picture of John Wesley's death.) It is easy to say that her language is at times almost flamboyant, that her sense of guilt is exaggerated, and her own importance magnified, but no one could question the joy of spiritual emancipation that came to her, and it remained with her through all the years of a long and useful life.

The case of Hester Ann Roe is typical of many thousands, and the journals which survive provide ample evidence of this widespread experience. There were many, however, who were illiterate, and the writing of a diary was an impossibility. None the less in these cases, oral tradition, crystallized in the records of the next generation, confirm the actual 'first sources'. Old Sarah M'Kim of Sligo, had never learned to read but she was 'familiar with the Word of God, and ready always to give an answer to every man that asked her a reason of the hope that was in her'. The young preacher, Mr. Lanktree, visited her. 'Sister M'Kim,' said he, 'when it is best with you, how do you feel?' 'Just on the verge of heaven,' she said with a smile that lit up her aged face. 'When it is worst with you, what is your experience?' Just as surely and joyfully she answered, 'Though He slay me, yet will I trust in Him'.[9]

The basis of this assurance was always in the love of God and never in the work of man. 'I now venture my whole salvation upon Thee, as God,' said Hester Roe, and countless others said almost the same. It was often a long-drawn struggle which brought these people to this point when their joy overflowed— a struggle and a joy which the Deist neither understood nor really knew. The crisis, as in the case of the medieval saints, came through long seasons of prayer. 'Prayer,' said the Deist, 'is illogical and absurd; God is not a man that he should change.' 'Wesley's answer was to teach men how to pray, and so to pray that whether God was changed or not, their relations to God were for ever changed.' That was the pronouncement made by Dr. H. B. Workman, in a memorable sermon preached at Cambridge during the Bicentenary Celebrations to mark the admission of John Wesley to his Fellowship at Lincoln College (1725–6).[10] They are the words of a great historian, spoken to a critical audience, and they remain his considered and generally accepted judgement on a fundamental issue of human life.

These experiences becoming more widespread as Methodism grew, met with fierce criticism and contempt. Some of the theologians scented a new attempt to greet this consciousness of personal relationship as an assurance of future perseverance. 'We speak of an assurance of our present pardon, not . . . of our final perseverance,' was Wesley's answer, as early as 6th October 1738, and he never weakened on the matter.[11] Others argued that it pre-supposed an arrogant claim based on personal piety or good works. It could be shown, again and again, that this was not the attitude of the typical Methodist, whatever might have been the case in the noisy affirmations of some people who were, in the technical sense 'enthusiasts' and fanatics. A man coming to Wesley in Bristol, asked to know if one 'could not be saved without the faith of assurance'. He answered: 'I never yet knew one soul thus saved without what you call "the faith of assurance"; I mean a sure confidence that, by the merits of Christ, he was reconciled to the favour of God.'[12] There can be no doubt from the whole teaching of Wesley and the general experience of the first generation of Methodists, as to where they believed the merit lay. They agonized in prayer, but there was no reference to any virtue in their agony—only in their Saviour's.

An extraordinary instance of a changed attitude on this particular point is quoted by John Wesley in his *Journal* (1st February 1748): 'I received an account of Mr. Towers of Leeds, who had even prayed that he might *not know* his sins forgiven, as believing it was the highest presumption; but, notwithstanding this, as he lay one night upon his bed, he did receive the knowledge of salvation by the remission of sins, and he declared it boldly to the confusion, at least, if not conviction of those who denied the truth.'[13]

The periods of conviction of sin presented the early preachers with serious problems, and they were not sentimental but severely practical in dealing with them. A woman, Jane Edge of Olerton, near Preston, told Robert Costerdine, travelling preacher from Haworth, that her sins were unpardonable, and she was determined to drown herself. Coolly he told her that he would like to be present when she did so, and would 'come to the water immediately'. She then changed her mind and said she would hang herself. 'Bring me a rope for her,' said Robert to her husband, 'for I am resolved to see what the Devil will be permitted to do.' Jane shrank from the test and Robert said, 'You know in your conscience you would be glad to meet me in Heaven.' 'Pray for me,' said Jane—and 'while he did so, the Lord removed the temptation, and she continued until five o'clock next morning praising God. Jane lived many years after this, and continued to the end a pious steady follower of Christ; and in death as in life, was enabled to witness a good confession.[14]

The danger of individualism and self-analysis was corrected by the healthy exchange of opinion in the fellowship-meetings, particularly in the class-meeting, and in the wider view of the divine purpose for the salvation of the world. This became more obvious as social service and missionary enterprise developed, but the joy of these people was deepened as they realized they could share in it themselves.[15]

Nor is it surprising that the element of fear played its part in convincing men of sin. Further reference must be made to this factor, but remembering Jane Edge it may be noted that punishment in the world to come was also associated with punishment here and now. There is an authentic account of an old lady, born in 1771, stating that as a girl of ten she was taken to the church at Swinefleet by her mother. 'She then saw a female standing in the church doing penance, having thrown over her a white sheet, and her hair combed over her face. This penance was performed during the time of divine service.'[16] The world in which the first Methodists lived had not entirely shaken off its medieval blanket!

There are many books which have been written in defence of the Methodist point of view, amongst which might be named Joseph Benson's *Defence of Methodism* and Edward Hare's *Doctrine of Assurance taught by Methodists*. Comparisons have been drawn between the views of Jeremy Taylor, Spangenberg, and John Wesley. The doctrine itself was amply expressed in Charles Wesley's hymns, which were sung by people who felt all they sang, and that the words were an expression of their own living experience.

In this brief summary two men, separated by a century and completely dissimilar in personal circumstance, shall bear their witness. The first, Thomas Jackson, President of the Conference in 1839, wrote on the occasion of the Centenary of Wesleyan Methodism: 'We may likewise observe the *depth* of the work so extensively and quickly wrought. Multitudes have been thoroughly convinced of sin; and shortly after, so filled with joy and love, that, whether they were in the body, or out of the body, they could hardly tell; and in the power of this love they have trampled under foot whatever the world accounts either terrible or desirable, having evidenced, in the severest trials, an invariable and tender goodwill to mankind, and all the fruits of holiness.'[17] The second witness is the Right Honourable Stanley Baldwin, speaking as Prime Minister nearly ninety years later, in 1928, at the Hundred and Fiftieth Anniversary of the Opening of Wesley's Chapel, City Road, London: 'Wesley's supreme legacy, as I see it, to this country was his conception of a practical religion for the ordinary man and woman. He aimed at finding —and here I come back to the calm mind of that century—

a reasoned balance between inward conviction and outward expression, individual conversion and collective worship.'[18]

The reality of the Methodist conception of Assurance as taught by Wesley and his preachers could not be hampered by the limitations of a Calvinistic creed. It is obvious to the student of the period that the differences between Whitefield and Wesley and, still more, the bitterness of later controversies, affected a few preachers and at times had a devastating effect on village communities,[19] and perturbed the Conference.[20] The cruder Calvinism which was accepted in the eighteenth century is almost meaningless today. 'To the twentieth century, Arminianism seems almost axiomatic, largely, of course, because the century starts with the postulate of the Fatherhood of God.'[21] It must always be borne in mind, however, that to the early Methodists it presented a very real problem, and the doctrine of election, in its most appalling setting, was always an alternative presented by well-meaning people. The influence of Wesley and his first followers was powerful in driving this strange and hard 'faith' from the field.[22]

It has often been said that conversion is 'a good old Methodist word', and it has certainly been well used by Methodists. It was inevitable that this should be so amongst a people who insisted above all else, on the possibility of the individual's conscious relationship with God. The idea of conversion was, as has been said, 'a natural corollary'. It meant the transformation of the whole being, and it implied the surrender of the will not to any human representative, but to God Himself in Christ Jesus. There were times when the Methodist presentation of this possibility was repellent and illogical, because of the stress laid on time and on the total depravity of human nature which involved little children in its cruel, if theoretical, toils.

A study of the conversion of John Wesley and his brother makes it evident that this change could be complex and protracted. The masterly exposition of this problem by Dr. J. E. Rattenbury is as complete as seems possible.[23] There is, however, so wide a range of personalities involved, even in the first generation of Methodists, that any kind of uniformity or approximation to the Wesley pattern can neither be expected nor desired. Some were first influenced by the crudest fears of physical torment, others grew gradually into a consciousness of the love of

H

Christ reaching down to their own small and insignificant lives. Though it is regrettable that a narrow interpretation of conversion had its evil results during the first years, it is astonishing to realize what a change it made to the life of England as a whole, and to so many individuals in particular. Whatever may have been the varying motives that brought men to face the issue, and however different may have been the manner of their conversion, the conditions fulfilled were exactly scriptural—repentance and faith—and the result of every true conversion was a life so transformed that the converted man or woman was consciously striving to 'live in Christ', as a new creature. The student need do no more than read the instances recorded in the *Journal of John Wesley* (indexed under the word Conversion) or scan the volumes of *The Lives of Early Methodist Preachers* to secure ample material on which to base his judgement. There is, however, a wider and less-known field in the lives of the ordinary Methodist people. A few instances must suffice.

A sailor's son, William Carvosso, born near Mousehole, Cornwall, in 1750, was early apprenticed to a farmer, and remained on the farm till he was twenty-one.[24] 'During this time,' he says, 'I was borne down by the prevailing sins of the age; such as cock-fighting, wrestling, card-playing and Sabbath-breaking . . . yet I was a regular attendant at my parish church. . . . In the year 1771 the Lord was pleased, in his mercy to convert my sister; and having tasted that the Lord was gracious, she came from Gwinear, a distance of twelve miles, to tell us of the happy news, and to warn us to flee from the wrath to come.' When William returned to his mother's cottage he was more than a little surprised to find a prayer-meeting in progress—'my sister on her knees praying with my mother and brothers. After she had concluded, she soon began to enquire what preparation I was making for eternity. I was quite at a loss for an answer.' Feeling, doubtless, that he must make some kind of amends for his dumbness, he promised to go to 'the Methodist preaching which was at Newlyn, in a room on the Maddern side of the river'. Only William Carvosso has the right to tell us what happened: 'As soon as I entered the place I steadfastly fixed my eyes on the Preacher, who was Mr. Thomas Hanson. His text was, "We are ambassadors for Christ, as though God did beseech you by us, we pray you in Christ's stead be ye reconciled to God". The word quickly reached my heart; the scales fell off from my eyes; and I saw and felt I was "in the gall of bitterness, and in the bond of iniquity". I had such a sight of the damning nature of sin, and of what I had done against God, that I was afraid the earth would open and swallow me up. I then made a solemn promise to the Lord, that if he could spare me I would serve him all my days. I now gave up my sins, and all my old companions at a stroke; and at once determined, if I could see anyone going to heaven I would join him. That night I had a hard struggle with Satan, about praying before I went to bed. . . .' In quaint phrase, but with absolute candour, William describes what was a very real battle to him. In the middle of his struggle he called out—to a very real Devil—' "I am determined, whether I am saved or lost, that while I have breath, I will never cease crying for mercy." The very moment I formed this resolution in my heart, Christ appeared within, and God pardoned all my sins, and set my soul at liberty. The Spirit itself now bore witness with my spirit that I was a child of God. This was about nine o'clock at night, 17th May 1771; and never shall I forget that happy hour.'—William Carvosso has spoken for himself. There is much that might be criticized, but criticism wilts before the record of the years that followed. He was a benediction to the countryside, and when, after long years of farming he retired, he spent his days visiting classes all over that part of Cornwall. Though he did not learn to write till he was sixty-five his journal is clear and concise, and contains amongst its most interesting features many accounts of men and women whom he led to God. To the first Methodists, to be converted meant to become at once an evangelist.

Instantaneous as the conversion of William Carvosso seems to have been, it stood the stress of the years. Amongst the most moving passages in his journal is the account of a visit to Mousehole on the fiftieth anniversary of his conversion.[25] 'This event was rendered the more abundantly gratifying and delightful, because it took place at the spot where I commenced, and in the presence of the three who set out in the way to heaven with me.' There they stood—four old men—Richard Trewarvas, M. Wright, William Carvosso and his brother Benedict, as he says 'After half a century . . . still kept by the power of God, through faith, with our faces Zionwards.' As they knelt there, giving thanks, one seems to catch a glimpse of the shadowy figure of the girl who tramped the twelve miles from Gwinear, fifty years before—to tell them of her Saviour.

Let old James Field report in his own words the story of the conversion of his brother and his own son: 'My brother is one of the greatest miracles of mercy that walks the earth. He was nearly thirty years in the army; was with the Duke through the Spanish war, a great sinner, a confirmed drunkard for thirty-four years. Nothing was of any use. I despaired of his ever being converted. But what is too hard for God? He was sent to Kinsale for coals, got drunk, and, sitting on one of the cars, fell off; and the car loaded with perhaps near a ton weight of coals, went over him. Not a bone was broken, although the road was newly gravelled. Was it not miraculous? This sobered him. He formed the resolution that he would drink no more strong drink. That is four or five years ago, and he has kept his resolution; but, best of all, he instantly turned to God, and suffered the good word of the Lord, which he heard in his father's house, to vegetate after forty years. He is now on the brink of eternity, praising God, and patiently waiting for his great change.'

That is an old soldier's account of his brother's conversion, and it might be studied closely with advantage, but it is the story of a late repentance. Let him speak of his son John, the younger of two boys whose father's prayers had been so often offered for them both: 'Blessed be God, Mr. Mayne's sermon last Sabbath reached the heart of my son John. The text was, "Ye cannot serve two masters". I never saw one in greater distress of mind. All desire for meat, drink, and sleep was taken away. This morning he was up, waiting for me, before it was light. I talked and prayed with him. He found comfort; but I was not fully satisfied that he had obtained peace with God until two o'clock, when having talked and prayed with him again, I found to my unspeakable joy, that God had graciously pardoned his sins in the morning. From the depths of terror and despair, he was raised to enjoy sweet peace in believing. Eternal glory to God! May divine grace be sufficient for him, even unto death!' The passage ends with these moving words: 'O my heavenly Father . . . help me to love Thee proportionately for the conversion of my dear John; and, for the sake of the blessed Jesus, bring all my family to experience the same salvation.'

There is, in this old veteran's private journal, the same sincerity and reality that one discovered in the account of William Carvosso. Lives were transfigured by a spiritual power which is inexplicable save on a Christian basis.

By contrast, Seth Evans, the husband of George Eliot's heroine Dinah, was a simple villager, whose life had been lived within the limits of Roston, a little Derbyshire village. In some fragmentary notes, attempting to describe his personal experience, he speaks of his early manhood as 'very dark and ignorant as regards divine truth'.[26] Hearing one day that 'the Methodist minister preached without a book' his curiosity was excited, and he went to hear 'the singular and gifted man'. The service was held at Snelston, and Seth went, as he would have gone to see some strange and freakish creature in a side-show on market day. His own description of what happened is the best material on which to form a judgement: 'While he was praying,' he writes, 'conviction first reached me. I was in great distress of soul; the anguish I suffered is indescribable. When he began to preach, I thought someone had told him of my state; every word seemed for me. I felt that I was the greatest sinner in the place. I continued in that state of mind six weeks, when praying in private, early one morning before going to work, the Lord, in great mercy, broke in upon my soul. I felt my load of sin removed; I felt peace and joy through believing, and I could then sing from my heart—

> My God is reconciled,
>   His pardoning voice I hear,
> He owns me for his child
>   I can no longer fear!

Those words 'I thought someone had told him of my state', are strangely reminiscent of John Nelson's account of a similar moment in his own life. Careful reading of these ingenuous diaries of the soul reveals constant parallels, which can only be accounted for by similarity in actual experience. Any question of plagiarism or imitation is ruled out, because even in cases where the journals were ultimately published, the delay was considerable. The only place where such experiences were exchanged was in the class-meeting which was entirely a local affair.

Conversion, amongst the first Methodists, was not always instantaneous or cataclysmic. Perhaps in their preaching, too

great a stress was laid on Time and this led to the belief in some
quarters that the experience must be the occurrence of one transforming moment. It is obvious from the facts that the time
factor was of little importance; the thing that mattered was the
quality of the experience—'the *fulness* of this consciousness of sin
and the Saviour'.

The father of Joseph Sugden had been converted under the
strong appeals of the Rev. John Grant, 'the walking Bible', as
he was called in Oakworth village. It was some time before
Jonas, remarkable for his caution, 'examined the principles of
Methodism' and was sufficiently satisfied to join the Society. In
1790 he attended the watch-night service and was 'made happy
in the love of God'. The friend who went with him wrote his
impression of the happening: 'There was no rapture, but there
was peace; no mighty agitation of the passions, but there was
the calm confidence of principle. The darkness had gradually
disappeared before the rising of the Sun of Righteousness, and
on that night the light of the Divine countenance shone on his
soul with great brightness.'[27] Though the circumstances were
less dramatic than in some cases, the consequences were the
same. Jonas Sugden eventually became a mill-owner whose
character was remarkable for its absolute honesty in all his
human relationships. The announcement which was once posted
at the entrance to Vale Mill, Bingley, was evidence that his
experience at the watch-night service—the climax of a long
period of calm but earnest seeking—was real and permanent.
The document was signed by Jonas and his three brothers and
was, at least, evidence of the stress they laid on character:
'*Notice.*—Jonas Sugden and Bros. wish and expect,—1st, That
every person in their employ attends some place of Divine worship every Lord's Day. 2nd, That every youth dependent on
those whom they employ, attends some Sunday and day-school,
from the age of six years and upwards. 3rd, That those who are
of proper age, and the parents and guardians of the young, make
choice of their own school and place of worship.'

Modern amenities, social, educational and religious, may make
such expectations seem quaint or even an infringement on the
freedom of the individual but, seen against the background of
English industrialism of the early nineteenth century, the document is significant. The biographer of Jonas Sugden having seen

the mill and the workpeople said: 'From the three brothers to the least of the girls who tends a frame, all appear to pursue their business with activity and determination. And yet we see no signs of languor; no countenance upon which a smile may not naturally play and not a particle of the brutality that an author to whom we shall afterwards refer, charges against the working classes of our manufacturing districts.' That is the unbiased judgement of a contemporary, and it points to an acknowledgement of the values of every individual, which could only have come to this mill-owner through the consciousness of his own personal relationship to God. To Jonas Sugden the men and women were not 'hands'. They were children of God and he knew it, because he had the witness of his own sonship.

The most noticeable feature in all the available records is that certain factors are common to each experience, whether the person concerned be educated or uneducated, rich or poor. There are many amongst these people who were unknown outside their parish, but there are others who had a definite place in much wider social groups, and some few who were national figures. The fact that some had lived sheltered lives and others been buffeted by the seven seas made no difference to the fundamentals of this experience they called conversion. To all of them there came a strong sense or conviction of sin, and a passionate desire for reconciliation with the God from whom they had estranged themselves. They found deliverance through faith in Christ, and began to live, new creatures in a new world. Variety in these experiences lay in secondary circumstances, never in fundamentals.

The life of Silas Told, written by himself, is reminiscent of the stories of Daniel Defoe. He was born in 1711 near the Hotwells, Bristol, and his parents were 'very creditable people'. One could hardly say that of Silas in his youthful adventuring. Though he appears to have had an astonishingly religious childhood his life at sea was tempestuous spiritually, as in every other way. 'When I was in petticoats, my sister Dulcybella and I wandered often into the woods and fields, fixing ourselves under the hedges, conversing about God and happiness. . . .'[28] It is difficult to realize that the man who had such memories of what seems today, religious precocity, records the wildest adventures sailing to the West Coast of Africa and carrying cargoes of wretched negroes to

the sugar and cotton plantations across the Atlantic. There are
few more graphic accounts of the brutality of the slave-trade
than the short chronicles of Silas Told. The effect on his own
character was inevitable. The child who sat in the fields with
Dulcybella, talking about God, grew to be the man who wrote:
'I can never sufficiently praise the Almighty for my happy
deliverance from the slave-trade, seeing it is one of the basest
practices under the sun. Surely an immediate curse from God
attends upon it, as few voyages are made to those parts in which
the crews are not thinned by poison, suicide, ill-usage, and every
species of destruction. God followed me with daily convictions
of sins; yet, having an evil precedent always before me, and the
corruptions of my own nature incessantly prompting me to sin,
I sometimes gave way thereto against the light of conscience,
knowing but very little of the corrupt fountain from whence
these currents flowed. I found that, when the bank was broken,
the breach was made wider and wider; and being at that time
between seventeen and eighteen years of age, my carnal passions
getting the dominion over me, I was oftentimes overcome with
swearing, drunkenness, and lewdness, as also divers other evils:
therefore, what with my terrified conscience, and disappointments in temporals, my life became completely miserable; and,
for about ten years, I continued in that unsettled state, sinning
and repenting; yet I never was without fear of death, hell and
judgement.'[29] It must not be supposed from this confession that
Silas Told was a weakling. He was, on the contrary, a good
seaman and faced storms, wrecks, and savage attacks by wild
men, black and white, with courage. By the time he was twenty-
nine he had a first-hand knowledge of the slave-trade, and had
played a part in that appalling traffic in which human lives were
counted of less value than a hogshead of rum. Soon he was to
become the respected master in Mr. Wesley's Charity School and
the most beloved unofficial chaplain to the condemned felons in
Newgate. Nothing less than a spiritual upheaval could have
made this possible. The change began when Charles Caspar
Greaves, a young bricklayer asked him to go to a Methodist
service. There 'was something in the countenance and behaviour
of this young man, very different to what I beheld in others . . .
yet I treated him with ridicule and contempt; and sometimes
cursed and swore at him, and told him his whole fraternity was

a mixture of false prophets and hypocrites. . . .'[30] But Caspar persisted: 'At twelve o'clock he asked me where I dined. I answered him very roughly, "In the hay-loft". He then said, "I will go with you".' They climbed the rickety ladder and the bricklayer took his Prayer-book and read a few verses from the Psalms. Then he began to talk to Silas, and urged him once more to come to hear Mr. Wesley preach. Once again the answer was a round of abuse, and Caspar said no more; 'but in that instant, God began powerfully to work upon my soul. Then the eye of my mind saw the Son of God sitting on His throne to judge the world, and such peace resting upon me as tongue cannot express.' The barrier was broken down and, there, as they sat on the trusses of hay, Silas poured out his soul to Caspar. Twice they went to the Foundery in the hope of hearing Wesley preach but were disappointed. Now, however, the pressure was coming from Silas, for the craving in his soul would not be denied. Next Sunday Caspar called for him 'precisely at four o'clock in the morning,' and he went with him to the Foundery. The superficial critic of conversion might be reminded of this, and be compelled to own that here is no question of mass meetings and halls overheated and over-charged with emotion encouraged by sweet music! Presently having walked down Cheapside they arrived at the Foundery, well before five o'clock. Silas looked about him and found it 'a ruinous place, with an old pantile covering, a few rough deal boards put together to constitute a temporary pulpit, and several other decayed timbers which composed the whole structure. . . . In one corner sat three or four old women, one of whom appeared like a statue, with her apron over her face, nor was she uncovered during the whole service. The enemy of souls immediately suggested that she was a hypocrite. My friend, Mr. Greaves, stood close behind, to prevent my going out, to which I was strongly tempted. . . .' Exactly at five o'clock, John Wesley entered. He was robed, and Silas was astonished that instead of a customary liturgical opening 'he began with singing a hymn, with which I was almost enraptured; but his extempore prayer was quite unpleasant, as I thought it favoured too much of the Dissenter'. The sermon was on the forgiveness of sins[31] and, for a moment, Silas suspected he was 'a Papist'.

Soon he was listening intently. He says plainly: 'I saw I could

THE EARLY METHODIST PEOPLE

never be saved without knowing my sins were forgiven; and the Spirit of God sealed every word upon my heart. At the close of the discourse, however strange it may appear, a small still voice entered my heart with these words, "This is the truth!" and instantly I felt it in my soul.' In Methodist phraseology 'the great transaction was done' and Silas Told, ex-slaver, was a new man in Christ Jesus. In spite of immediate domestic opposition, and the obvious difficulties such sudden transformation would create, he continued from that hour a faithful and increasingly useful and happy servant of God.[32] When he died, thirty-nine years later, a contemporary wrote: 'After having done all the good in his power, he cheerfully resigned his soul into the hands of the heavenly Father', and many a poor soul 'cast off' at Tyburn gallows would have testified to the blessing of his ministry in their last mortal hour. It would be difficult to explain away 'conversion' even if there were but the record of Silas Told.

In an entirely different environment, the instance of Darcy Brisbane, Lady Maxwell might be cited. She came of ancient stock, and climbed sometimes, as a small child, into an old oak elbow-chair which bore the family arms, carved in 1357 on its worn back.[33] Her life became eminent for its piety, and the record of her good works has its assured place in Scottish history. She was by no means the least important of a circle of friends which included Lady Henrietta Hope, Lady Glenorchy, Lady Mary Fitzgerald, and Elizabeth Ritchie, but she had a sense of social and spiritual responsibility which demanded the best of her time and energies. Her tastes were simple and her whole life marked by generosity. In her correspondence she reveals much that is indicative of spiritual perception and growth in understanding, but the account of her conversion is contained in one poignant sentence. She lost her husband in less than two years after their most happy marriage. Six weeks after his death her little son died, and she was left a lonely widow at nineteen years of age. To her most intimate friend she said: 'God brought me to Himself by afflictions.' Her whole life reveals how near and intimate that relation was, and her letters make it quite plain that in the hour of her greatest need, she began to know the joy of her Lord. 'Having brought me into the wilderness, He spoke comfortably to me; drew me with the cords of love . . . taught me, as I could bear them, the lessons of His grace; He informed my judgement, but first affected my heart. Without this, I should have gone heavily on, if at all.' With it, she became a woman who served her day and generation, with all her heart.

Criticism has sometimes been passed on these private journals on the ground that they reveal their writers as self-centred and morbidly introspective. There is little justification for this, as a rule, so long as the whole record be taken into account. In many cases to begin with the earlier sections describing the preface to conversion and to end with the pages dealing with the crisis itself would be to obtain a wrong impression of the experience and the writer. The sequel often lies beyond the scope of the journal. The crisis was of supreme importance to the individual concerned, and since it changed the rest of his life he can be forgiven for dwelling on the small details which seem to a later generation boring and ego-centric. A fair estimate can only be obtained by considering the life as a whole. What kind of a man did the converted person become? Did he remain self-centred or did the transformation send him out to 'brother all mankind'? In the majority of cases the answer would be that the 'conversion' affected his whole life afterwards. As soon as he was sure that he was 'right with God' he desired above all else, to help his fellows towards the inner peace he now enjoyed. The fact that his personal journal, so often, spoke less of his subsequent service is surely to the writer's credit. To record one's own good deeds is not the habit of a real Christian. This means, then, not only that such journals must be read in their entirety, but also that they must be considered in their proper setting and, wherever possible, checked by external evidence of a life well-lived.

Amongst the more detailed records that survive are the diary, letters and memoirs of Henry Longden, a sturdy Yorkshire Methodist.[34] He was born in Sheffield in 1754. 'Although my parents had had nineteen children, none of them were living when I was born,' he writes, and explains that he grew up a spoilt child, because of the natural anxiety that he, too, would not long survive. It was a comfortable and pious home, but he became wilful and reserved. The result was that his schoolmaster treated him 'brutally' and he accepted all punishment in silence. 'I had made considerable progress in the Latin tongue,' he records, and adds, a little inconsequently, 'when my father,

by some bruises upon me, became acquainted with my treatment at school,' he was removed at once, and soon after, was
apprenticed to a razor-maker in Sheffield, at the age of fifteen.
For the next three years he was restrained from the wilder
excesses of his fellow-apprentices by the thought and influence of
his mother. Then, on her death, he gave way to the temptations
which surrounded him. He was a sturdy fighter, and 'became
the champion of Sheffield'—apparently amongst the apprentices.
How far his description of his conduct is exaggerated, it is difficult
to judge, for he maintained even in this period what he calls
'a high sense of honour' though the phrase is used rather as the
modern talks of 'playing the game'. At nineteen he was drinking
hard, for he confesses that at 'Attercliffe feast on a Sabbath
afternoon . . . a few of us drank five pints of gin in a short time'.
He was brought home 'insensible' and for some weeks it was
uncertain whether he would recover. Not long after, he broke
his apprentice's bond and ran away to join the army. His father
followed him and although he had already enlisted, secured his
discharge and persuaded him to return home. He completed
his apprenticeship and marvelled, in later years, that he survived
the dissipations of his youth. There was, however, in his heart
an unswerving devotion to his mother's memory and to his
father's increasing need. 'Being now of full age, I sat down
seriously to consider the course of my future life. To continue
in the business I had learnt, would have been the most profitable;
but when I recollected the age and growing infirmities of my
father, and the gratitude and affection which I owed him as
a son, I resolved to offer him my services to conduct and manage
his business. He accepted my offer with readiness and great
affection.' As he watched the old man failing he became anxious
about his spiritual well-being! Presently he found himself, a
stranger from God, praying for his father, who was 'in uncertainty and darkness'. There is something strangely moving in
the thought of the youth, who, himself, was in greater uncertainty,
praying not for himself but for the old man. 'And when we
arose from our knees', he says, 'we were both much affected.
Ever after this my father's views relative to the method of
salvation were altered, and he became a man of prayer.'

Presently Henry Longden married, and his diary reads 'for
which union I shall have cause to praise God in time and in

eternity'. Six weeks later his father died, and the bereavement again forced him to consider his own spiritual condition. 'I was an enigma to myself. I felt in my soul a painful void.' Visiting two neighbours who were dying he was impressed by the tragic death of the one and the triumphant passing of the other. He decided to accept the advice of the latter, and went straight from his funeral to the service at the Methodist Chapel. He had, of course, never been to such a place before and he was immediately impressed. 'The Preacher, Mr. John Peacock, was a plain man, without any parade', he records in his diary. 'His deportment was solemn, without affectation; his prayer was simple, but it opened heaven; his preaching was unadorned, but mighty by the power of God. He felt what he said, and he could not restrain tears from running down his cheeks. I observed the congregation were often in tears also. The men sung with all their hearts, and the women sweetly sung the repeats alone: the men sat on one side, and the women on the other. I thought, Where am I?—this worship is pure, simple and spiritual; nor did I think there had been a people so primitive and apostolical upon earth. In the fullness of my heart I said, "This people shall be my people, and their God shall be my God for ever".'

The impression was so deep that he told his friends that he meant now to serve God, since he felt that to be the most reasonable end in life. They tried in vain 'to shake his resolution. He went regularly to the preaching services, had family prayer at home, prayed in private and, in short, considered himself to be a reformed character, and a very good Christian.' With a view to joining a class, he interviewed the class-leader and asked him wistfully whether a man might know that his sins were forgiven. The leader answered without hesitation, assuring him it was so and that he spoke from his own experience, giving him many scriptural proofs. But Henry Longden—reformed character though he believed himself to be—was not convinced. 'The veil was on my heart,—I could not understand him.' Nevertheless, he joined the class, and was promptly told by his leader that he was not sufficiently conscious of his sins. 'I would seriously recommend you to pray earnestly to God to give you a sense of the burden of your sins,' he said. So for a time he continued uncertainly, becoming gradually aware of his real plight. 'I saw the tenor of my life had been an act of daring contempt of the

Majesty of heaven, and myself an enemy of God.' So he continued to pray, but his mental and spiritual agony increased,
because, he said afterwards, he was praying for deeper conviction
rather than for deeper faith. His friends deplored his melancholy. Newcomers to the preaching services found deliverance,
and he remained in bonds. Then a class-member put him in a
dilemma. 'It must be either God's fault or your fault,' he said,
and the hard-headed Yorkshireman admitted the point. He
pressed home his advantage: 'I know you have broken off every
sin, have left your old companions, and have sought the Lord
earnestly, with many tears: all which are essential to salvation.
You have been mighty in grief . . . and you have trusted in this,
as a plea for the mercy of God, instead of pleading in faith the
death and mediation of Jesus Christ, as the only ground of your
hope and plea for pardon. If you were to seek salvation a
thousand years, without the precious name of Christ, it would
not, it could not avail.' They were hard words, and they may
not command universal approval, but they brought Henry
Longden to his senses! He saw that neither his tears nor his
prayers could atone for his sin. He groped his way to the little
class-meeting resolved to make open confession of his new faith.
For a time he 'had a mighty contest with the powers of darkness', then suddenly his Leader asked him how he fared. In a
moment, in the fullness of his heart he cried out, 'I will believe,
I can believe, I do believe: glory be to God'. So there came to
him after long struggling a love and joy and peace he had never
known before. There is something that reminds one of John
Bunyan in the full and frank record he has left. It must not be
imagined that it is the account of a man selfishly concerned with
the salvation of his own soul to the exclusion of all else. Long
before he thought of his own personal salvation he was praying
for his father, and as soon as he realized his relationship with
Jesus Christ he began to serve his fellows with an intensity which
never lessened till the end of his life.[35] For many years the
Yorkshire countryside knew and loved him as a great under-
shepherd of souls.

The truly converted man becomes, himself, an evangelist.
That may be taken as axiomatic of the early Methodist conception
of conversion.

It had been so with John Wesley himself and it was no passing emotional reaction. Twenty years after the crisis in Aldersgate Street he wrote from Ireland to Ebenezer Blackwell[36] and the words almost burn the paper in their passion: 'I have now gone through the greatest part of this kingdom, Leinster, Ulster and the greatest half of Connaught. Time only is wanting. If my brother could take care of England, and give me but one year for Ireland, I think every corner of this nation would receive the truth as it is in Jesus. They want only to hear it; and they will hear me, high and low, rich and poor. . . .' This is the cry of a heart young and eager, with a youthfulness of zeal which time cannot touch, and it is not an experience peculiar to John Wesley.

In her simple little journal Mary Titherington, a class-leader of Liverpool, describes how a person came to her in distress. 'She wanted to be saved, but having got the notion of some Calvinists, she seemed desirous to be saved as a stock or a stone. I shall never forget the burden I felt in prayer while she held that opinion. My body sunk under it, so that I did not recover for three or four days.' Day after day she dragged her frail little body to houses where men and women were in spiritual darkness, and wrestled in prayer for their souls![37]

Before Lady Hope set out on a long journey by coach to Bristol she received a letter from her friend Lady Maxwell.[38] It contained advice as to her opportunities for personal evangelism in the inns at which she would be staying. The advice was, of course, based on her own practice, but it is, to say the least of it, an unusual attitude for a notability to take in the eighteenth century! 'As you pass along, endeavour to make all nature a scale to lead you up to its great and adorable Author. Having arrived at the inn, retire immediately, and for a few minutes strive to pour out your heart to the Hearer of prayer. After thanking Him for His mercies by the way, make a fresh surrender of yourself, and all you have and are, and pray for a sweet sense of His presence with you in that place. Entreat also for mercy to those who abide in the house, or occasionally resort to it. Plead for inclination and courage to attempt doing them some good, either by books, or conversation, or both, as opportunity offers, or circumstances permit. If at mid-day, let a portion of God's word be read, either by yourself or with your company. Should a Minister be with you, request him to engage in prayer, and invite the people of the inn to join with you. If there be not a Minister present, do it by turns yourselves with your two maids; and let this rule be invariably followed every morning and evening. If you stay above one day in a place, endeavour to find out some of the Christians that are in it, and strengthen their hands by taking notice of them; and to spiritual counsel add, if need be, and as particular circumstances call for it, a supply of temporal wants.' So the letter continues and proclaims itself to be the outpouring of one who was herself a true evangelist.

There is ample evidence to prove that this passion for souls was the inevitable outcome of a personal experience of the love of Christ, and it affected the lives of people both inside and outside the Methodist Societies. When James Morris was preaching at Coolymain in Wexford in 1756, it happened that Augustus M. Toplady was in the congregation. His father had been a major in the army, and on his death the widow brought her son to Ireland as she wished to claim part of an estate there. The surprising fact is that they should find their way into the little preaching service. Once there it could be guaranteed that they would hear a sermon evangelistic in its appeal. This is what Toplady, the gifted but critical author of the hymn 'Rock of Ages' wrote about the event, which was of such significance to him, and to thousands who have sung the inspired prayer. 'It was from Ephesians ii. 13 that Mr. Morris preached on the memorable evening of my effectual call by the grace of God, under the ministry of that dear messenger; and under that sermon I was, I trust, brought nigh by the blood of Christ, in August 1756. Strange that I, who had so long sat under the means of grace in England, should be brought nigh to God in an obscure part of Ireland, amidst a handful of God's people met together in a barn, and under the ministry of one who could hardly spell his name.' It was surely James Morris who shared in the writing of the hymn, for it would be difficult to imagine its existence apart from that earlier experience.[39]

But this evangelism was not confined to preaching, for the truly converted person proclaimed the 'Good News', consciously or unconsciously, by the manner and quality of his life. When Thomas Marriott, baker of Norton Folgate, went out regularly every evening, his new journeyman-baker was curious to know which public-house he favoured! His workmates told him it was the preaching-house at the Foundery! The young Scotsman,

Alexander Mather, was intrigued by the fact and went to see for himself. Later, hearing John Wesley at West Street Chapel, he was converted and became one of the most distinguished preachers in Methodism, if not indeed, in England. That is a statement of the bare facts, but there are details which call for comment. The engagement of Alexander Mather had happened in an unusual way. Old Thomas Marriott, needing a young journeyman to serve in his bakehouse, heard of a possible applicant. Quite naturally he prayed for guidance, as was his custom. Then he set out to inquire about the person of whom he had heard. 'He had scarcely left the house on this errand before his attention was attracted by a decent-looking young man in an apron, dressed as a baker. Going up to him, and finding he wanted a place, he engaged him at once.'[40] So the links appear between the prayer, the regular worshipping at the Foundery, and the certainty of personal appeal in the preaching. These things, by the grace of God, changed Alexander Mather from an out-of-work baker, interested in the best available public-house, to a man whose apostolic ministry had eventually a nation-wide influence.

This kind of thing was happening constantly all over the country. When Wesley came to Potto in 1761 he found a little Society strongly established. The central figure was Mrs. Moon, to whom he wrote many letters, and whom he counted an intimate friend, but her Christian life and influence were the result of a nameless evangelist. 'John Wesley also preached at Potto', says Tyerman, 'where Mrs. Moon resided . . . whose conversion had been brought about by an old woman, a Methodist from Birstal, who came to the house of Mr. Moon to card his sheep "doddings", and to spin them into linsey woolsey yarn.'[41]

Such examples might be multiplied indefinitely, and the mass of evidence is so great that it is impossible to dismiss it all under the cynical, or even patronizingly tolerant, heading of 'coincidence'.

The experience was not confined to those who were trained by John Wesley or Adam Clarke, and so might be expected to reproduce their theological theories. It appears again and again, in the lives of men who, with robust simplicity, attempted to explain to themselves the meaning of the spiritual forces which had driven, or led them, through tremendous struggles to an ineffable peace. Tradition still preserves the story of John Nile,

I

the Cornish farmer of Botternell. Deeply convinced of his sinfulness, he 'roamed his fields praying for Divine forgiveness'. That
painstaking chronicler, Herbert Bolitho, describes what happened: 'Looking over a hedge, he saw a man stealing his turnips,
gathering them in a sack. He challenged him with "Hullo there,
wot be 'ee about?" Startled, the guilty man replied, "Oh,
maister, maister, do 'ee fergive me; I'll never do it agen, I won't.
If you'll only fergive me this wance, maister!" It must be
remembered even turnip-stealing might have meant transportation. "Fergive 'ee," exclaimed Nile, "wey that's wot I waant
the Lord to do fur me, and if I waant the Lord to fergive me
I mun fergive thee!" That moment he received the assurance of
the pardon he so earnestly desired. Lifting the sack on the man's
back, he said, "Take the turnips and go home with mun, but
don't 'ee steal any more. If you waant any come to me and I'll
give mun to thee." So the thief went home penitent and relieved',
says Bolitho, 'while John sought his resting place with rejoicing.'
It is a simple, straightforward story with something in it which
recalls the New Testament.[42]

The examples cited represent a cross-section of Methodism in
its first fifty years. They have been selected from many types
in the hope that they will make plain that conversion, with its
consequent urge to evangelize, was the usual experience of all
early Methodists. The fact that the implications of this spiritual
visitation were worked out by John Nile in a turnip-field and by
Lady Maxwell in the select coterie at Edinburgh only strengthens
the reality. How far the plan of salvation, as they understood it,
fitted the theories of the schoolmen is only of academic interest.
These people had a living experience and because it *was alive* it led
to further revival. There was a quickening of the spirit of the
English people and every competent historian of the eighteenth
century has recognized it as a fact that cannot be denied. In
using the word revival, however, it must not be assumed to refer
only to mass movements or to be the outcome of mass emotion-
alism. In the first fifty years it was more often a natural, if sudden,
blossoming. It began on prepared ground in the class-meeting
or the lovefeast, and occasionally even in a Quarterly Meeting.

Soon after Seth and Dinah Evans were married such a movement took place in the village of Roston where they first lived.
The simple words in Seth's diary give some idea of what

happened: 'It was a blessed revival; the holy fire ran through our class and prayer meetings. Seven or eight at one meeting found peace with God. I well remember one man, an overseer, who obtained pardon; he was so powerfully wrought upon that he could neither stand nor kneel; he was so happy and full of joy. . . . He lived a consistent life and died a happy death.'[43] It was a modest enough beginning, but when later a revival 'broke out' amongst the lead miners at Wirksworth 'there was a most powerful shaking amongst the hardest and worst of sinners'. One effect of this was seen in the awakening of a social conscience in the whole area.

At Micklefield in Yorkshire great things began in 'a solitary barn, which stands in Mr. Wade's farm, Sturton Grange', where a prayer-meeting was held on Sunday mornings and Monday evenings. As the blacksmith of Aberford put it: 'The power of the Lord was present to wound and to heal.' The barn was filled with expectant people night after night. Two colliers from Garforth had been tramping the countryside, holding services which resulted in 'the conversion of hundreds of persons during that summer'.[44] The year, 1794, was memorable in the history of that part of Yorkshire for it purified the life of the villages and the effect on many of the villagers was permanent.

In Halifax, in 1793, a revival began at Greetland, 'which for many years had been proverbially dead'. In a letter to Dr. Coke, Charles Atmore wrote: 'It was in a lovefeast that an uncommon measure of the spirit of prayer was given to my dear fellow labourer, Brother Lomas, and also to many of the people.'[45] Feeling that this was a divine visitation the little group of men and women returned to their respective Societies and told the members what had happened. There is nothing cheap or sensational in Charles Atmore's calm description. 'We have added about seven hundred persons in our circuit since last Conference; the far greater part of whom, there is reason to believe, are truly converted to the Lord, and can rejoice in Him as their Saviour and Redeemer. The work has commonly been carried on in prayer-meetings: which were singularly owned of God.' Another account of the same series of events gives a more vivid impression. After describing at length the lovefeast at Greetland, it continues: 'The good which had already been done did not end here; each individual returned to their homes with the holy fire burning

and glowing in their hearts. With zealous simplicity they related
the great and mighty wonders the Lord had done to their souls.
. . . The fire stole from heart to heart and speedily the whole
circuit was under a similar influence. . . . Every Methodist
found employment; prayer meetings were resorted to with
unspeakable ardour, and not infrequently were they kept up
through the whole of the night. The chapels were crowded, and
the general inquiry was, "What must I do to be saved?" '[46]

There are many similar accounts, amongst them one which is
particularly detailed occurs in the Memoir of Henry Longden
and records his own transition from being a puzzled spectator to
becoming an active participant in the revival at Sheffield in
1794–5.[47] It is valuable in so far as it gives a contemporary
reaction to events that were much more unusual at the time
than was the case in the first half of the next century.

To imagine that all the early Methodists were swept off their
feet by tidal waves of uncontrolled emotion is to get an entirely
false picture. Many of them were critical of sudden harvests and
though they were prepared to separate all good wheat from the
tares, men like Thomas Tatham of Nottingham were quick to
perceive the tares. In writing enthusiastically about the revival,
he was glad that the saintly William Bramwell, the 'superintendent
preacher' and one of the greatest evangelists, was a man of sound
judgement. 'Now Mr. Bramwell', he says, 'was by no means of
a censorious disposition, yet he seemed to possess the gift of dis-
cerning the spirits and dispositions of men. I have frequently
known him detect religious impostors.'[48]

It would be absurd to deny that in some of the later revivalism,
in the first half of the nineteenth century, there were elements
that rightly earned the severe strictures of the *Quarterly Review*
and less reputable journals. On the other hand, the good that
was accomplished so outweighed the occasional excesses that the
revivals were amply justified by their final results. In the earlier
period there is less to criticize, and the simple fervour of the
writers commands acceptance. When Thomas Vasey wrote from
Whitby to Mary Barritt in 1798 he tells her of quarter-day at
Gainsborough:[49] 'The dales are flaming. . . . The fire hath
caught, and runs from one dale to another. I dined at the
farmer's last week, who had six children converted in twenty-
four hours. The first week after I left you at Whitby, and went

into my circuit, I found the new converts standing their ground
well: thanks be to God! I know not which to wonder at most,
the good done, or the continued good, deepening and widening.
Thank the Lord for both. There are fourteen families in one
dale, all now in society, except the little children. We have added
one hundred and forty-five in Whitby alone, since Christmas. . . .'

Statistical records are only of secondary value in studying the
people who passed through these experiences. It would be easy
to select instances of unbalanced and hysterical reactions, but,
generally speaking, in the midst of these manifestations of spiritual
power, they gained a new poise, and went back to their daily
problems with fresh hope and a sense of the divine companioning.
They were confident that they had been with God and talked
with Him. It was not the magic of the crowd which had cast
a spell over them. Rather, as C. H. Crookshank says in reference
to a revival while Conference was in session in Dublin in 1790,
'One man, though surrounded with many, seemed as much alone
with God as if he were in a desert'.[50] That was an essential in
the Methodist experience. Whenever and however conversion
took place, it was, in the last analysis, an affair between the
individual and God; there was no human intermediary, no
salvation by proxy.

It has been suggested that all these personal experiences were
either imaginary or the result of suggestion, directly or indirectly
made, through the teaching of the Wesleys with their 'assistants'.
No one who is prepared to sift the available evidence could be
satisfied to describe the experience of so many people, in such
widely different circumstance, as the result of imagination. In
the first place it would be unreasonable to suppose that
such similar reactions occurred through the combination of
entirely dissimilar elements. In the second place it must be
emphasized once more, that the result in lives so transformed
that they are lived not only on an increasingly higher level, but
with so much greater usefulness to the community, cannot be
accepted as the result of mere imagination. Nor is it a satisfactory
explanation of the great majority of 'cases' to say they were
imitative—the consequence of Wesley's preaching, for often he
was a hundred miles away when the revival occurred.

It was not always connected with sermons or expositions of
any kind. Here is a description of the character of an Irish lady,

Mrs. Slacke of Annadale, Co. Leitrim: 'I never knew a more decided follower of the Saviour than was this truly lovely woman. With an elegant person, were united in her all that results from a liberal education, sound judgement, an enlarged knowledge of Divine truth, deep experience in the things of God, a cheerful and lively address, and a spirit sweetly tempered by love to God, and zeal for His glory.' These are the words of an unimpeachable witness.[51] How did this woman develop such a character? Was it from an imaginary experience or by some subtle, suggestive process? In point of fact she had a place in fashionable Irish society, and came up to Dublin in 1780 for the season. She had arranged a round of social engagements, and had no other idea in mind when she entered the house of Alderman Exshaw where she was to be a guest. When alone in her apartment she repeatedly heard sounds which she could not understand. They appeared to come from a room above. Either out of curiosity or nervousness she stole upstairs and listened at the door of the room from which the sounds had come. To her astonishment she heard the voices of men at prayer. Obviously she could say nothing about her adventure. Next night the same thing occurred and, this time, she listened with a strange unrest. Presently she crept back to her room to try to pray. The three young apprentices, Bennett Dugdale, Matthias Joyce, and Robert Napper, had no idea that as they offered their humble prayers, a lady of fashion listened eagerly that she might learn the secret of their deep-seated joy. It was not long before she found herself kneeling with the despised Methodist Society in Whitefriars Street chapel. In their midst she found—not a doctrinal formula nor an eloquent sermon, but a personal Saviour. That, at any rate, is what she believed, and what she said quite bravely to an astonished husband when she returned to Annadale.[52] From that day her whole attitude to life was changed. Through all the years that lay ahead she was to move, unostentatiously but benevolently, amongst her neighbours. How could the prejudices of her husband withstand the witness of her gracious life? He, too, joined with her in opening their house and their hearts to those who needed the sympathy or shelter it was their joy to give.

Even if one stripped the experience they called conversion of every theological significance, it would still be difficult to dismiss it as unreal, when so many thousands of people ceased to live selfishly and became constructive and positive in their neighbour-liness. There was, of course, a far deeper significance in the initial stages of the new experience, and it could not be satisfied with a mere change into an altruistic way of life. 'Man is both a fallen and sinful creature', says Nicolas Berdyaev, 'split into two and longing for wholeness and salvation, and a creative being called to continue the work of building the world and endowed for the purpose with gifts from above.'[53] When the first Methodists claimed they knew the joy of personal forgiveness, they began to realize that present salvation was only a stage in what must be a progressive growth in grace. Because they knew themselves as free, spiritual beings and believed they had personal relationship with God Himself, the idea of new creative activity began to appear.

The next stage in their experience has been termed the doctrine of Holiness, Christian Perfection or Perfect Love. In Wesley's works it appears, quite naturally, as 'a corollary of his appeal to experience'.[54] The possibility that a son may be conscious of his relationship to a worthy father involves the further possibility that such consciousness may be complete—a condition which should bring great joy and absolute confidence. The invaluable work by Dr. R. Newton Flew on *The Idea of Perfection in Christian Theology*, and *The Path to Perfection* by Dr. W. E. Sangster have surveyed the theological aspects, critically and completely.[55] It is only necessary to deal briefly here with the incidence of the doctrine on the lives of a few representatives of the people called Methodists.

'Wesley's doctrine of Christian perfection has been inad-vertently stigmatized as a theological provincialism of Method-ism,' says Professor George Croft Cell, and he maintains that it is an original and unique synthesis of the Protestant ethic of grace with the Catholic ethic of holiness. This statement may be accepted whole-heartedly, whilst admitting that the conception of the doctrine by the early Methodists varied greatly. At times it becomes in their journals what Dr. Sangster calls 'the artless words of those early followers of John Wesley who claimed that the gift of holiness had been given to them'. There are instances, however, where the record bears marks of a distinct and personal appreciation, which is not necessarily coloured by the teaching or preaching of Wesley or any other. The experience in such cases, is quite distinctive, yet has the same qualities of which Wesley's statement of the doctrine speaks.[56]

Some confusion has been caused by the use of at least five different terms to denote the doctrine. Holiness, Perfect Love, Christian Perfection, Sanctification, and Entire Sanctification are all used, though in the case of the last two there is the suggestion of successive stages. Most theologians have been still more perplexed when they have tried to use severely analytical methods to confine such an experience within the limits of theological terms. The mere suggestion of entire sanctification makes the ordinary man hesitate, and there is something not unpraiseworthy in this attitude. He knows himself too well, he feels, to believe that for him there is such a possibility. Certainly he shrinks from claiming any title to perfection. This attitude Wesley himself shares with him. There is no account of his ever having publicly claimed that he himself had the experience, though the entry in his *Journal* for 24th December 1744 makes humble confession of a moment of supreme blessedness. He had been ill the previous day, and on Monday morning, he wrote, 'I was again as a dead man; but in the evening, while I was reading prayers at Snowsfields, I found such light and strength as I never remember to have had before. I saw every thought, as well as action or word, just as it was rising in my heart; and whether it was right before God, or tainted with pride or selfishness. I never knew before (I mean not as at this time) what it was "to be still before God".'[57]

In their critical consideration of this silence, Dr. Bett, Dr. Flew, and Dr. Sangster all find it to be a difficult problem. In Dr. Bett's opinion it was the publicity of Wesley's life which caused his personal hesitation. Few men have been more opposed to iron curtains round even the most intimate spiritual experience, and the candour of his *Journal* is almost as complete as that found in the voluminous *Confessions of Leo Tolstoi.* Yet this point of publicity is important. Was it that Wesley feared that any such personal claim made by him might hurt the Societies? It would have been so easy for the antagonistic elements to quote 'a thousand insignificant and innocent words and actions', and by distorting and exaggerating them point the finger of scorn at the whole of his work.[58]

There may also have been in his heart something of that very shyness of anything suggesting spiritual 'boasting', which is so distasteful to the man of today. Was there, as Dr. Flew asks, some 'half-conscious suspicion that avowal would be perilous to the health of his soul'?[59]

Both these contentions are sustained by the fact, as Dr. Sangster points out, that Wesley on one occasion actually seemed to disclaim the experience.[60] When Dr. William Dodd had launched a bitter personal attack against him, he answered: 'I tell you flat I have not attained the character I draw.' It would probably be going too far to call this a denial or disclaimer. The character of the ideal Methodist or the ideal Christian, as Wesley portrayed him, still remained for him and all his people an unrealized ideal. If he meant, however, by Christian perfection the knowledge that there was nothing consciously in one's heart that was contrary to the will of God, those who knew him best would have unquestionably said that for him there had been such a moment.

In considering the less reserved confessions of some of the rank and file it must be remembered always that their leader urged them to expect, to seek and to record the experience. Again and again he heard or read their claims, corrected or approved them, by word or letter, and often rejoiced with them in their triumphant joy. Is this really inconsistent? Is it not the natural thing for a father who has won the V.C. or achieved some notable academic distinction, to say nothing about his own victories, but to encourage his son and to rejoice, quite loudly, about that son's success? In the affairs of the spirit it does not seem unnatural, that Wesley should have been modest, even to the point of reticence.

The personal accounts of many early Methodists are detailed and quite definite. In examining them one is compelled to conclude that, when they speak of sanctification they describe a real experience, and to be quite sure in one's own heart, that if these people reached such a stage, then John Wesley, also 'attained'.

Perhaps for the sake of the Church, and his own sake, he remained silent about himself, but there can be no question that he rejoiced with a great joy in the blessings experienced by his children in the Gospel.

Though he has been accused of credulity he hesitated to accept any easy profession of the experience of sanctification amongst the members of the Societies, without submitting it to close scrutiny and often to searching oral examination!

There is an entry in his *Journal* for 2nd December 1744 which shows a cautious but real acceptance. Writing in London, Wesley says, 'I was with two persons who believe they are saved from all sin. Be it so, or not, why should we not rejoice in the work of God, so far as it is unquestionably wrought in them? For instance, I ask John C., "Do you pray always? Do you rejoice in God every moment? Do you in everything, give thanks? In loss? In pain? In sickness, weariness, and disappointments? Do you desire nothing? Do you fear nothing? Do you feel the love of God continually in your heart? Have you a witness, in whatever you speak or do, that it is pleasing to God?" If he can solemnly and deliberately answer in the affirmative, why do I not rejoice and praise God on his behalf? Perhaps because I have an exceeding complex idea of sanctification or a sanctified man. And so, for fear he should not have attained all I include in that idea, I cannot rejoice in what he has attained.'[61]

As his own views became more definite, so did his examination of the evidence. When Thomas Walsh was with him in London, he helped John Wesley in a most exacting test. 'I desired all those in London who made the same profession (of being fully sanctified) to come to me altogether at the Foundery that I might be thoroughly satisfied.' The questions were put, and it should be remembered that the questioners were Thomas Walsh and John Wesley—of whose intelligence and discernment there could be no question. This was Wesley's verdict: 'They answered every one without hesitation and with the utmost simplicity, so that we were fully persuaded they did not deceive themselves. In the years 1759 to 1763 they multiplied exceedingly in London, Bristol and elsewhere. In London alone I found 652 members of our Society who were exceedingly clear in their experience, and of whose testimony I could see no reason to doubt. I believe no year has passed since then wherein God has not wrought the same work in many others; and every one of them has (without a single exception) declared that his deliverance from sin was instantaneous—that the change was wrought in a moment.'[62]

It is not always easy to decide how far the influence of Wesley urged the people to make such professions, and how far it restrained them. He himself grew increasingly convinced that Christian Perfection or Sanctification should be a present experience, and that it was Methodism's responsibility to emphasize the fact.

'The more I converse with the believers in Cornwall', he writes in 1762, 'the more I am convinced that they have sustained great loss for want of hearing the doctrine of Christian Perfection clearly and strongly enforced. I see, wherever this is not done, the believers grow dead and cold. Nor can this be prevented but by keeping up in them an hourly expectation of being perfected in love. I say an hourly expectation; for to expect it at death, or at some time hence, is much the same as not expecting it at all.'[63]

When he is in Bristol in September 1765 he comes to a similar conclusion: 'Monday the 30th and the two following days I examined the society at Bristol, and was surprised to find fifty members fewer than I left in it last October. One reason is, Christian Perfection has been little insisted on; and wherever this is not done, be the preachers ever so eloquent, there is little increase, either in the number or the grace of the hearers.'[64]

It became evident that the preachers were either shy of the doctrine which had undoubtedly been cheapened by the language and behaviour of some who professed to have the experience, or were themselves not clear about its significance. On 25th March 1772 he writes to his brother Charles in evident perplexity: 'I find almost all our preachers in every circuit have done with Christian perfection. They say they believe it; but they never preach it, or not once in a quarter. What is to be done? Shall we let it drop, or make a point of it?'[65]

There could be little doubt as to what his own answer would be to the question. Whatever the name to be given to the experience, it was too real a fact in the lives of many people for Wesley to 'let it drop' or relegate it to the background of his teaching. When he reached Launceston on 15th August 1776 he was disappointed at the situation and convinced of the reason that progress was not being made: 'Here I found the plain reason why the work of God had gained no ground in this circuit all the year. The preachers had given up the Methodist testimony. Either they did not speak of Perfection at all (the peculiar doctrine committed to our trust), or they spoke of it only in general terms, without urging the believers to "go on unto perfection", and to expect it every moment. And wherever this is not earnestly done, the work of God does not prosper.'[66]

At times he was obviously exasperated at the folly of some of the people. 'In the evening I preached at Yarm', he writes;

'but I found the good doctrine of Christian Perfection had not been heard of there for some time. The wildness of our poor brethren in London has put it out of countenance above two hundred miles off; so these strange advocates for perfection have given it a deeper wound than all its enemies together could do!'[67] He was constantly trying to correct mistaken ideas or interpret experience. 'All this week I endeavoured to confirm those who had been shaken as to the important doctrine of Christian Perfection, either by its wild defenders, or wise opposers, who much availed themselves of that wildness.'[68]

Even William Grimshaw had objected to the term 'sinless perfection' as being 'a grating term—even to those who are desirous to be truly holy in heart and life'. In a letter to John Wesley he deplores 'strange, fulsome, offensive, unscriptural expressions and representations', but when he heard him preach on 'Be ye perfect, as your Father which is in heaven is perfect' the two friends found themselves in agreement. 'Mr. G[rimshaw] afterwards told me that this perfection he firmly believed and daily prayed for, namely, the love of God and man producing all those fruits which are described in our Lord's Sermon upon the Mount.'[69]

In spite of extravagances and misinterpretations, in spite even of impostures, the experience was too widespread to be denied and too fundamental to be destroyed by ridicule or contempt. He would be a strange critic who could read the intimate confessions of so many obviously sincere people, and conclude they were empty vapourings. It would be more reasonable to say that in them are movements of the Spirit, too great to be confined within the limits of a theory and too varied to be brought down to a common denominator. In attempting to reduce such experience to a formula there is always the danger of imprisoning the soul. It must be admitted that sometimes the language seems grotesque and the ecstasies of joy hysterical, but even an Isaiah fails to convey the whole of his vision through the medium of words. However sublime his language it holds but part of that many-splendoured thing. However carefully conceived the theological definition, it cannot hold the heart-throbs of the spirit set free! Whatever the dangers Wesley had to face, who shall say that he was not wise in accepting the risks rather than rejecting or ignoring the living realities? The experience would not be denied, whatever the decisions of the preachers and teachers might be!

There is nothing unreasonable or artificial in Henry Longden's account of what followed his conversion.[70] For some months he bore his witness to his new allegiance. He 'dared not suffer sin to pass unreproved. Whether rich or poor, I had no alternative, but instantly "in the name of our God, I set up my banner".' Quaintly enough, but very honestly he writes: 'I took a hazel-stick in my hand, to have in readiness, if I should hear any boys blaspheme the name which I so much venerated; that at least, if I could not beat Satan out of them, they should not sin in my hearing with impunity.' So he struggled to 'defend the Ark' with very primitive weapons! Then his Class-leader asked him an awakening question. 'Do you think that God can save you from all inbred sin?' He replied, 'I know God can do everything; but I do not expect that he will save me, or any of his servants to that extent and degree before death: I think he will suffer these enemies to remain, for the trial of my faith and constancy.' The leader did not argue but lent him a treatise on *Christian Perfection*. He read the book with candour, mixed with prayer, and records his impression: 'I saw from the Lord I was not in the most excellent way: the remains of self-will and unbelief, of pride and anger, were within me. . . .' Immediately he confided in some of his 'religious companions' and discovered they were in a similar condition. They decided to meet in band and seek what they were confident they lacked. 'As soon as I had received a clear conviction of the necessity of entire sanctification, I saw the word of God had comparatively been a sealed book to me. The prayer of the great Apostle for the Thessalonians, "The very God of peace sanctify you wholly", taught me that those Christians for whom he prayed were sanctified in part by the Spirit of adoption, in that moment when their sins were pardoned. He asks entire sanctification, as a blessing which was to be received in time, in life, in health; because the blessing, in common with all other spiritual blessings in Christ Jesus, must be received in answer to the prayer of faith, *now*; and not as something to be wrought in a succession of years by the hoary hand of time; neither gradually by the performance of a succession of religious duties, nor suddenly by the iron grasp of death, as I had before vainly imagined.' So he continued, seeking this fuller experience of the grace of God! Quite simply he describes its coming: 'One evening, at our band, the presence of God peculiarly over-shadowed us. . . . We were presently baptized with the Holy Ghost and with fire. Being purged from all iniquity, we fully and heartily gave up our bodies and souls to be the Lord's for ever.'

It is a simple, straightforward statement of fact, as far as Henry Longden is concerned, and it does not imply the beginning of a static condition, or any kind of self-complacency. After spending himself ceaselessly and unselfishly in the service of his fellows, he is writing, twenty years later, these words: 'We had a time of much love and union at my band: it appears, unless I labour hard, I shall be left far behind.'[71] Five years after, the entry in his journal reads: 'I am sweetly at liberty . . . I expect all, and seek all, my happiness in God. . . . But my state of mind is not what I could wish it to be. I want to live at the fountain-head, evermore thirsty for God, that I may be filled. . . . I am almost dejected, that I am but yet a dwarf!'[72]

As he reached the end, he said to two friends from the country: 'I can testify the faithfulness of God. He comes nearer and nearer to me in my affliction . . . the promises are not yea and nay, but all yea and amen in Christ Jesus. . . . I renounce my labour for Christ and his church, as very imperfect and full of infirmities. I have been an unprofitable servant. I rest my all upon the boundless mercy of God, and the infinite merits of Jesus Christ.'[73]

There is no arrogant self-assurance, but there is not a shadow of doubt or fear, nor had there been through the long years of his devoted service and joyful living. The experience that came in the little band-meeting had been progressive, not final, though at the time it had been complete.

That doughty old Cornishman, Richard Trewarvas, pilot of ships and of souls, had no doubt about the date of his conversion —13th July 1771. 'I then had a sure trust and a firm confidence in God's mercy, that for Christ's sake he had blotted out my sin, nor did I ever doubt of it afterwards.'[74] His biographer, Richard Treffry, says that for the next ten years he maintained 'an untarnished character in the sight of the world'. Then, and not till then, 'he experienced a full deliverance from the power and domination of inward sin; and a total renewal of his heart in righteousness'. This is how Richard Trewarvas himself describes it: 'God has at last given me the victory through faith in Christ Jesus my Lord. O happy change! It is now become my great business to live for eternity. Praised be the Lord, I enjoy his constant smile, and peaceable reign in my soul. He condescends by his Spirit to live and dwell in my poor worthless heart. He hath implanted that divine principle in my soul, whereby I am enabled to govern my affections, to subject my will and desires, and keep within due bounds all the passions of my soul. God hath now taught me that most excellent lesson, in every circumstance of life, and under every dispensation of his providence, to be content. A morsel of bread in God's way is more desirable and satisfactory than all the accumulated wealth and treasures of earth and sea in the way of sinners. Divine peace, and sweet content, day and night reside in my soul. . . . O wondrous grace! O boundless love! Praised be the God of my salvation; he hath delivered my soul from every painful anxiety of life, and gloomy idea of death.' Here again is something quite definite and distinct from the experience of which he speaks in 1771. The ten years reach a climax in a new joy, which though described in simple language, has a directness and conviction not to be denied.

The experience of William Carvosso, a friend of Richard Trewarvas, is just as definite, and quite uninfluenced by reading books on Christian Perfection. There is nothing vague or uncertain about time or circumstance. Of his conversion he says: 'The Spirit itself now bore witness with my spirit that I was a child of God. This was about nine o'clock at night, May 7th, 1771; and never shall I forget that happy hour.'[75] He and his brother Benedict joined the little class at Mousehole. For three months he continued 'in the same happy frame of mind'. Then he discovered he had to fight enemies within his soul. 'Having never conversed with anyone who enjoyed purity of heart, nor read any of Mr. Wesley's works, I was at a loss both with respect to the nature, and the way, to obtain the blessing of full salvation. . . . Though I had not much time for reading many books, yet I blessed God I had his own word, the Bible, and could look into it. This gave me a very clear map of the way to heaven, and told me that "without holiness no man could see the Lord". . . . I never had one doubt of my acceptance; the witness was so clear, that Satan himself knew it was in vain to attack me from that quarter. . . . What I now wanted was "inward holiness" and for this I prayed and searched the Scriptures. Among the number of promises, which I found in the Bible, that gave me to see it was my privilege to be saved from all sin, my mind was particularly directed to Ezekiel xxxvi. 25–27: "Then will I sprinkle clean water upon you, and ye shall be clean; from all your filthiness, and from all your idols, will I cleanse you. A new heart also will I give you, and a new spirit will I put within you, and I will take away the stony heart out of your flesh, and I will give you an heart of flesh. And I will put my spirit within you, and cause you to walk in my statutes, and ye shall keep my judgements and do them." . . . I saw clearly the will of God was my sanctification. The more I examined the Scriptures, the more I was convinced that without holiness there could be no heaven.' The longed-for experience did not come easily. 'I well remember, returning one night from a meeting, with my mind greatly distressed from a want of the blessing. I turned into a lonely barn to wrestle with God in secret prayer. While kneeling on the threshing-floor, agonizing for the great salvation, this promise was applied to my mind, "Thou art all fair, my love; there is no spot in thee". But, like poor Thomas, I was afraid to believe, lest I should deceive myself.' For a fortnight he continued on the sharp threshold of what was to be the new experience. 'At length,' he continues, 'one evening, while engaged in a prayer-meeting, the great deliverance came. I began to exercise faith by believing, "I shall have the blessing now". Just at that moment a heavenly influence filled the room; and no sooner had I uttered or spoken the words from my heart, "I shall have the blessing now", than refining fire went through my heart, illuminated my soul, scattered its life through every part, and sanctified the whole. I then received the full witness of the Spirit that the blood of Jesus had cleansed me from all sin. I cried out, "This is what I wanted! I have now got a new heart." I was emptied of self and sin, and filled with God. I felt I was nothing, and Christ was all in all. . . . This happy change took place in my soul, March 13th, 1772.'[76]

The remarkable thing about William Carvosso's account is that it describes a lonely quest. There seems to have been no human guidance, but the man wrestling in prayer in the darkness and solitude of the old barn, Jacob-like, won through. His joy was no vague ecstasy: it was God's answer to his passionate desire. 'Soon after this', he says, 'Mr. Wesley's pamphlet on Christian perfection was put into my hand. I do not know that I had seen any of his works before. On reading this little work, I was filled with amazement, to think that a man could read my heart in such a manner. This tended greatly to establish me in the truth of the Gospel.'[77]

There can be no doubt about the reality of his experience nor about the humility of his joy. It taught him how to live, and it taught him how to die. His son's account of his last days is a most moving document. 'At times, for hours together, he is sustained in the highest Christian triumph. . . . During this extraordinary confession unto salvation, two things appeared especially conspicuous; namely his great jealousy for the honour and glory of God, in guarding against every word that might have the slightest appearance of self in it; and his eager desire that no part of the truth of God might be denied, of which God had made him a living witness.'[78] Farmer and fisherman, a humble and happy Christian, William Carvosso, died as he had lived, triumphantly, singing 'Praise God from whom all blessings flow.' He did not finish the verse—on earth! It was sixty-four years since the blessing came which transfigured him—and it had no ending.

The classification of such experiences is always arbitrary and, even when it is made, its usefulness is questionable. The blessings of salvation cannot be mass produced and they are never automatic even in a world that prides itself on having entered the Machine Age. There were times when John Wesley grew impatient of the narrowness of definition and was prepared to judge by results—which is neither unscriptural nor illogical. In March 1760 he was in Leeds and gives an account of what happened there: 'Having desired that as many as could of the neighbouring towns, who believed they were saved from sin, would meet me, I spent the greatest part of this day [Wednesday, 12th March] in examining them one by one. The testimony of some I could not receive; but concerning the far greatest part, it is plain (unless they could be supposed to tell wilful and deliberate lies), (1) that they feel no inward sin, and to the best of their knowledge commit no outward sin; (2) that they see and love God every moment, and pray, rejoice, give thanks evermore; (3) that they have constantly as clear a witness from God of sanctification as they have of justification. Now in this I do

K

rejoice, and will rejoice, call it what you please; and I would to God thousands had experienced thus much, let them afterward experience as much more as God pleases.'[79]

It is a relief to read those words: 'I will rejoice, *call it what you please*' for they reassure one that the 'examiner' was a human being, with an open mind and an eager heart. Did it matter very much if the examinees were a little confused about the distinction between justification and sanctification? Was it not a good thing, that, after conversion, they were disturbed by the presence of pride and hatred lurking still in the secret places of the soul? Was it not an even better thing that they arrived at a new stage in their experience, when they were suddenly sure that there was no longer anything consciously contrary to the love of God in their hearts? In his searching analysis of the witness of Wesley's followers, Dr. Sangster finds five general characteristics. 'Love', he says, 'is the key. All conscious sin had gone. It [the experience] normally begins at a definite moment. The blessing carries its own assurance with it. The element of asceticism is usually there.'[80] Some of these points will be considered later,[81] but Dr. Sangster, we feel, rightly refuses to let the issue be confused by arguments about terminology. The words 'perfect love' appeal to him (and to us) more than other terms such as 'sinless perfection' or even Christian perfection, but like Wesley he is determined to rejoice in the peace of God in human lives. Thinking of ordinary and even obscure people he knows, he says, 'It was plain to see almost in their faces that here was a stream of sanctity, and one might venture to add we will rejoice, call it what you please.'

There were those, however, who were not content with any simple tests, but condemned all 'claims' as being based on unreality. At Huddersfield in 1779, Wesley saw the result of such an attitude: 'I saw a melancholy sight indeed! One that ten years ago was clearly perfected in love, but was worried by Mr. ——, day and night, threaping him down he was in a delusion, that at length it drove him stark mad. And so he continues to this day. Observe! it was not Perfection drove this man mad, but the incessant teasing him with doubtful disputations.'[82]

Meanwhile there were preachers who maintained the reasonableness of the experience and, in many cases, were unconscious exemplars of their teaching. Men as varied in temperament as John Nelson,[83] Captain Webb[84] and 'Sammy' Hick[85] were quite definite in their acceptance of the doctrine and the fact. When John Bennet met John Nelson in 1742 he was in doubt, but the stone-mason convinced him by quoting St. Paul and St. John. 'I pulled out my Bible and shewed him the words; and when he had read them, his countenance changed, and he cavilled no more.' Thousands of people heard 'Sammy's' favourite sermon on 1 Thessalonians v. 16–23 and believed. There was no possibility of mistaking his position. 'But this state of holiness is not without its trials,' he said. 'O no! you must not think that the battle is over, or that the work is done; for as soon as you step into this gospel liberty by *faith*, you may get out of it by *unbelief*. Take care then that you do not fall from your stedfastness.' Just as surely as he denounced the idea of finality, so he proclaimed the completeness of the victory. 'Some folks believe that sin will never be destroyed, but by death they make death a mightier conqueror than Jesus Christ.' He clinches his argument by an unexpected reference. 'Old mother Church . . . teaches us to pray "that the thoughts of our hearts may be cleansed by the inspiration of the Holy Spirit": and if the thoughts be cleansed, we are sure the words will be good and the life holy.' There is no extravagance in such a statement, and the crowds who gathered to hear the blacksmith of Aberford were never encouraged by him to make outrageous 'claims'.

At the same time such preachers welcomed every evidence of a real 'experience'. In one of his letters to Wesley, John Nelson wrote an account of Hannah Richardson of Briestfield. She had been 'the bitterest persecutor in the town', vowing that she would 'help to stone to death' the Methodist preacher, should he return. Eventually she was persuaded to hear Charles Wesley preach at Dewsbury. 'That day God begot her by His word', wrote John Nelson, 'so that she could never rest till she found Christ in her own heart.' For the next two years she was 'a steady follower' and then there came a moment when she says, doubt 'damped the love of God in my soul for two hours. But the Lord is come again, and now I am fully assured He does take up all the room in my heart. He has sanctified me throughout, body, soul, and spirit. I am a witness for Jesus Christ that He is a greater Saviour than Adam was a sinner.'[86] Here the preface to the experience is short, unlike that of William Carvosso, but it cannot be too strongly emphasized that the time factor is the least important circumstance. Even advocates of the doctrine have often laid too great a stress upon a period of hours or years. It is the complete tenancy of the heart and mind by the welcome Guest which brings the blessing. Of five men and six women who, as Wesley said, after he had 'talked with them . . . "rejoice evermore, pray without ceasing, and in everything give thanks". I believe they feel nothing but love now: what they will do, I leave to God.'[87] It was the immediate fact of their complete consecration which thrilled him. The durability of the experience depended on the quality of their lives on each new day.

It must not, of course, be assumed that either Wesley or his more thoughtful preachers rested content with accepting facts without making any attempt to interpret them. In *A Plain Account of Christian Perfection* John Wesley set out his own views in 1725 and published *Farther Thoughts on Christian Perfection* in 1763. It is not our present concern to discuss in detail his own theological development of the doctrine, but rather to notice his reaction to the experience of the people. The interpretation of such experience played its part in helping them, in later years, to understand better what had happened and was then happening. Nor was Wesley the only interpreter. In a letter to Alexander Mather, Lady Maxwell wrote in 1796: 'It was with satisfaction I perceived you had taken up your pen in defence of that important branch of doctrine and experience, so little known by many Christians, and experienced by fewer,—entire sanctification. Is the small manuscript treatise upon that subject, a sight of which you favoured me with some years ago, never to see the light? I wish you would go forward in the strength of the Lord, and furnish us with a little volume; complete, both as to doctrine and experience. It would, at least, be strengthening to those whose minds have been so far enlightened as to believe the former and enjoy the latter in a small measure'.[88] It is evident from the rest of the letter that she felt 'the precious truth' should be known beyond the bounds of Methodism, and that Alexander Mather being 'a master of the subject' could help towards that end. Her knowledge of the extent of the experience was perhaps limited by the cold reception given to the doctrine in Scotland, where Robert Carr Brackenbury had been told: 'You must not preach such doctrine here. The doctrine of Perfection is not calculated for the meridian of Edinburgh.'[89]

The development of Wesley's views is seen best in his correspondence on the subject. His letters range from more formal statements to non-Methodists, to intimate personal communications to his preachers and his friends. There are three which might be quoted, with advantage. The first, written to Lawrence Coughlan, on 27th August 1768, contains the passage: 'You never learned, either from my conversation or preaching or writings, that "holiness consisted in a flow of joy". I constantly told you quite the contrary: I told you it was love; the love of God and our neighbour; the image of God stamped on the heart; the life of God in the soul of man; the mind that was in Christ, enabling us to walk as Christ also walked.' The whole letter deserves the closest study but it reaches its climax in the definition of the much criticized word 'perfection'. 'This perfection cannot be a delusion, unless the Bible be a delusion too; I mean, "loving God with all our heart and our neighbour as ourselves".'[90]

The second letter was written 5th April 1758, from Dublin. The recipient was not Miss Hoar, as Crookshank suggested,[91] but Elizabeth Hardy of Bristol. (The mistake arose because of the mention of Thomas Walsh, who was not, however, in Dublin at the time, but was ill in Bristol and did not leave there till 13th April.) It is evident that Miss Hardy had been perplexed and annoyed by the attitude taken by some preachers on the doctrine of Perfection. One had said 'A believer till perfect is under the curse of God and in a state of damnation. . . .' Another insisted, 'If you die before you have attained it, you will surely perish'. Wesley completely repudiated such statements. 'By "perfection" I mean "perfect love" . . . I am convinced every believer may attain this; yet I do not say he is in a state of damnation or under the curse of God till he does attain. No, he is in a state of grace and in favour with God as long as he believes. Neither would I say, "If you die without it you will perish": but rather, Till you are saved from unholy tempers, you are not ripe for glory. There will, therefore, be more promises fulfilled in your soul before God takes you to Himself.'[92] The letter continues to explain other mistaken notions of the doctrine. Like many correspondents, the writer to whom he is replying, was evidently concerned about the whole matter, and troubled because she found it impossible to accept crude and cruel expositions.

The third letter, written to an unnamed Irish lady in June 1769, refers to sharp differences of opinion between James Morgan and Thomas Olivers, but it contains another statement on the meaning of the term 'Christian Perfection'. 'By Christian Perfection', he says, 'I mean (1) Loving God with all our heart. Do you object to this? I mean (2) an heart and life all devoted to God. Do you desire less? I mean (3) regaining the whole image of God. What objection to this? I mean (4) having all the mind that was in Christ. Is this going too far? I mean (5) walking uniformly as Christ walked. And this surely no Christian will object to. If any one means anything more or anything else by perfection, I have no concern with it. . . .'[93] This is a plain statement, in simple language, and it explains the kind of experience realized by many of the early Methodists. They believed in holiness not as a theory but as a life in which Christ was all and in all. One of Wesley's most intimate friends in the London Society was George Clark. Born in 1711, he was converted in 1746 and became a most useful leader with no less than three classes. In a letter written to John Wesley on 29th July 1774, he told him that he first received the blessing of 'entire sanctification' in 1762, that is to say sixteen years after his conversion.[94] He felt that the Societies were not progressing as they might because the preachers were not preaching the doctrine, and he reminded John Wesley that he had himself said, 'Give up the doctrine of entire sanctification, and you will easily slide into formality.'

There were many who refused to 'give up the doctrine' because like George and Adylena Clark, they could not deny a reality in their own lives. Their own accounts of the experience were often published in the *Arminian Magazine*, and those which concern the first fifty years of Methodism are to be found for the most part in issues up to 1835. The hymns of Charles Wesley, sung by all the Societies, were expositions of spiritual experience, and thus included an interpretation of Christian Perfection. Even the most illiterate learnt the hymns by heart and so had, at their command, a compendium of practical theology.[95] The better-known journals and diaries of people like Elizabeth Ritchie (Mrs. Mortimer), Hester Ann Roe (Mrs. Rogers) and Mary

Bosanquet (Mrs. Fletcher) contain full and carefully written records of the various stages in the writers' spiritual pilgrimage. Reference has been made to some of the lesser-known records which witness the same confession. They are not all of equal merit, either in style or content, but most of them have the authentic marks of personality and sincerity.

There were some Methodists who like Wesley, made no 'claim' to the experience, yet had in their hearts a love so unselfish, robust, and active that the observer might well have added the epithet 'perfect' which they so carefully avoided. Such a man was Samuel Drew of St. Austell, a metaphysician who was sometimes styled the English Plato and who enjoyed an intimate friendship with Dr. Coke and Adam Clarke. His philosophical writings were welcomed by a wide circle of competent critics and he was offered a professorship at London University in 1830, which he felt unable to accept. His biographer, his eldest son, wrote of him: 'His Christian experience . . . was without any material fluctuation. Sustained by a vigorous faith which rarely exhibited a symptom of weakness, an even tranquillity marked his course. He knew very little of depression or of ecstasy. By him the apostolic benediction, "Let the peace of God rule in your hearts", seemed to have been fully realized; and to many of his friends, who at seasons, appeared to feel "more abundant joy", he was the means of administering consolation and comfort, when "the bright shining of their Lord's countenance was for a time withdrawn".'[96] Who would question the joyfulness of such a life? The findings of Samuel Drew are worth consideration. Writing to a relative on the subject of faith he said: 'Between our *safety* and our *enjoyment* there is an essential difference. Our safety depends upon the genuineness or *quality* of our faith; our enjoyment, upon its strength or *quantity*. Forgetting this distinction, many mourn when they have more reason to rejoice. Our safety is connected by faith with the efficacy of the atonement; and, if faith be genuine, though, through its weakness, our enjoyment may be little, yet, as it unites us to the Saviour, our felicity in an eternal world will be secure, even while we pass the time of our sojourning here in fear.'[97]

In answer to a question asked by his son, Samuel Drew wrote: 'Secondly you ask, "How shall I know when I am thus saved?" . . . I admit, with you, that the common answer, "By the witness of the Spirit", is vague and indefinite; and perhaps a particular definition is impossible. There are, however, certain characteristic marks which are properly descriptive, although they convey no definition of the thing. First: The soul that experiences the salvation of God feels gratitude towards him for every spiritual blessing. Secondly: This gratitude is accompanied with a degree of love towards him—and we love him because he first loved us. Thirdly: Gratitude implies confidence in his mercies; and this confidence is faith, whether prospectively or retrospectively exercised. Fourthly: This gratitude leads to obedience, not from a dread of punishment, but from a sense of duty and obligation. Fifthly: The gratitude is accompanied with internal peace; and peace presupposes a removal of condemnation. These are marks of a spiritual salvation. But in what degree these *must* be experienced, so as to form a distinguishing criterion, perhaps none but God can discern. If we feel these marks in any degree, let us be thankful; and, through the exercise of thankfulness for past mercies, we shall assuredly have more.'[97]

There is not a wide gulf between the philosopher's attempt to help his dearly-loved son, and the word of an old Yorkshire local preacher to Roger Crane, who, 'in a state of penitence' could find neither peace nor joy. 'Brother,' he said, 'you are inverting the order of God. Remember, it is believe, love, obey; and you are trying to obey, love, and believe.' That was a red-letter day, in 1777, for Roger Crane who 'saw the way of salvation in its simplicity, and consciously laid hold upon the living Saviour'.[98]

When all the stages of spiritual experience are analysed, and all the test questions asked and answered, the most convincing proof, humanly speaking, is in the transfigured life. If the relationship between the individual and his Maker, and between the individual and his neighbour, becomes one of love, anxious to serve, it would be difficult to question the reality of the experience. That, in the end, was the practical conclusion of John Wesley.

In his *Journal* (21st April 1764) he writes: 'I visited one who was ill in bed, and, after having buried seven of her family in six months, had just heard that the eighth, her beloved husband, was cast away at sea. I asked, "Do not you fret at any of those things?" She said, with a lovely smile upon her pale cheek, "Oh, no! How can I fret at anything which is the will of God?

Let him take all besides; He has given me Himself. I love, I praise Him every moment." Let any that doubts of Christian perfection look on such a spectacle as this! One in such circumstances rejoicing evermore, and continually giving thanks.'[99] It may be that her interpretation of the will of God is open to question—but who could question the love and the faith which gave to her, even so, a joy unspeakable?

The arguments as to the 'how' and the 'why' are no longer of first importance. The facts speak for themselves in lives so transformed that no outward circumstance, nor even a childlike inability to explain, can contradict them, still less deny them altogether. The first witness of Christian Perfection in Wednesbury was, according to Wesley, Elizabeth Longmore. In recording the preaching of her funeral sermon on Sunday, 18th March 1770, he says, 'I gave some account of her experience many years ago. From that time her whole life was answerable to her profession, every way holy and unblameable. Frequently she had not bread to eat; but that did not hinder her "rejoicing evermore". She had close trials from her poor, apostate husband, in the midst of sharp pain and pining sickness. But she was superior to all; still seeing her Father's hand, and "in everything giving thanks". Her death was suitable to her life.

> No cloud could arise,
> To darken the skies,
> Or hide for a moment her Lord from her eyes.

All was noonday. She praised God with every breath till He took her to Himself.'[100] Those last two sentences might well have been written later to describe the passing of John Wesley himself —who never even 'claimed' the blessing, he so surely enjoyed and was so quick to recognize in his fellows.

It is inevitable that a brief survey of so vast a subject should leave much unexplained or undefined. That an experience of such radiant joy should seem to begin in paroxysms of misery is in itself astonishing. But did it begin in penitence or is not Dr. Barry right when he says, 'You cannot have any genuine sense of sin (in its full religious connotation) until you have seen some vision of God's glory'?[101] That was surely how the experience began. The early Methodists realized their sinfulness only when they had begun to realize the love of God in Christ Jesus.

When, long after conversion, they confessed a still deeper penitence, it was neither hypocrisy nor hysteria. The clearer a man's
vision of Christ, the fiercer the light that beats upon his own sin
or the more conscious he is of his present failure. To quote Dr.
Barry again: 'The farther a man has advanced, by the grace of
God, in the recognition of goodness, the clearer his insight into
its real demand and the keener his sense of his own unworthi-
ness'.[102] That indisputable fact explains the spiritual struggles
which sometimes took place long years after a conversion of whose
reality there could be no doubt. The goal before them was holiness and the good they sought 'none other than God Himself'.
They realized—wonder of wonders—in their own hearts a present
conscious life in Christ. The more they understood its possibilities and obligations the more they longed for holiness. Even
the blessed state of having nothing, as far as they knew, contrary
to the love and will of God in their hearts was no longer
unattainable. They sang together:

> All things are possible to God,
>   To Christ, the power of God in man,
> To me, when I am all renewed,
>   When I in Christ am formed again,
> And witness, from all sin set free,
> All things are possible to me.[103]

The song was a prayer, and their mounting faith expected its
answer. Nor did they hope in vain. Hymn after hymn expressed
what, in so many cases, their own words were quite incapable of
saying. Even as they prayed for a heart to praise their God,
a heart from sin set free, the last bonds were broken, and a new
life began. In many a barn or little cottage-room the battle was
fought and won—but the victory always came while they were
on their knees. With mighty faith and lowly hearts they prayed,
not for a vain-glorious exaltation, but for that perfect love which
should cast out their fear and every other evil thing.

> Humble, and teachable, and mild,
> O may I, as a little child,
>   My lowly Master's steps pursue!
> Be anger to my soul unknown,
> Hate, envy, jealousy be gone;
>   In love create Thou all things new.[104]

There was no trace of arrogance in such a plea, but if the answer came by the grace of God shed abroad in their hearts, why should any man be astonished or critical of their unbounded joy?

Nor as they gathered together and sang of their deliverance was there any sense of a finality which would free them from all future carefulness. It was liberty that had been given to their souls, but it was not licence. Once more they were singing and their prayer is for all the tomorrows:

> With me O continue, Lord!
>   Keep me, or from Thee I fly;
> Strength and comfort from Thy word
>   Imperceptibly supply,
> Hold me till I apprehend,
> Make me faithful to the end.[105]

This was the holiness for which they longed and, when for a moment, they realized it in their hearts, they rejoiced with a great joy, and rose from their knees to take the news of God's great love to their neighbours, for perfect love must set out at once to serve its Giver and all mankind.

NOTES

1. *Methodism*, Dr. H. B. Workman, p. 54. (Cambridge University Press, 1912.)

2. *Studies in Mystical Religion*, Rufus Jones, Introduction, p. xxxiii.

3. *Memorials of Early Methodism in Easingwold*, J. R. (London, 1872.)

4. *Lives of Early Methodist Preachers.*

5. Speech by Sir William J. Ashley at Wesley Bicentenary, Lincoln College, Oxford, 27th March 1926. Quoted in *W.H.S.*, XVI. 32–4.

6. Transcript of Minutes of Cork Leaders' Meeting, in *Memoirs of James Field*, p. 187. (Museum, London, 1851.)

7. *A Family Memorial*, p. 14. (Privately printed, London, 1877.)

8. *The Experience of Mrs. Hester Ann Rogers*, pp. 1–31. (Mason, London, 1840.)

9. *History of Methodism in Ireland*, C. H. Crookshank, II. 113.

10. Report in *W.H.S.*, XV. 154.

11. *Journal of John Wesley*, II. 83.

12. ibid., p. 333–4.

13. ibid., III. 330–1.

14. *Methodism in Preston*, Richard Allen, pp. 21–2. (Toulmin, Preston, 1866.)

15. See Chapters IV, also *More About the Early Methodist People*, Chap. I.

16. *Methodism in Marshland*, George West, p. 96. (London, 1886.)

17. *Centenary of Wesleyan Methodism*, Thomas Jackson, p. 164.

18. Speech recorded in *W.H.S.*, XVII. 24.

19. *Methodism in Lincoln*, p. 55. 'John Cennick's Journal', *W.H.S.*, VI. 130.

20. Bristol Conference, 1771, *W.H.S.*, XIX. 81.

21. *Methodism*, Dr. H. B. Workman, p. 111.

22. 'Account of Thomas Day', *W.H.S.*, VII. 106–8.

23. *The Conversion of the Wesleys.* (Epworth Press, London.)

24. *Memoir of Mr. William Carvosso*, edited by his son, pp. 5–10. (Mason, London, 1860.)

25. *Memoir of William Carvosso*, pp. 65–6.

26. *Seth Bede*, chiefly written by himself, pp. 10–11. (Tallant, London, 1859.)

27. 'Commerce and Christianity', *Memorials of Jonas Sugden*, Hamilton, pp. 11–12. (Adams, London, 1858.)

28. *The Life of Silas Told*, written by himself, p. 22. (City Rd., London, 1789.)

29. ibid., pp. 115–16.

30. ibid., pp. 117–18.

31. St. John xii. 13.

32. *More About the Early Methodist People*, Chap. I.

33. *The Life of Darcy, Lady Maxwell*, pp. 1–4, 6ff.

34. *The Life of Henry Longden*, pp. 1–31. From his Memoirs and other authentic documents. (Mason, London, 8th edition, 1846.)

35. See Chapter VII.

36. *Letters of John Wesley*, IV. 21. See also *History of Methodism in Ireland*, I. 130.

37. *A Short Account of Miss Mary Titherington*, Henry Moore, pp. 51–6. (R. and J. Richardson, York, 1819.)

38. *Darcy, Lady Maxwell*, pp. 78–9.

39. *History of Methodism in Ireland*, I. 117.

40. *City Road Chapel*, G. J. Stevenson, p. 572.

41. *Life and Times of Wesley*, Luke Tyerman, II. 409. See also *History of Methodism in Darlington*.

42. *Truly Rural, Lights and Shadows on the History of North Hill Circuit (Cornwall), 1743–1946*, Herbert Bolitho, p. 37. (Whitehead, Leeds, 1947.)

43. *Seth Bede*, pp. 22–31.

44. *Memoirs of Samuel Hick*, pp. 10–11.

45. Letter dated 20th June 1794. Charles Atmore to Dr. Thomas Coke.

46. *Methodism in Halifax*, p. 192.

47. *Memoirs of Henry Longden*, pp. 70–4.

48. *History of Wesleyan Methodism in Nottingham*, p. 96.

49. Letter from Thomas Vasey to Mary Barritt (later Mrs. Mary Taft). Quoted in her *Memoirs*, pp. 65–6.

50. *History of Methodism in Ireland*, II. 17.

51. *Memoir of Rev. A. Averell*, p. 166.

52. *History of Methodism in Ireland*, I. 343–4.

53. *The Destiny of Man*, N. Berdyaev, p. 49.

54. *Methodism*, Dr. H. B. Workman, p. 114.

55. *The Idea of Christian Perfection in Christian Theology*, Dr. R. Newton Flew. (Oxford University Press, 1934.) *The Path to Perfection*, Dr. W. E. Sangster. (Hodder and Stoughton, 1943.)

56. *A Plain Account of Christian Perfection*, John Wesley.

57. *Journal of John Wesley*, III. 157.

58. *The Spirit of Methodism*, Dr. Henry Bett, p. 161. (Epworth Press, London.)

59. *The Idea of Perfection in Christian Theology.*

60. *The Path to Perfection*, p. 31.

61. *Journal of John Wesley*, III. 154.

62. *Works of John Wesley*, VI. 464.

63. *Journal of John Wesley*, IV. 529.

64. ibid., V. 149.

65. *John Wesley's Letters*, V. 314.

66. *Journal of John Wesley*, VI. 120.

67. ibid., V. 17.

68. ibid., V. 35.

69. ibid., IV., 469–70.

70. *The Life of Henry Longden*, pp. 34–6.

71. ibid., p. 106.

72. ibid., p. 140.

73. ibid., pp. 167–8.

74. *Memoirs of Richard Trewarvas, Senr.*, pp. 67–9.

75. *Memoir of William Carvosso*, p. 9.

76. ibid., pp. 12–13.

77. ibid., p. 14.

78. ibid., pp. 174–7.

79. *Journal of John Wesley*, IV. 372.

80. *The Path to Perfection*, pp. 124–30.

81. See Chapters IV, V, VI, etc.

82. *Journal of John Wesley*, VI. 232.

83. *Methodism in Manchester*, p. 20–1.

84. *Journal of John Wesley*, VI. 296.

85. *Memoirs of Samuel Hick*, pp. 53–7.

86. Letter to John Wesley from John Nelson (December 1757). Quoted in *Journal of John Wesley*, IV. 246.

87. *Journal of John Wesley*, IV. 343.

88. *Life of Darcy, Lady Maxwell*, p. 265.

89. *Journal of John Wesley*, VI. 240.

90. *John Wesley's Letters*, V. 101–3.

91. *History of Methodism in Ireland*, I. 127.

92. *John Wesley's Letters*, IV. 10–13.

93. ibid., V. 139–41.

94. *Arminian Magazine*, 1787.

95. See Chapter XIV.

96. *Life of Samuel Drew*, by his eldest son, pp. 299, 422. (Longman, Rees, Brown, Green and Longman, London, 1834.)

97. ibid., p. 484.

97. ibid., Appendix, p. 517. Letter of Samuel Drew to his eldest son, St. Austell, 15th February 1815.

98. *Methodism in Preston*, Richard Allen, p. 27. (Toulmin, Preston, 1866.)

99. *Journal of John Wesley*, V. 66.

100. ibid., 356.

101. *The Relevance of Christianity*, F. R. Barry, p. 190. (Nisbet, London, 1931.)

102. ibid., p. 189.

103. Hymn by Charles Wesley (*Methodist Hymnbook*, 548).

104. ibid. (*Methodist Hymn Book*, 553).

105. ibid. (*Methodist Hymn Book*, 545).

CHAPTER IV

FELLOWSHIP

THE profound and progressive spiritual experience of the first Methodists was better understood and more wisely directed because it was shared. The dangers which always beset the path of the solitary mystic were avoided and mistakes corrected by the fellowship they enjoyed together. This developed naturally, and its constitutional history need not, here, be considered in detail. Though the class-meeting has been described as the germ-cell from which the complex organization of the Methodist Church has grown, it did not come into being at once.

During the first few years it frequently happened that a villager walked miles to hear John Wesley or John Nelson preach, and returned home with heart aflame. All he could do was to gather his neighbours together to pray and read the Bible, and form a very primitive and uninstructed Society. The visits of the travelling preachers were inevitably few and far between, and the few struggling souls needed guidance, discipline, and pastoral oversight. At this crisis the sense of family developed, and saved the situation. In his own familiar language Dr. Fitchett once reminded a Canadian audience that 'there are two ideas of the religious life. There is the tramcar idea and the fireside idea. In the tramcar you sit beside your fellow-passenger. You are all going in the same direction, but you have no fellowship, no intercourse with or interest in one another. . . . Then there is the fireside, where the family meet together, where they are at home, where they converse one with another of common pursuits and common interests, and where a common relationship binds all together in a warm bond of love and fellowship. . . . Methodism stands for the fireside idea.'

Though it was a few years before the severity of the first 'bands' yielded to a warmer and more intimate fellowship in the class-meeting, the time came when the latter was perhaps the most important feature in Methodism. For the next fifty years and more the little village Societies were saved because of the classes which were the 'fireside' round which the members of the 'family' shared a common experience and kept their sacred tryst. In a 'Plan of the Travelling and Local Preachers in the Leicester Circuit' issued in 1807, fourteen villages had only one preaching service each fortnight.[1] This was partly due to the fact that, in a few cases, the members still attended the Parish Church in the morning, but the main reason was that there were so few preachers available. To these isolated communities the opportunity for regular Christian fellowship meant more than the practice of 'private pieties' for it made them members of a living organism. They learned that 'the highest end of Christian communion is attained when it enables us to find God in the souls of other people'.[2]

The first step towards fellowship was the creation of 'bands' on the model of the Moravian groups John Wesley had known in Georgia, and, later, in the Religious Society which met in Fetter Lane, London. These groups of between five and ten people, either male or female, single or married, met in separate 'bands', and were visited by John and Charles Wesley as they had opportunity. They were composed of people who sought to deepen their spiritual experience, and the two brothers did their best to guide and, where necessary, rebuke them. As they grew in numbers it became quite impossible that any two men, travelling so far afield, could give them adequate oversight. At the end of 1738 John Wesley drew up a set of rules which contained eleven questions to be answered by those seeking membership, and five others to be asked at every weekly meeting.

It is difficult to imagine the effect produced by the regular repetition of these inquiries. 'What known sins have you committed since our last meeting? What temptations have you met with? How were you delivered? What have you thought, said, or done, of which you doubt whether it be sin or not? Have you nothing you desire to keep secret?' Such was the formidable questionnaire, and it has been characterized as 'an indication of the still unhealthy tone of Wesley's piety'.[3] It was certainly an attempt to create a circle of 'inner fellowship', but if nothing beyond this first plan had emerged, the future of Methodism would have been gloomy indeed.

After the formation of the United Society in Bristol in October 1739, and in London in December 1739, and the subsequent separation from Fetter Lane, the development was more definite. By 1744 it is evident that the United Societies consisted of 'awakened persons', whilst the 'Bands' were formed of those who claimed to have received 'remission of sins'. The Select Societies were made up of Band members 'who seemed to walk in the light of God', whilst the Penitents were those who had made 'shipwreck of faith', but were still allowed to remain in a kind of probationary fellowship. In 1744 the Rules of the Band Societies were republished, and 'Directions' as to personal conduct were made quite definite.[4]

It is important to realize that the members of the 'Bands' were people whose spiritual experience was more advanced than the ordinary member of the United Societies, but that the members of the 'Select Societies' had reached a still further stage. There is no doubt that Wesley himself placed a very high value on the Band meeting. In 1768 the preachers were directed: 'As soon as there are four men or women believers in any place, put them into a *band*. In every place where there are bands, meet them constantly and encourage them to speak without reserve.' As late as 1788 he writes to William Simpson who was then an 'assistant' in the Yarm Circuit: 'You should speak to every believer singly concerning meeting in band. There were always some in Yarm Circuit, though not many. No circuit ever did, or ever will flourish, unless there are bands in the large Societies.'[5] It might be assumed that he was thinking of the severer discipline and closer oversight which the 'Bands' afforded. Was there not, perhaps unconsciously, a more personal reason? Was there any other Methodist whose life had, humanly speaking, a greater loneliness than his? Essentially a leader, suffering the isolation which is a consequence of leadership, and with no home life such as his brother Charles enjoyed, he needed human fellowship as much as the loneliest shepherd on the northern hills. Amongst the members of a Band he was more likely to find congenial company than in any other group, with the exception of the 'Select Societies'. The first of these he had formed in London.[6] He had been meeting, on Monday mornings, a small group of people who longed to walk 'in the light of God's countenance'. There is a note of wistfulness about his account: 'My design was, not only to direct them how to press after perfection, to exercise their every grace, and improve every talent they had received, and to incite them to love one another more and to watch more carefully over each other, but also to have a select company, to

L

whom I might unbosom myself on all occasions without reserve, and whom I could propose to all their brethren as a pattern of love, of holiness and of good works.' Amongst these special little groups he could feel free, and it is probable that to them, he spoke of his hopes and fears, of his victories and defeats, more intimately than to anyone else. They were people bound not so much by rules as by three 'directions'. All that was said was in confidence and never to be repeated. In all 'indifferent things' they agreed to submit to the minister. And each member bound himself to bring all he could spare to the common stock.

The words 'Select Societies' would not find favour with the people of today, but they conveyed neither a sense of superiority nor exclusiveness to their members. When he was waiting, storm-bound, on his way to the Isle of Man, John Wesley was able to join such a group at Whitehaven. Of the meeting he wrote: 'I was pleased to find that none of them have lost the pure love of God since they received it first. I was particularly pleased with a poor negro. She seemed to be fuller of love than any of the rest. And not only her voice had an unusual sweetness, but her words were chosen and uttered with a peculiar propriety. I never heard, either in England or America, such a negro speaker (man or woman) before.'[7] Perhaps it was easier for him to hear the sweetness in such a company, where there was no colour-bar and no jealousy or intrigue. 'Everyone here (i.e. in a Select Society) has an equal liberty of speaking, there being none greater or less than another. I could say freely to these, "Ye may all prophesy one by one (taking that word in the lowest sense), that all may be comforted." And I often found the advantage of such a free conversation, and "that in the multitude of counsellors there is safety". Any who is inclined so to do is likewise encouraged to pour out his soul to God.' There were times when a 'Select Society' was a quiet refuge for this lonely man.

The Bands with their severe 'Rules' seem to a later generation more artificial, and all the questions and questioning an encroachment on individual freedom. They do not, however, appear to have produced such an impression on their members, nor is there any record of objections being raised when the 'Rules' were rea in Conference. A Liverpool Methodist, Mary Titherington, wrote in her journal, in 1799: 'Mr. Barber read the Band rules in the Band. I felt much humbled that I had not paid stricter attention

to them; and much gratitude to God and his people for bearing
so long with me, and promoting me to honour among them,
notwithstanding all my inconsistencies. I felt also a desire that
wherein I came short in times past, I might bear with others as
I had been borne with.'[8]

Though the Bands and the Select Societies fulfilled a purpose,
they did not provide fellowship for the great majority of the
people. It was only when the idea of the class-meeting was born,
in 1742, that Methodism had its family hearth round which all
could gather, whether they were beginners or veterans, and feel
themselves at home, their Father's welcome guests. This was the
'crowning glory' and it has done more than any other Methodist
organization to influence the world. In a memorable judgement
Dr. R. W. Dale said: 'Methodism made one striking and original
contribution to the institutions of the Church, in the Class-
meeting. Never, so far as I know, in any Church had there been
so near an approach to the ideal of pastoral oversight as the
Class-meeting, in its perfect form, provides; and it also provides
for that communion of saints which is almost as necessary for the
strength and joy and the harmonious growth of the Christian
life as fellowship with God.'

Like many 'miracles' it came about in a natural and unspec-
tacular way. The first Methodist Society was founded in London
in December 1739, and a graphic account is given by John
Wesley himself: 'In the latter end of the year 1739, eight or ten
persons came to me in London, who appeared to be deeply convinced of sin and earnestly groaning for redemption. They
desired (as did two or three more the next day) that I would
spend some time with them in prayer and advise them how to
flee from the wrath to come. . . . I appointed a day when they
might all come together, which from thence forward they did
every week, namely on Thursday, in the evening . . . their
number increasing daily. . . . This was the rise of the United
Society, first in London, then in other places.'[9] The date of the
first meeting has been established by Thomas McCullagh as
27th December 1739.[10] The nature of this first 'United Society'
was clearly defined in the Preamble to the Rules. It was 'a company of men having the form, and seeking the power of godliness;
united in order to pray together, to receive the word of exhortation, and to watch over one another in love, that they may help

each other to work out their salvation'. Even while the numbers remained small it was difficult for John or Charles Wesley to meet them regularly, because they were both so often riding far afield. Soon the numbers grew to such an extent that it became impossible for them to have a close personal knowledge of all the members even in London, still less of those in the country. At the beginning of 1742 there were eleven hundred in the London Society, in spite of the fact that they had been repeatedly 'sifted' so that the returns were genuine.[11] No man could have striven harder to keep in touch with every individual, but even John Wesley was compelled to admit the task beyond his powers.

On Monday, 15th February 1742, he met the United Society in Bristol, 'to consult on a proper method for discharging the public debt'.[12] The modest 'Room' in the Horsefair was ill-built, and needed constant repair. Money had been borrowed for its erection and John Wesley had made himself responsible for its repayment. In the meeting, as might be expected in a great sea-port, there were several ships' captains. Amongst them was Captain Foy, whose identity has not been finally established. (The strongest case seems to be made out for Captain John Foy, master of a ship trading between Bristol and London[13] but W. A. Goss shows that either Matthew or William Foy, both master mariners, or Captain Edward Foy the commander of a frigate in 1712, are possibilities.)[14] If there must be some uncertainty about the rest of his history there is nothing vague about his contribution to Methodism. As the little group sat facing Wesley's question: 'How shall we pay the debt upon the preaching-house?' the sea-captain spoke, tersely enough, but to the point. 'Let every one in the Society give a penny a week, and it will easily be done.' They heard him with some astonishment. Many were poor and even a penny every week was out of the question. 'True,' said the captain, 'then put ten or twelve of them to me. Let each of these give what they can weekly, and I will supply what is wanting.' The man who is prepared to back his convictions with himself and his possessions, generally carries the day, but Captain Foy had done something much more than meet a single financial crisis. Indeed, there was nothing new about the weekly contribution of a penny, for that was already the method adopted for meeting the needs of the poor, but as Dr. Simon has pointed out, he had established a new principle.[15]

The richer members were pledging themselves to give of their wealth, sufficient to meet any deficiency due to the smallness of the contributions made by the poor. It was a recognition of the honour and privilege of 'the family'. Here was the germ that was to develop into a fellowship that reached not only to the depth of the pocket but, presently, to those deeper depths of the soul.

The meeting having accepted Captain Foy's suggestion, decided that 'the whole society should be divided into little companies or classes—about twelve in each class'. One can be fairly sure that John Wesley himself suggested the word class, for it is obviously the Roman *classis* which he has in mind, when he writes the account in his *Journal*.[16] One person in each class was to be appointed to collect the pennies and bring them to the steward weekly. So the little meeting ended, with no one realizing what had happened! Not even John Wesley himself foresaw what great thing God would make of man's humble effort. The persons appointed called on the members of the 'little companies' and made some astonishing discoveries. A domestic quarrel, a man 'in drink', another bowed down with a secret sorrow—these revelations accompanied the collection of the twelve pennies. Wesley saw, immediately, the tremendous possibilities. Here was an opportunity, not merely to clear a debt, but to solve his most pressing problem. These collectors of pennies might become the sub-pastors who, by their regular contacts, could do much to guide or comfort or, where necessary, reprove every individual in each Society. It was, at first, a dimly-seen vision, but he was never the man to be satisfied with a dream. As he rode into Wales and presently back to London, the dream was already becoming reality.

On 25th April his *Journal* records: 'I appointed several earnest and sensible men to meet me, to whom I showed the great difficulty I had long found of knowing the people who desired to be under my care. After much discourse, they all agreed there could be no better way to come to a sure, thorough knowledge of each person than to divide them into classes, like those at Bristol, under the inspection of those in whom I could most confide. This was the origin of our classes at London, for which I can never sufficiently praise God, the unspeakable usefulness of the institution having ever since been more and more manifest.'[17]

Though the original 'classes' brought such welcome results the developments which soon followed were, perhaps, the most important in the whole history of Methodism. Wesley had been greatly influenced by reading Cave's *Primitive Christianity: or the Religion of the Antient Christians in the first age of the Gospel*. He studied it, page by page, in Georgia, and it guided him when he wrote the 'Rules' in Newcastle. His constant desire was to mould his Societies on the lines of the first Christian communities. The formation of the first 'classes' in Bristol and London marked a definite stage in the achievement of his ideal. It soon became apparent that there were objections to the visitation of the members in their houses. It took time which the leaders could not spare and it was not always convenient to the members, especially such as were 'in service' and could not easily leave their duties to talk with their visitors. There were occasions when it was necessary to bring the members together to solve a problem which affected several of them. The obvious solution was that they should all meet once a week, under the direction of the leader.

At first the meetings were somewhat stiff and formal. Though they began and ended with the singing of a hymn and with prayer, the intervening hour was occupied by the leader in 'conversing' with those present, 'one by one'. This meant that he stood before each one, and, as in the band meetings, asked personal and direct questions about their 'spiritual condition'. Some of the original members of Society objected to the innovation, no doubt with good reason. An ideal leader might be able to follow this plan with little suggestion of the inquisitorial in his technique, but the leaders themselves were only beginners. When their apprenticeship was ended, the classes were gradually transformed. They became the opportunity for real fellowship which had been so sorely needed. Instead of resembling courts of inquiry, they were family circles, where problems might be solved and experience shared, and where every member felt that there was One in the midst to guide and to bless. In Wesley's own words is to be found the most satisfying summary: 'It can scarce be conceived what advantages have been reaped from this little prudential regulation. Many now happily experienced that Christian fellowship of which they had not so much as an idea before. They began to "bear one another's burdens", and naturally to care for each other.'[18] Whilst the class-meeting was evolving, he showed himself patient and reasonable to its critics. 'We are always open to instruction; willing to be wiser every day than we were before, and to change whatever we can change for the better.'[19]

The Societies began to accept the new development, and from 1742 to 1746 the change was affected so that as Dr. Simon says 'in 1745–6 it had become the established usage'.[20]

The weekly class-meeting, called by William Grimshaw the parish-class, was the medium for deepening the intimacies of Christian fellowship in countless ways. In these gatherings conversions took place, experiences were exchanged and interpreted and, at times, a Pentecost broke on their eager spirits.

There was no hesitation in adapting times to local needs. By April 1742 in the Society at the Foundery there were sixty-six leaders though the number of members in each class was at most of six or seven. At that time no man 'led a class of females'. Mostly the classes met at eight o'clock in the evening because the majority of members worked long hours and could not get to the Foundery earlier. A few of the women's classes met at four o'clock.[21] It was evidently not the general custom for classes to meet in the afternoon, for it is recorded as an item of special interest that in 1788 Miss Mary Hudson, a valuable member of Society in Halifax, being unable to attend the evening class-meeting, persuaded Mr. Godwin, the preacher stationed there, to 'establish, principally on her account, a class at his own house on a Monday afternoon'.[22]

As will be seen later, the creation of class-leaders made pastoral oversight much more thorough, but there were those who resented the idea of personal questioning, and even went so far as to compare the class with the confessional. The idea persisted long after the death of Wesley, and may have been justified in cases where leaders had a wrong conception of their functions. In a *Memorial of Thomas Bush* the author, writing while the criticism was still a live issue, refers to the comparison drawn between class-meeting and confessional: 'The one is private confession to a priest, the other is conversation among fellow Christians. The one exceedingly minute, extending to every thought, word, and act,—the other such as a sound judgement will dictate. . . . Pardon a man cannot give; advice and comfort, Christians are well qualified to afford. And their united prayers secure a mutual blessing. . . .'[23]

The more the class-meeting became a fellowship where there was complete confidence, respect and a growing affection, the less the idea of an inquisition was justified. It would always have been easier to understand the critics focusing their attention on the 'Bands' rather than on the typical class-meeting, which became more and more the family circle, and less and less the law court.

In 1764 'the large and ancient village of Mousehole' near Penzance experienced a revival of religion. It was decided to establish a class-meeting to gather together the new converts. The houses were scattered and it was difficult for people to leave their young families and tramp into Newlyn, so 'a class was formed in John Harvey's house, where the first Methodist sermon was preached. This was a day of small things', wrote Richard Treffry, 'but God did not despise it. The members were few, and in the estimation of the world despicable. But they were a little band of love; they took sweet counsel together, and they strengthened each other's hearts in God.'[24] The fellowship deepened and since love not only meets opportunities but makes them, it sought to aid not only the members of 'the family' but, through the family, the homeless wayfarer. Whether his loneliness was physical, mental, or spiritual the class members welcomed him to the fireside whose fires were as sacred as those of the altar. In Mousehole there lived George Badcock, 'a little slender man, of a low voice and admirable spirit. . . .' He had arrived there in the height of a storm, but let him describe the event in his own words: 'We were driven by the fury of the storm ashore on the beach, and stripping off our clothes, as our boat went to pieces, we struggled to the land. The night was very dark, and the wintry wind pierced us through: there was a light flittering to and fro, not far from us; it was a will-o'-the-wisp in the marsh, that would lead us to our doom; and I told my companion so, but he said it was a light in a cottage window, at Ludgvan, and that he would go to it, for we could not live until the morning, cold, naked, and wounded, as we were by the rocks. He left me, and was found the next day stifled in the marsh. I strove to keep life in me, by walking up and down all that miserable night. O how solemnly did the sea break upon the shore! It was like a dirge; for I knew that my companion was lost. O how precious was the first dawn of light, when I found I was on the green, St. Michael's Mount on my right, and Penzance two miles on the left, to which I crawled as well as I could! In the first house

I came to, the people were still asleep; but they rose and received me kindly. This preservation induced me to think very sadly and seriously of my state; and then it led me earnestly to cry to God for mercy. I joined the religious people that first met at John Harvey's: we were few; and when we gathered together in the great kitchen, we looked like a little band that had struggled to the shore, while the waves still roared behind us; but the day of salvation had broke upon us.'

Was it John Bunyan or Daniel Defoe or some strange combination of the two who seemed to be inspiring honest George Badcock? Or was it more truly the spirit of that family circle which had saved him from the fury of the storm that battered his body, and the fiercer tempest that was making shipwreck of his soul? Many a year he lived in Mousehole, afterwards, and learned to share the peace he knew, with all who were troubled and afraid.

The class at Mousehole was typical of such groups all over the country. One of the first leaders appointed in the north of England was John Dale, of Gateshead Fell, and for many years he met his class in his own house. His grandson, John Dungett, 'a weakly child', often stayed with his grandparents and many years after, when he himself was a respected class-leader and local preacher, wrote down his memories. He was often allowed to remain in the room while the class was meeting, and describes his grandfather taking his seat, after singing and prayer, and calling 'the members one after another, who came and stood before him while he enquired how their souls prospered, and conversed with them about their experience of the grace of God.' This seems to be an example of the earlier methods which gradually changed, but it certainly succeeded then, perhaps, as in many other cases, because of the common sense and spiritual insight of the leader. In his journal on 25th February 1816, John Dungett, the grandson, thirty-six years of age records: 'I was sent for today to see my grandmother. I found her very weak; but blessed be God she is waiting in faith for the messenger. After preaching, I met the class which was my grandfather's twenty-nine years ago; and there are yet three which met with him. . . .'[25]

Whether the evidence be sought in Mousehole or Gateshead, in the lonely villages or the industrial centres, the conclusion is the same. The class-meeting was more than 'a stroke of genius' on the part of Wesley or any other man; it was the gift of God to needy people who grew in grace because they gathered in eager and expectant fellowship. It was not uniformity of procedure which mattered most but rather the sharing of experience and the readiness to accept the guidance of God whenever and however it was given to their ready minds and hearts.

They sang together with great thankfulness:

> What troubles have we seen,
> What conflicts have we passed,
> Fightings without, and fears within,
> Since we assembled last!
>
> But out of all the Lord
> Hath brought us by His love;
> And still He doth His help afford,
> And hides our life above.[26]

In prayer and thanksgiving they learnt to face life joyfully and usefully, and, when the time came, they faced death with invincible courage and a sense of triumph through faith in their Lord. It was a characteristic of Charles Wesley that he selected pictures which caught the imagination of almost every section of the community. It is, for example, thrilling to stand with George Badcock and Richard Trewarvas, old seafarers who knew the way of the sea, and hear them singing when the years had thinned out the little class and they themselves were looking for the end of the voyage:

> There all the ship's company meet
> Who sailed with the Saviour beneath,
> With shouting each other they greet,
> And triumph o'er trouble and death.[27]

There is nothing mawkish or sentimental about the ringing notes. The sailors do not croon—they shout, for the love that has bound them to one another and to their Captain is a robust love of which none need be ashamed.

The character of a class was determined to some extent by the character of the leader. The special functions of a class-leader were defined in the *Rules of the Society*, and on various occasions John Wesley expounded these in detail. In 1744, at the First

Conference, it was agreed that the leaders themselves should be examined as to their methods, that they should keep in close touch with the preachers, and attend a weekly leaders' meeting. These early arrangements were subsequently modified, but no findings of Conference had so powerful an influence on the development of leadership as had John Wesley himself, who met each new situation with a personal letter or by talking with the people concerned. Three examples will serve to show the trend of his advice and instructions.

In 1747 he examined the classes at Gateshead and seemed to be conscious of the fact that people had been questioning his ability to 'distinguish the precious from the vile' in his attempts to 'purge the societies'. His experience on this occasion convinced him that he could do this on two conditions: 'first, courage and steadiness in the examiner; secondly, common sense and common honesty in the leader'. They are virile qualities, and they indicate the kind of person he intended should be entrusted with the responsibility of leading a class. If the leader has common sense he can answer the questions asked about the behaviour of his members, and if he has common honesty he will. That was Wesley's attitude. It was, as he says, 'the general tenor' of the life of the individual that was in question.[28]

If it should appear that he was too concerned with the part to be played by leaders in helping to discipline the Societies, it should also be remembered that no true fellowship could exist where hypocrisy was tolerated or where double-dealing remained unrebuked. The class-meeting, like the family, demanded complete loyalty on the part of the members to one another, and, above all, to the Father in whose love their unity and kinship was based.

In 1771 the Society in Dublin was distressed by a dispute, which had gone on for some years, as to the relative authority of preachers and leaders. Over a hundred members had been lost, and in April John Wesley decided to take a firm hand. He read a paper to the leaders in which he declared that their 'sole business was (1) to see each person in his class once a week; to inquire how their souls prosper; to advise, reprove, comfort or exhort them; (2) to receive what they are willing to give toward the expenses of the society; and, (3) to meet the assistant and stewards once a week.'[29] It was a rather harsh document and, though strong measures needed to be taken, the action of Wesley at this juncture did not heal the wounds. He insisted that 'in the Methodist discipline the wheels regularly stand thus: the assistant, the preachers, the stewards, the leaders, the people. But here the leaders, who are the lowest wheel but one, were got quite out of place.' This was a somewhat arbitrary and unnecessary gradation, made perhaps under considerable provocation, and Dublin did not understand it. A study of the first Methodist class-leaders does not leave the impression that they assumed any particular authority in discharging what was accepted, often in great humility, as a spiritual office. Perhaps one of the reasons why Wesley definitely forbade any of his preachers leading a class[30] was that he felt the necessity of maintaining the scale of authorities defined in Dublin. It would have been an anomaly for one man to be the second 'wheel' and 'the lowest wheel but one' at the same time.

A final example of the way in which he strove to keep up the standard of both leadership and membership is seen in his letter to Joseph Benson, who was stationed at Newcastle in 1776: 'We must threaten no longer, but perform. In November last I told the London Society, "Our rule is to meet a class once a week, not once in two or three. I now give you warning: I will give tickets to none in February but those that have done this." I have stood to my word. Go you and do likewise wherever you visit the classes. Begin, if need be, at Newcastle, and go on at Sunderland. Promises to meet are now out of date. Those that have not met seven times in the quarter exclude. Read their names in the Society, and inform them all you will the next quarter exclude all that have not met twelve times—that is, unless they were hindered by distance, sickness, or by some unavoidable business.

'And I pray without fear or favour remove the leaders, whether of classes or bands, who do not watch over the souls committed to their care "as those that must give account".'[31]

Again it is necessary, before passing judgement on what seems a strangely severe document, to remember that to have admitted laxity in the classes and above all in the lives of the 'leaders' would have been to discredit the very things for which Methodism stood. Cases of indifference to the fellowship, and instances of smuggling and spirit-drinking had come to his notice in London

and Newcastle. His immediate resolve was to stamp out such
evils, and first of all the Societies must be freed from all suspicion.
He felt that action must be swift and drastic, and unworthy
leaders be deprived of their leadership at once, lest the whole
fellowship suffer.

For the most part the first Methodist class-leaders were men
and women of exemplary character, and their diaries show that
it was something much more than fear of disciplinary action
which kept them faithful to their charge. Class-leading was to
them a vocation and demanded utter loyalty not merely to a set
of 'Rules' but to the Lord and Master who had called them.
They found their highest joy in the cure of souls committed to
them, and they accepted the responsibility of their office as
a most sacred trust.

In November 1777, Elizabeth Ritchie (afterwards Mrs.
Mortimer) was appointed a class-leader, and her friend Agnes
Bulmer wrote: 'She entered on her charge, impressed with its
importance, and deeply sensible of her incompetency to fulfil its
duties without much Divine assistance.'[32] There lay the secret
of all successful class-leading. The men and women who under-
took the task went from their knees to each class-meeting.
Through the week they had prayed for each member daily, and
they came to them fresh from the presence of God. What Agnes
Bulmer describes as 'habits of reflective and consistent piety'
were coupled with fervent zeal and charity that could 'expand
itself beyond the circle of its own immediate interests to sym-
pathize with others in their difficulties, cares and sorrows'.

The first Methodist in Scarborough thought little of the fourteen
miles she had to go to Robin Hood's Bay to meet her class.
Riding on a donkey old Mrs. Bozman was as regal a figure as
Queen Elizabeth declaiming at Tilbury. Indeed she would have
held that her work was more important.[33]

The scholarly and artistic Henry Brooke, friend of Wesley and
Fletcher, was described as having 'tasted the good word of God,
and the powers of the world to come; his soul was ever burning
with the flame of divine love . . . and he earnestly longed for the
salvation of others. . . . Abiding in such a spirit, and resting as
under the shadow of the Almighty, he was proposed as a leader
of a Class in the Methodist Society.'[34] The cultured Dublin
artist made an ideal leader. He went to his class 'with the

advantage of a superior understanding and a well-cultivated mind, and was a giant in the spiritual combat—his strength daily renewed by his continual waiting upon God. There is a charm about his personality, as described by a contemporary, which challenges some of the superficial caricatures claiming to portray the early Methodists. 'In him', wrote Dr. D'Olier, 'were sweetly blended the rare combinations of natural vivacity without levity —sublime devotion without a tincture of austerity—a strong and aspiring mind with the most condescending manners and invincible meekness—large acquirements of knowledge without the parade of learning—and for reviling and contradiction, in the true Spirit of his Master, he returned nothing but blessing.'

It would be difficult to find three personalities differing more completely than Elizabeth Ritchie, Mrs. Bozman and Henry Brooke, yet all three were class-leaders busying themselves in the same high calling and ministering to little groups of people.

In a Lincolnshire village the squire, William Lambe of Aubourn Hall was persuaded to allow a preaching service in the house of one of his tenants. He came to the service himself, and presently twelve members joined together to form a class. The squire himself became its first leader, and the local historian says quite simply 'the class prospered in his hands till the day of his death'.[35]

In Somerset an old class-leader, living in Ditcheat, left in manuscript an account of his life. In it is his own idea of the purpose of the class-meeting and, by implication, the duty of a leader. 'Upon the whole', he says, 'I think this to be the most useful means (excepting preaching) that we (Methodists) enjoy; it is instructive, it unites us together, it stirs us up to press forward; the enemy's schemes are brought to light and defeated and our souls in general abundantly comforted and strengthened.'[36] The record is dated 1784 and is a fair indication of the progressive spiritual fellowship which had developed from the first suggestion made by Captain Foy in the 'Room' at Bristol.

The leaders often retained their office as long as they lived, though they sometimes moved from one class to another. Ideally the family circle contained all age-groups but in practice there was something to be said for the younger leaders dealing with youth, and the more mature gathering about them the older members. When the whole Society met together there was still the sense of 'family'. In the villages the problem scarcely existed because there was often only opportunity or occasion for one class.

The *Memoir of Mr. William Carvosso* has as a sub-title 'Sixty Years a Class-leader in the Wesleyan Methodist Connexion', and it is perhaps the most detailed account of class-leading in existence. When he decided to give up his little farm at Ponsanooth, he records his decision in his diary: 'From this moment I saw my way clear; I was entirely freed from the world, and resolved to give up my few remaining days wholly to the service and glory of God.' There was nothing selfish about the act, for it gave him an opportunity to commence a 'ministry' in Cornwall which helped to change hundreds of lives. He became a kind of travelling class-leader. Month after month, and year after year, he wandered from Mylor to Mousehole, from Redruth to Camborne and Plymouth, then back to St. Austell and Ponsanooth. Little villages like Breage and Sparnock welcomed him—not as a preacher but as a class-leader, coming to see how they fared. 'He is an instance of the wisdom exemplified by the Founder of Methodism in employing such a class of men in gathering and building up the Church of God. . . . In many places when it was known that he was to meet a class, and the room admitted of it, crowds from other classes would come to listen to his deep experimental instructions, and to catch the fire of his spirit. His visit to a Society was often regarded as a sort of era; for the expectation of the people, and the fervour of his soul, when they met "together in one place with one accord" often conspired to bring more than ordinary influences from above. He was never harsh in meeting a class, but he would blend great fidelity with fervent, melting compassion; so that, however close he came, he would rarely give offence.'37

The visitation was an opportunity for happy fellowship, but it was also a crusade, for William Carvosso, like so many of his contemporary leaders, had a passion for souls. Again and again men and women found the peace that passes understanding, in the class-meeting. 'I went to Ponsanooth; and while meeting one of the classes, we had a very gracious visitation from above. One who had been for four years seeking the Lord, after a severe struggle with unbelief, was enabled to believe with her heart unto righteousness, and boldly testified that she had received forgiveness of sins.'38 '. . . I believe I never had greater pleasure in meeting classes; in labouring to prop the feeble knees, strengthen the hands that hang down, and press on believers to all the depths of humble love.'³⁹ '. . . After a tour of seven weeks among various societies, I have returned in health and peace; having scarcely felt an hour's pain or indisposition since I left home. In meeting classes, visiting from house to house, singing and praying, and talking freely of the great things of God's kingdom in the heart, I have had many blessed opportunities, melting times, and precious seasons with the people of God.'⁴⁰ What a visitor he was! Whilst there was nothing austere or forbidding about his coming, there was something much more than a social contact—something of positive value to the souls and the bodies of those to whom he came. 'By a few minutes' conversation and prayer the whole scenery of the sick man's apartment was often changed: it was, in fact, turned from darkness to light.'⁴¹

So he continued his triumphal progress—guiding, inspiring and healing, yet remaining always one of a great family.

Nor was he alone in such leadership. In many ways Henry Longden, of Sheffield, resembled him. At first he had been hesitant about accepting the office of class-leader, protesting to the Preacher who called for his answer: 'A Class-Leader ought to be a father in Christ; a man of sound and deep experience; well acquainted with the workings of the human heart, and the devices of Satan. . . . He ought to lead the people forward . . . till he delivers them up to the great Shepherd and Bishop of souls, "blameless, without spot, or wrinkles, or any such thing". He should also be so exemplary that like a true captain, he may lead the way himself, and meekly, but confidently say, "Follow me!" '⁴² The preacher pointed out to him that the maturity of a father in Christ came only with the years, and here, in a leaderless class was a little flock waiting for him, as he was. 'I was much affected', writes Henry Longden. 'I durst not refuse; but with many tears, and much trembling, I engaged in what I considered by far the most important office amongst the Methodists. The first objects of my attention were to convince the people of the necessity of punctual attendance, to conform to all the rules of the society, and to acquaint myself with every member, as much as one man may know another; and when I had used every human effort of which I was capable, then frequently to commend them to God in my closet.'⁴³ So he became a leader, not at all perturbed if, in the discipline of Methodism, he was on 'the lowest wheel but one'! His class-meeting was 'a little company' which learned to share experience, resources, and responsibility, and, through their living fellowship, to minister to the needs of their neighbours. Like Thomas Bush of Aldbourne and William Carvosso of Ponsanooth he devoted his later and more leisured years to visiting other classes farther afield. He had become a local preacher but 'to preach the gospel was only part of his work, as an under-shepherd of Christ's flock. He had interviews with the Class-leaders of the respective societies; inquiring faithfully of each the state of his personal experience, his manner of leading his class, the attendance of the people, their growth in holiness, and the increase of their numbers; and if any of the members were sick, he would visit them, accompanied by the Leader'.[44]

Instance after instance might be quoted to show this lofty ideal which was ever in the minds of the leaders of the early Methodist classes. Remembering that they wrote in the idiom of their own day, and that phrases which suggest to the modern an embarrassing pietism were part of current speech and did not necessarily imply anything that could be called smug or self-satisfied, these men seem to have striven to translate, in their own lives, the Sermon on the Mount. Mistakes they made, and were swift to acknowledge in the very classes they led which, after all, is an acid test of their sincerity.

The old soldier, James Field, was so successful in his leadership that he found himself obliged to give up one of his *five* classes. The pastoral oversight of a hundred members was becoming difficult. 'I am confined to business', he writes, 'cannot visit except at night, and this is an unseasonable time, for the members cannot easily be seen, and I always get cold going from house to house; so that the most essential branch of a Leader's duty is unfulfilled by me.' He was growing an old man, but it was a grief to reduce his classes to four, with eighty-four members! To make up for what he felt were his deficiencies, he wrote several letters, with questions and advice, to be read when he was absent. A kind friend offered him a 'confidential situation' at Ballincollig, but he declined it, saying he 'could not give up his classes in Cork, so long as he was able to meet them'.[45] What is even more convincing, his classes would not give him up—so he went

M

his rounds in the evening, cold or no cold, till the end. Though
he did not cover so wide an area as William Carvosso, he made
it his business to write personally to new leaders when they were
appointed in Cork or the surrounding district. The letters were
very human documents, full of warm-hearted interest and
common-sense advice. A class-meeting, he felt, should not last
more than an hour, but should begin 'exactly at the hour
appointed—if only two are present. Four or two double verses
are quite enough to sing. Your prayer should especially concern
your class . . . except in rare instances, speak your own experience,
but be short and comprehensive; and exhort others to speak similarly. . . . If you would be useful, you must "bear all things".
Let nothing offend or move you though it comes from your
dearest friend. . . . Give none up who have the least spark of
spiritual life in them. Remember what they cost Him who hates
putting away. . . .'[46] It must have been a great grief to that fifth
class when James Field could no longer lead it, for he was a man
with a great 'concern' for his members, and for the whole
family of God.

It should be noticed that in the function of leadership, the
class-meeting provided a great sphere of service for the women
of Methodism. Though some few of them preached during
Wesley's life-time[47] the work of class-leading called out the best
in some of the finest characters amongst the women of the day.
The more familiar personalities—Elizabeth Ritchie, Hester Ann
Roe, Agnes Bulmer, Mary Bosanquet, and many others—have
left records of their spiritual experience which give some idea of
the kind of subjects they considered in their classes.

In Lady Maxwell's diaries there are passages which show the
value of the fellowship to her as a member, and the opportunities
she realized as a leader. 'I have to remark now, more than ever,'
she writes to Alexander Mather in 1796, 'the fulness of the Divine
presence in our little class-meeting here; and something still more
remarkable, (as there is often only myself and sometimes two or
three Preachers,) there is, for the time, an uncommon power given
me to express my own experience'.[48] This freedom of self-expression
did not end with the little group to which she belonged in Edinburgh. She was deeply troubled about the iniquities of the
slave-trade and she determined to enlist the intelligent sympathy
of the Society in the question of emancipation. In a letter written

by Mrs. Bridgman, daughter of the Rev. William West, there is
an account of the way she seized the opportunity. 'Lady Maxwell,
was wonderfully solicitous for the salvation of all mankind. When
we were stationed in Edinburgh the last time, her Ladyship
instituted what was called a Compact. The design was, in the
first place, that the members should pray for each other; and,
secondly, that on every Wednesday forenoon, between the hours
of eleven and twelve, each should offer up earnest prayers and
supplications to Almighty God for the spread of the gospel. And
it was a frequent question with her Ladyship when we met, "Do
you remember the Compact?" '[49] Here, as in the other cases
that have been cited, there is the vital principle established of
the lesser fellowship reaching out to the larger until, in prayer,
it embraces all mankind. The little class in Edinburgh was prophetic of that small group of men today who in their concern for
the peace of the world, conceived the 'Big Ben Silent Minute'
with its act of daily 'recollection'.

The first 'race' of class-leaders were, undoubtedly, men and
women whose lives were purifying and enlightening to their
fellows, bringing to the lonely a new and vital friendship and
transforming what Maeterlinck calls a sense of 'lostness' into the
living experience of salvation through faith in Christ. 'I cannot
repeat all the good things I heard from Mrs. Crosby, Mrs. Downe,
and others,' said Mrs. Frances Pawson. 'I can only add, that
those little parties, and classes, and bands, are the beginning of
the heavenly society in this lower world.'[50]

As they sang, their lives were knit together by the love of God,
which guided their thoughts and their energies to the succouring
of all mankind.

> O let us stir each other up,
>   Our faith by works to approve,
> By holy, purifying hope,
>   And the sweet task of love.
>
> You on our minds we ever bear,
>   Whoe'er to Jesus bow;
> Stretch out the arms of faith and prayer,
>   And lo, we reach you now.[51]

It was the custom for the senior Preacher in a Circuit to keep
a complete list of the members of Society, and send a copy to

John Wesley or the Conference. From early *Stewards' Books* still in existence it seems that the usual time at which these details and annual statistics were prepared was the June visitation of the classes.[52] From this list the *class-paper* was prepared, and this was superseded eventually by the *class-book*.[53]

The custom of issuing Band tickets was in operation as early as 1741, for Wesley records in his *Journal* that he met the Bands at Bristol on 24th February of that year, and struck from the list of members of the United Society the names of all 'disorderly walkers. . . . To those who were sufficiently recommended, tickets were given on the following days.'[54] Though it has been suggested that such tickets were used in the Moravian Societies as 'certificates of membership', definite proof of this is lacking. It has been pointed out that the metal tokens issued to admit persons into the meetings of the Moravians in England did not denote membership. Class tickets were probably first introduced in 1742, but the whole question of their origin and purpose has been critically discussed by F. M. Parkinson and J. G. Wright and it is only necessary to record some of their conclusions.[55] In order 'to separate the precious from the vile' John Wesley determined to meet the classes at the Foundery, as he says, 'at least *once in three months*, to talk with every member myself. . . . To each of those whose seriousness and good conversation I found no reason to doubt, I gave a *testimony under my own hand*, by writing their name on a TICKET prepared for that purpose; every ticket implying as strong a recommendation of the person to whom it is given, as if I had wrote at length, "I believe the bearer hereof to be one that fears God and works righteousness".'[56] These tickets were acknowledged as a kind of passport to Methodist Societies everywhere, and as Wesley naïvely continues: 'They also supplied us with a quiet and inoffensive method of removing any disorderly member. He has no new ticket at the quarterly visitation, or as often as the tickets are changed, and hereby it is immediately known that he is no longer of the community.' Once again it is evident that Wesley was basing his structure on the plan of apostolic Christianity, for the class ticket was a 'commendatory letter'. In their earliest forms they varied in shape and size as well as in design. Some were engraved on wood, others on copperplate. Until 1750 they were usually adorned with emblems—a vase of flowers, an angel flying in the clouds and blowing a trumpet, a dove, a crown, and other pictorial devices. Later a more elaborate picture was printed— Christ in the clouds having a crown in the right hand and a cross in the left, the Saviour washing the feet of a disciple, and, amongst those most criticized, a picture of the Crucifixion. This kind of emblematical ticket continued till 1750 when, according to J. G. Wright, texts of Scripture began to replace the emblems, though these did not entirely disappear till 1764. Some of the devices used resembled those on the title-pages of some of Wesley's earlier books, and suggest that he had an eye to the economies in publishing! How far the disappearance of the emblem was due to criticism or to further economies it is impossible to say. The printing was done with black, red or blue ink and sometimes the design was repeated. In 1765 Conference agreed: 'Let there be one ticket everywhere, and the form sent direct from London, and so in every succeeding quarter.' The tickets became more simple in design and contained a text of Scripture, room for the member's name and the preacher's initials or signature, and a large alphabetical letter. This last-named feature was due to a somewhat quaint usage. The tickets were essential for admission to Love-feasts, Covenant-services and Society-meetings. In the earliest days men were duly appointed as Ticket Examiners. The alphabetical letter was a convenience to these officials, who could see at a glance whether the ticket was out of date or a current issue. A metal token is in existence bearing, in the centre, the date 1787, with the words 'Wesleyan Methodist Church' encircling the figures. It is generally assumed that this was used for admission to Holy Communion, especially in Scotland.

The first Methodist class-books are an evidence of the scrupulous care with which many of the leaders kept their records. By the courtesy of Dr. Bonsall it has been possible to examine closely a MS. devised and written, in beautiful copper-plate writing, by Thomas Goulding, the first class-leader in Upwell.[57] He was a schoolmaster and was a member of the Methodist Society for more than fifty years. The first entry in the book was made in 1796 when Thomas Goulding was thirty-seven years of age, and the last is dated 1823. The writer died in 1837. In addition to a careful record of the names and attendances of the members, the comments are in the nature of a diary which gives some indication of the joys and sorrows of the little company, and of the hopes and fears and invincible faith of the Leader.

The short, carefully-written preamble runs: 'In opposition to those who call the proud happy, they that fear the Lord assemble themselves together, to speak of the goodness of God, and the Lord hearkeneth and heareth it, and a book of remembrance is written before him for them that fear the Lord, and that think upon his name. And they shall be mine, saith the Lord of Hosts, in that day when I make up my jewels; and I will spare them, as a man spareth his own son that serveth him. Then will be discerned the difference between the righteous and the wicked, between him that serveth God and him that serveth him not.' (The capitalization has been preserved here as in the original manuscript.)

The first page of this improvised 'class-book' contains the names of thirteen members: Thomas and Ann Goulding, Richard Edwards, Mary Vincent, Thomas Lister, David and Sarah Johnson, Mary Palmer, James Newgent, Catherine Lister, William James, Sarah Trower and Catherine Lister Junior. Of these, nine were married people, one was a widow, two were spinsters, and James Newgent was a boy. The class met on Sundays, and the Leader's comment on the quarterly record from 18th December 1796 to 12th March 1797 is: 'This Quarter a few came to us, but finding that the laws of religion opposed sin, they could not bear such hard dealings and so withdrew.' One surmises that Thomas Goulding had not hesitated to tell them their faults 'plain and home', as Wesley would have put it. The subsequent pages recount the story of the class in some detail. Since the day of its meeting was always Sunday, there were occasions when it was suspended in order that the members might go to the Love-feast or 'to hear preaching' at Wisbech. 'But I suppose the true reason is to get rid of class duty, so much easier is it to hear another speak, than to delineate our own character', is the Leader's comment at the foot of the page. In 1798 things were not going well. 'But the worst of our troubles came through scandalous members, some of which we cast off.' Some persecution broke out and 'the Preachers as well as people were molested by some of the baser sort who were hired to insult us'. Persecution continued, and though the number of hearers at the preaching and prayer-meetings increased, the little class shrank to seven members and the average attendance was only fifty per cent. of the member-ship. 'Yet some of us who could walk tolerably well used to travel sixteen miles upon the Sabbath day to hear preaching until the Lord was pleased to favour us again.' In 1802 the class was gathered together once more, and nine members made almost complete attendances in the June to September quarter. Next year the numbers rose to eighteen and the class was divided, so that Joseph Moul could lead those who lived at the far end of the town. For the next three years the Leader's comments are omitted, but the amount of the 'Quarterage' is faithfully recorded. It averaged £1 16s. 5d. per quarter and was made up almost entirely of 'class and ticket money'.

When all was peaceful and the class was gathering new members, the little company was disturbed by a sensational happening which must be reported in the words of Thomas Goulding himself: 'Between the sixth and thirteenth of July, 1806, a very alarming circumstance happened; which brought us into great confusion, insomuch that I supposed we should all be destroyed and that without remedy. One of our members, William Stafford by name, was in company with some of his fellow Labourers, washing some sheep, and as he professed to be a Methodist, those who were with him said they would dip him and wash away his sins, and make him clean. Stafford remon-strated against their proceedings; and desired them to let him alone and go on with their work. But being deaf to all entreaties, and of the baser sort, they still continued their railing and very much abused him, which he bore with great calmness all the fore part of the day. As they were returning to their work after Dinner they threatened him and said he should be thrown into the soak pen and washed. He again admonished them to let him alone for he didn't choose to be so served. But they swore they would do it, and being upon their watch for an opportunity they at length found one, for while he was busied with his work the shepherd went behind him and threw him into the water which so irritated Stafford, that upon his recovery and getting out of the water, he snatched up a scrubbing rake and gave the Shepherd a blow upon the back of his head and knocked him down, which blow proved mortal, for he never spoke afterwards and in a few hours died.

'When this unpleasant news reached mine ears, what a mighty

consternation was I in. What trembling took place! I could think of nothing but that the cause must certainly fall and that we should all be immediately destroyed.

'The Sunday following this sad event, was our monthly meeting, and as we had to go thro' the Village, it being very long, being so much confused could not tell how to get thither to meet with our Brethren who were as much confused as we were. At length we resolved to go by the back lanes, and being impressed with so much sorrow I could not lead the Class.

'I entreated them who were present to postpone the Class meeting, and hold a prayer-meeting, to which they all gave their consent, during which time I felt somewhat refreshed. In the course of a few days Stafford was apprehended and imprisoned until the February following, and then was arranged (*sic*) at the Bar, took his trial, while he stood trembling, amazingly. There were but one witness, who appeared against him, and that was one who saw the blow struck, and who also joined with the shepherd to abuse Stafford. But he being a very base fellow and had been arranged twice at the bar himself and imprisoned for committing rapes, he was not suffered to speak, thus Stafford was cleared, and many was disappointed who wished for his death. This instance seems to me to be a Judgment upon the persecution, Prov. xxix. i.'

The tragedy had evidently shaken Thomas Goulding, as can be seen by the occasional grammatical mistakes in his recording —though the copper-plate writing is as good as ever. Unfortunately as the class was struggling to recover itself, it received another blow. One of its members, William Abraham, 'being much more taken with the Luxuries of life than with religion, gave so much way to his carnal inclinations as to get shamefully drunk, and made himself an object of ridicule for all the sons of Bacchus who were there present'. His Leader was discouraged and committed to a battle in his own soul. Had he failed in leading his class? Beating back his depression, he took action and, in his entry, there is a blend of strength and gentleness which commands respect: 'I could not find myself concerned in the guilt of Abraham's sin. I could not prohibit it, neither did I delight in it. I looked again to the strong for strength and found it. Blessed be his Holy name. I suspended the unworthy member for five weeks: but out of compassion to his worthy

partner made intercession to the travelling preacher to have him
admitted into Class again, though with very little hope of success.'

In spite of discouragements the class grew steadily until it had
twenty-three or twenty-four members, not only on 'the book' but
attending very regularly. At the end of 1807 the Leader's comment is: 'Notwithstanding our having been favoured with preaching for upwards of Seventeen years, we could never obtain the
privilege of having the Sacrament administered amongst us until
this Quarter, which administration was performed by a Mr.
John Brownell.'

In 1808 there were thirty-one members, though the year ended
a remarkable record. The little Society had been in existence for
eighteen years and not one member had died, but now they lost
three in quick sequence. Year after year Thomas Goulding ruled
his big blank pages into sixteen columns recording the number,
name and 'state' of each member, with the record of the attendances for thirteen weeks. The last of such entries was in 1823
when the members numbered nineteen, of whom three had
belonged to the class in 1796.

From 1809 the comments grew shorter until they ceased altogether in 1816. Some of them refer to the preachers with whom
there was not always the happiest relationship. There is continual evidence of the Leader's care for the members and of his
determination by exhortation and discipline, to keep up the
standard of their individual and corporate life. The Napoleonic
wars were still dragging on, and the strain had its effect, even on
rural England. 'When shall we have better days?' asks Thomas,
and answers his question, 'When we walk more circumspectly'.
Sometimes he laments the laxity in prayer, and more often the
sins of drunkenness and covetousness. On 2nd December 1810,
he is happier, for on this day the Chapel 'which was begun on
June 25th', was opened, and the little Society which had so often
been 'buffeted and disquieted' could now worship God in peace.
Three years later his class had so grown in numbers that it was
divided into three, and he mourned the loss of many of his old
members. 'I seemed as it were to be left alone, having only a
few young ones to train up for God and heaven. May the Lord
give his blessing to them, and to me, and teach me how to lead,
and them how to follow.' The last two comments were recorded
in the December quarter of 1816, and the March quarter of the

following year. They were written in a post-war England, and each refers to 'the pressure of the times'. How far economic confusion affected the class and its leader is not clear, but it was certainly a factor in the lives of the little community. Though for the last six years the commentary ceases, the records continue to speak for themselves. They reveal, in the consistency of the attendances, and in the careful register, that amongst all 'the family circle' there was a bond which did not break. Days of exaltation and distress came to them, but through the years they grew into a conscious kinship with the great family of God's children in heaven and on earth. One can almost hear them singing,

> We meet, the grace to take
> Which Thou hast freely given;
> We meet on earth for Thy dear sake,
> That we may meet in heaven.[58]

It is not easy to take leave of the big book with its thick leaves, and its worn grey cover—the book to which Thomas Goulding entrusted the secrets of his heart. His niece, Mrs. Seaton, wrote in his Concordance a short record of his life which ended '. . . He died on Monday and was buried on the Sunday following, attended by an immense concourse of people. May I follow him so far as he followed Christ and may my last end be like his. So prays Mary Seaton.' Those words were written by the great-grandmother of Dr. Bonsall whose generosity in sharing the intimacies of the book maintains the tradition which began, nearly a hundred and fifty years ago, in the little class at Upwell.

The fellowship of the class-meeting was undoubtedly one of the most precious things in the lives of the first two generations of Methodists. Their love for the little circles to which they belonged led them to endure all kinds of physical hardship that they might enjoy it.

In 1744, John Maden, stirred by the sermons of 'Scotch Will' Darney joined with nine others in a class at Walsden, near Gawksholme, and for twelve months tramped every week a distance of five miles each way to the meeting. It was a wild moorland path which led from his cottage amongst the hills to the tiny village in the valley, and he had to toil hard all day on the rough land which he farmed. Neither weariness nor winter storms hindered him, and as he climbed those steep hills, carrying his horn lantern, he came home each week, singing for the joy in his heart.[59]

The little Society at Swanage longed for a visit from John Wesley but his route to the west did not come nearer to them than Salisbury. Nothing daunted, Mary Burt set out in October 1774, carrying her baby in her arms, to ask him to come to preach to them. It was a 'walk' of forty miles, but she succeeded in her mission.[60] On 12th October he arrived. 'When we came to Corfe Castle, the evening became quite calm and mild. I preached in a meadow near the town, to a deeply attentive congregation, gathered from all parts of the Island.'[61] The tired woman who had doubtless been driven back, with her baby, in John Wesley's chaise, had achieved her purpose. Perhaps more than the rest of the little circle, she realized their backwardness and their possibilities. 'I afterwards met the society, artless and teachable and full of good desires', John Wesley continues, 'but few of them yet have got any farther than to see "men as trees walking".' They were helped that day towards a new and deeper experience because of the vision and determination of Mary Burt—one of themselves! She was thirty-three at the time of her great adventure, and must have been a member of society for two years, for she died in 1826 at the age of eighty-five, having then completed fifty years in membership.[62]

The thrill of the class-meeting was more than a passing phase in the experience of most of the members. The 'family' grew up together in the knowledge and service of their common Lord, and membership was often life-long.

When Ann Darvell died at Farlington, in the ninety-fourth year of her age, she had been a class-member for seventy-three years.[63]

In London, Mrs. Phillis Burland reached the age of ninety-two, having lived all her years in Tabernacle Walk, close by the old Foundery. She 'continued her membership for seventy years . . . and her sun went down in a clear sky, and her end was peace'.[64]

A young man named Hugh Fauls was amongst the first members in Clones. 'So highly did he prize the communion of saints that for upwards of seventy years, except when ill or absent from home, he was never once absent from class.'[65]

In face of such examples, which are typical of a great number, it is ridiculous to dismiss the class-meeting as the product of a passing emotion or to comment, contemptuously, that it was a gathering of neurotics who shut themselves in a selfish circle to practise morbid introspection. Some of the more intimate pages of self-revelation in the personal journals may astonish or shock our modern susceptibilities, but it cannot be too strongly emphasized that the love of which they spoke and sang was, at its best, a virile and self-sacrificial quality which sought to give rather than to get. If the modern forms of Christian fellowship can reach the heights and sound the depths of those groups of friends so surely knit together, the outlook for the future will brighten into the glory of a new day for all mankind.

The class-meeting was essentially a gathering of the friends of Jesus, who, because of that friendship shared a common life as surely as the several branches of one vine.[66] What could be a finer testimony to such relationship than the simple description of a humble member in Frome? 'Mrs. Seagram never lost a friend but by death.'[67] Perhaps the most sceptical would have paused to think again if they could have heard the little class to which she belonged singing:

> Why hast Thou cast our lot
>   In the same age and place,
> And why together brought
>   To see each other's face;
> To join with loving sympathy,
> And mix our friendly souls in Thee?
>
> Didst Thou not make us one,
>   That we might one remain,
> Together travel on,
>   And bear each other's pain;
> Till all Thy utmost goodness prove,
> And rise renewed in perfect love?

Widow Seagram had known what it was to endure fierce persecution for her faith. She had borne the indignity of imprisonment, had been stripped of all her household goods to pay an iniquitous fine, but, strengthened by Christian fellowship, she had so maintained her faith and her friendliness that 'even the openly wicked and profane respected her and were

constrained to admire the excellence which they were unwilling
to imitate'.

Membership in any Methodist class was a sufficient passport
to any other class in the country—or, presently, in the whole
world. When John Brunskill came from Cumberland to London,
he joined the Society at City Road Chapel. For many years he
was Surveyor-General and Examiner in the Excise, and so constantly travelling. 'When away from home, he made it a rule in
every town to find out a Methodist class-meeting once in the
week, and in this way he met in class in nearly every county in
England.'[68] Remembering the strain of travel at the end of the
eighteenth century one feels his achievement is evidence of the
value of such fellowship to a cultured and responsible man
of affairs.

Some time after the inception of the class-meeting, services
began to be held for the recognition of new members. In 1780
John Valton records in his journal: 'This day [31st December]
I received several new members that had been upon trial (in
Manchester). I had them all in front of the congregation, and
read the substance of the Rules to them. Gave them a suitable
exhortation, and finished the ceremony with a hymn and prayer
adapted to the occasion, and God made it a gracious season
indeed.'[69]

The Preachers were convinced of the increasing value of the
Class-meeting, but sometimes inefficient leadership or laxity
amongst the members prevented true fellowship. This was particularly true of Scotland where the whole idea was at variance
with tradition—a fact which the English preachers stationed
there did not seem to understand: 'The people here come out to
Sermon pretty well and last Sabbath we had two new members
at the Class. I am going to put our Rules in execution here more
than usual. Our discipline has been so very lax, the Class-papers
always give me pain when I look them over; there are numbers
of them meet their Class once or twice a Quarter. I told them
the other day I would have no such Members amongst us;
I would put them all out of Society who neglected them thus
except a good reason could be assigned for their being absent.
It is probable this will make our small number still smaller, but
then we shall have fewer Triflers amongst us. And a few diligent
earnest souls will afford us more comfort and satisfaction than a

crowd of Laodiceans.'[70] This extract from a letter written by Joseph Sanderson to Samuel Bardsley in 1782 scarcely does justice to the Scots members. Though they attached the highest importance to attendance at the Sacrament of the Lord's Supper, they were accustomed to quarterly attendances, and the idea of a weekly meeting for fellowship probably appeared an unnecessary innovation.

There was, however, a certain amount of laxity in other places, and John Wesley felt that such slackness often revealed a weak spiritual 'experience'. Amongst his most intimate friends was Ann Bolton, who lived with her brother at Blandford Park, near Witney. His many letters to her include one, written from High Wycombe in 1790, in which the following passage occurs: 'From the time you omitted meeting your class or band you grieved the Holy Spirit of God, and He gave a commission to Satan to buffet you; nor will that commission ever be revoked till you begin to meet again. . . . Woman, remember the faith! In the name of God, set out again and do the first works! I exhort you for my sake (who tenderly love you), for God's sake, for the sake of your own soul, begin again without delay. The day after you receive this go and meet a class or a band. Sick or well, go! If you cannot speak a word, go; and God will go with you. You sink under the sin of omission! My friend, my sister, go! Go, whether you can or not. Break through! Take up your cross. I say again, do the first works; and God will restore your first love.'[71] Written in the last year of his life, to a most-beloved friend, there is an urgency and directness about these words which emphasize the value Wesley placed on the class-meeting. In its fellowship lay the possibility of revival and new growth for the individual or the whole Church. One can easily imagine the return of Ann Bolton, depressed and anxious, to the 'family circle' to which she had so long belonged. As she entered the little room, they were singing one of the hymns that had meant so much to her and to them all:

> Thee we expect, our faithful Lord,
>   Who in Thy name are joined;
> We wait, according to Thy word,
>   Thee in the midst to find.

. . . . .

Whom now we seek, O may we meet!
  Jesus the crucified,
Show us Thy bleeding hands and feet,
  Thou who for us hast died.

Cause us the record to receive,
  Speak, and the tokens show—
O be not faithless, but believe
  In Me, who died for you![72]

It would be difficult in the midst of friends who sang with such confident expectancy, for Ann Bolton or any other, to remain unmoved. In fellowship depression vanished, the burden of sin was loosed, and even the weak grew stronger—not because they had met one another, but because together they had met God.

NOTES

1. *History of Wesleyan Methodism in Melton Mowbray and the Vicinity*, Josiah Gill, Junr. (Warner, Melton Mowbray, 1909.)

2. Professor Tasker. Quoted by Brian Wibberley in *Marks of Methodism*, p. 42. (Whillas and Ormiston, Adelaide, 1905.)

3. *Life and Times of John Wesley*, Luke Tyerman, I. 210.

4. See Chapter IV.

5. *John Wesley's Letters*, VIII. 57.

6. 'A Plain Account of the People called Methodists.'

7. *John Wesley's Journal*, VI. 277–8. See also III. 208.

8. *A Short Account of Miss Mary Titherington*, Henry Moore, p. 37. (R. and J. Richardson, York, 1819.)

9. Preamble to 'The Nature, Design and General Rules of the United Societies', 1743.

10. *W.H.S.*, III. 166–72.

11. *Wesley's Works*, I. 335.

12. *John Wesley's Journal*, II. 528. For account of the United Society at Bristol in 1741, see *W.H.S.*, IV. 92–6.

13. *W.H.S.*, III. 64–5.

14. ibid., XIX. 65.

15. *John Wesley and the Methodist Societies*, Simon, pp. 63–4. (Sharp, London, 1923.)

16. *John Wesley's Journal*, II. 528, footnote.

17. ibid., p. 535.

18. 'A Plain Account of the People called Methodists', *Wesley's Works*, VIII. 254.

19. ibid.

20. *John Wesley and the Methodist Societies*, J. S. Simon, p. 312. (Sharp, London, 1923.)

21. *City Road Chapel*, p. 29.

22. *Methodism in Halifax*, p. 178.

23. *Christian Stewardship Exemplified, a Memorial of Thomas Bush, Esq.*, late of Lamborne, Berks, anonymous, p. 31. (Mason, London, 1849.)

24. *Memoirs of Mr. Richard Trewavas, Senr.*, Richard Treffry, pp. 14–16. (Mason, London, 1839.)

25. *Memoir of John Dungett of Newcastle-upon-Tyne*, J. Heaton, pp. 7–8, 50. (Mason, London, 1833.)

26. Charles Wesley (*Methodist Hymn Book*, 709).

27. ibid., 973.

28. *John Wesley's Journal*, III. 284–5.

29. ibid., V. 404–6. Full text from original MS. in *W.H.S.*, XI. 19–22.

30. Letter from John Wesley to John Cricket (10th February 1783), *Letters of John Wesley*, VII. 166.

31. *Letters of John Wesley*, VI. 208.

32. *Memoirs of Mrs. Elizabeth Mortimer*, pp. 57–8.

33. *W.H.S.*, III. 107.

34. *Life of Henry Brooke*, Isaac D'Olier, LL.D. (Dublin, 1816.)

35. *History of Methodism in Lincoln*, A. Watmough. (Mason, London, 1829.)

36. MS. diary (probably by John Goodfellow), *W.H.S.*, XX. 75–80.

37. *Memoir of Mr. William Carvosso*, written by himself and edited by his son, pp. 155–6.

38. ibid., p. 45.

39. ibid., p. 103.

40. ibid., p. 107.

41. ibid., p. 157.

42. *Life of Henry Longden*, p. 49.

43. ibid., p. 50.

44. ibid., pp. 68–9.

45. *Memoirs of James Field*, pp. 98–102.

46. ibid., pp. 122–6.

47. *More about the Early Methodist People*, Chapter IV.

48. *Life of Darcy, Lady Maxwell*, p. 267.

49. *Life of Darcy, Lady Maxwell*, p. 302.

50. *The Experience of Mrs. Frances Pawson*, p. 109.

51. Charles Wesley (*Methodist Hymn Book*, 722).

52. See details of Stewards' Book, Haverfordwest, 1781; Grimsby Circuit Register, 1769–85; Horncastle Circuit Register, 1786, in *W.H.S.*, XV. 61; and Stewards' Book, Cork, 1785, in *W.H.S.*, IX. 59.

53. *Methodism in York*, Lyth, p. 155.

54. *John Wesley's Journal*, II. 429.

55. *W.H.S.*, I. 129–35, and V. 33–44.

56. 'Plain Account of the People called Methodists', John Wesley (1748).

57. MS. in possession of the Rev. Dr. B. S. Bonsall.

58. Charles Wesley (*Methodist Hymn Book*, 718).

59. *Methodism in Rossendale*, p. 41.

60. *Methodism in Dorset*, Dr. J. S. Simon. (Weymouth, 1870.)

61. *John Wesley's Journal*, VI. 41.

62. Memorial Tablet in Wesleyan Methodist Chapel, Swanage.

63. *Early Methodism in Easingwold*, p. 75.

64. *Methodist Magazine*, 1836, p. 886.

65. *History of Methodism in Ireland*, I. 194.

66. St. John xv.

67. *Brief Annals of the Frome Methodist Society*, S. Tuck, p. 28. (Tuck, Frome, 1814.)

68. *City Road Chapel*, p. 462.

69. John Valton's MS. Journal, *W.H.S.*, VIII. 21.

70. Letter from Joseph Sanderson (Edinburgh, 2nd October 1782), *W.H.S.*, X. 148.

71. *John Wesley's Letters*, VIII. 246.

72. Charles Wesley (*Methodist Hymn Book*, 719).

N

CHAPTER V

PERSONAL CONDUCT

IN considering the behaviour of the early Methodists as individuals and as members of the community as a whole, it must be remembered that for a long time they accepted the guidance of John Wesley and his immediate associates. The 'Rules' gave explicit instructions, which when observed, ensured general uniformity in personal conduct. The casual reader of the diaries and other contemporary records almost invariably comes to the conclusion that this resulted in narrowness and what has been sometimes called 'unhealthy piety'. This judgement does not do justice to the facts. In the first place moral conditions in the eighteenth century were such that any revival of religion demanded immediate and violent changes. A quiet and leisurely transition was impossible, and it was inevitable that the 'revolution' in morals should sometimes result in extremes bordering on an asceticism that seems to us unnatural and even contradictory to the teaching of the Gospels. These pietistic excesses gradually adjusted themselves to the healthy Christian norm.

In the second place such 'narrowness' was not confined to Methodism or the Methodists. In the life of the Venerable Robert Peck of Loughborough there are numerous examples of the severe standards and youthful piety of an Anglican. In 1782 Robert Peck was born at the Angel Inn, Loughborough, and as a boy in the 'Free School' made a close friend of George Davies who subsequently became Bishop of Peterborough. In a series of letters written as a schoolboy there are many passages which are in the pattern of the Methodist diaries. 'O how sorry I was to hear this news', he writes to one boy who had been bullying another. 'I went directly to a throne of grace to pray for your welfare; and as I look upon myself to have the care of both your souls, it would be sin in me if I did not tell you of it.'[1] In his next letter to the same boy he says: 'O my dear R., remember what an infinite friend you have beyond the sky, Jesus Jehovah. . . . O consider it in your heart. I will gladly lend you my hand to help you on; for, dear R., I am over you in the Lord, and you

are over J. B. Correct him when he sins if you have an opportunity, and let him join you in your prayers; I give him to your
care.' These letters were written when he was twelve years old.
At thirteen he was writing sermons and prayers, and he left three
volumes of manuscript sermons which he had completed before
he was seventeen. At this time he was a member of the Loughborough Parish Church, and would have undoubtedly taken
Holy Orders had his 'means and opportunities' permitted. There
are many similar examples notably in the journals of Hester Ann
Roe (Mrs. Rogers) whose father was a clergyman. At six years
of age she was expected to give an account 'every Sabbath evening of the sermons and lessons she had heard at church', say
a portion of the catechism and recite the Collect for the day.
She trembled 'lest Satan should be permitted of God to snatch
her away body and soul', because she had been thinking of
childish stories when saying her prayers. At eight she was forbidden to read novels, to learn to dance or to 'go on visits to
play with those of her own age'. In spite of such severity, almost
unpardonable to us today, life in the vicarage at Macclesfield
does not seem to have been unhappy.[2]

In the third place, though the 'Rules' appear to fence in the
life of the ordinary person, almost as rigidly as the regulations of
a monastic order, John Wesley frequently indicated that he
approved a tolerant attitude to those who differed from him.
'It is the glory of the people called Methodists that they condemn none for their opinions or modes of worship', he wrote to
Mrs. Howton at Worcester. 'They think and let think, and
insist upon nothing but faith working by love.'[3]

The text of the *Rules of the Society of the people called Methodists*
was first published on 1st May 1743. Following the preamble
which describes the origin of the United Society and outlines the
duties of Leaders, it defines the condition of membership and
lays down specific rules for personal conduct. These are as
follows, and may be taken as a suitable basis on which to form
some conception of the behaviour of the first Methodist people:

4. There is only one condition previously required in those who
desire admission into these Societies, viz. '*a desire to flee from the
wrath to come, to be saved from their sins*'. But wherever this is really
fixed in the soul it will be shown by its fruits. It is therefore

expected of all who continue therein, that they should continue to evidence their desire of salvation,

FIRSTLY, By doing no harm, by avoiding evil in every kind, especially that which is most generally practised.

Such is

The taking the name of God in vain;

The profaning the day of the Lord, either by doing ordinary work thereon, or by buying or selling;

Drunkenness; *buying* or *selling spirituous liquors*, or *drinking them*, unless in cases of extreme necessity;

Fighting, quarrelling, brawling; brother *going to law* with brother; returning *evil for evil*, or *railing for railing*; the *using many words* in buying or selling;

The *buying* or *selling uncustomed goods*;

The *giving* or *taking things on usury*; *i.e.*, unlawful interest;

Uncharitable or unprofitable conversation, particularly speaking evil of Magistrates or of Ministers.

Doing to others as we would not they should do unto us;

Doing what we know is not for the glory of God, as—

The *putting on of gold or costly apparel.*

The *taking such diversions* as cannot be used in the name of the LORD JESUS.

The *singing* those *songs*, or *reading* those *books* which do not tend to the knowledge or love of GOD;

Softness, and needless self-indulgence;

Laying up treasures upon earth;

Borrowing without a probability of paying, or taking up goods without a probability of paying for them.

5. It is expected that they should continue to *evidence their desire of salvation,*

SECONDLY, By doing good, by being in every kind merciful after their power; as they have opportunity, doing good of every possible sort, and as far as possible, to all men:—

To their bodies, of the ability that God giveth, by giving food to the hungry, by clothing the naked, by visiting or helping them that are sick or in prison;

To their souls, by instructing, *reproving*, or exhorting all they have any intercourse with; trampling under foot that enthusiastic doctrine of devils, that 'we are not to do good, unless *our heart be free to it*'.

By doing good especially to them that are of the household of faith, or groaning so to be; employing them preferably to others, buying one of another, helping each other in business; and so much the more, because the world will love its own, and them *only*.

By all possible *diligence* and *frugality*, that the Gospel be not blamed.

By running with patience the race that is set before them, *denying themselves, and taking up their cross daily*; submitting to bear the reproach of Christ; to be as filth and off-scouring of the world; and looking that men should *say all manner of evil of them falsely, for the Lord's sake*.

6. It is expected that they should continue to evidence their desire of salvation,

THIRDLY, by attending all the ordinances of GOD; such are,

The public worship of God;

The ministry of the word, either read or expounded;

The Supper of the Lord;

Family and private prayer;

Searching the Scriptures; and

Fasting or abstinence.

7. These are the General Rules of our Societies: all which we are taught of God to observe, even in His written word, the only rule, and the sufficient rule, both of our faith and practice. And all these we know His Spirit writes on every truly awakened heart. If there be any among us who observe them not, who habitually break any of them, let it be made known unto them

who watch over that soul, as that they must give an account. We will admonish him of the error of his ways: we will bear with him for a season. But then if he repent not, he hath no more place among us. We have delivered our own souls.

May 1, 1743.   John Wesley.
                                                          Charles Wesley.

The Rules fall naturally into sections of which the first is concerned with the avoiding of evil. Certain practices are judged to be harmful and these all members of Society were expected to renounce. Some difference of interpretation is noticeable in the lives of the first two generations of Methodists, but there was no great margin of possible variation. The passing of the years brought relaxation on some points, but generally speaking the members kept the 'Rules'.

The first of the prohibitions concerns blasphemy. In his sermon preached before *The Society for the Reformation of Manners* in 1763, John Wesley gave advice as to the treatment of profanity. 'A mild admonition is given to every offender, before the law is put in execution against him.'[4] He wrote in the same vein to George Merryweather of Yarm in 1766. 'So far you may fairly go. You may mildly reprove a Swearer *first*. If he sets your reproof at naught, *then* you ought to proceed as the Law directs.'[5]

On the question of Sabbath Observance the Rules were emphatic. There are those who condemn this rigid Sabbatarianism, maintaining that Wesley made Sunday a day of boredom. One of these critics goes so far as to say that if Methodism had helped to revive 'the older Anglican tradition which expressed itself in The Book of Sports' it would have been better for the country.[6] Such an opinion is certainly against the evidence, and though modern conditions have complicated the problem there is still value in the story of the struggles of those who tried, so valiantly, to keep the Fourth Commandment as they understood it.[7]

The tradesman was often compelled to risk his business for conscience' sake. In Exley, Halifax, John Iredale kept a grocer's shop, and it had long been customary for the country people to leave their baskets outside his door when they came to church on Sunday mornings. He filled them with the goods ordered and had them ready as they returned after the service. When John was converted—under the preaching of the saintly Venn at Elland parish church—he decided he must end the practice.[8] Some of his customers left him. 'This was a severe trial . . . the storm, however, was of short duration . . . and his business increased.' It is interesting to notice that his conscience was aroused by Mr. Venn and not by Mr. Wesley.

Bakers were faced with a special problem, but Alexander Mather, coming to London took a firm stand, by protesting to his master against Sunday labour. 'I dare not commit sin by breaking the Sabbath,' he said. All the bakers in the locality worked on Sundays, and Mather's employer was in a difficult position. Rather than lose a good workman, he put the case to his neighbours and competitors. All but two agreed to give up Sunday labour altogether—which does not seem, from the workman's point of view to enforce a duller day![9]

In order to relieve barbers of Sunday work, Conference directed that no members of Society should have their hair dressed on Sunday.[10]

The solving of the problem often entailed a struggle between loyalties. In 1795 Mary Taft wrote an account of a young butcher in Thirsk, who realized that to obey the 'Rule' might involve not only himself but his mother who was dependent on him. Her words describe the situation with dramatic simplicity: 'During the week he was much tempted, and particularly distressed with this thought: "I must sell no more meat on the sabbath-day, and the best of my customers send for it then; and if I do not let them have it, probably they will not come on the Monday, so my meat will spoil, and I shall not be able to pay my way, and so become a scandal to religion." Again he thought, "I have taken my dear mother to keep; I could take a spade and work in a ditch for myself, but I cannot bear that she should come to want." He took the right method, laying his case before the Lord, and in earnest prayer seeking for wisdom and strength.'[11] The clash of loyalties—to customers, to his mother, and to religion —was resolved by this newly-accepted supreme loyalty. 'When sabbath came, he rose early, went to his shambles door, and told his customers as they came, that he could not let them have any meat that day, but in the morning he could supply them as they pleased. Some cursed, others said he was mad, and his mother was quite displeased at him; for she then knew nothing of the

quite unconvinced that its result was merely the creation of a
'dull day'. (In a book of virile reminiscences, Sir Harold Bellman
reviews a life of widespread activities and innumerable contacts
on five continents, and then recollects his early days. His description of the Methodism he knew at the beginning of the twentieth
century, contains this comment: 'Sunday was the day for best
clothes, button-holes, music, happy fellowship and good cheer.'[16]
Not even so complete a cosmopolitan as he finds the memory of
a 'Sabbath well-kept' dull or regrettable.)

The prevalence of drunkenness in the latter half of the
eighteenth century was little short of a national disaster. More
particularly the importation of gin and the production of spirits
sold at a relatively low price, filled the debtor's prisons and
lowered the moral level of life as a whole. There could be only
one rule for the Methodist people at such a time. 'Spirituous
liquors' were banned. 'Distilled liquors have their use', said
John Wesley in a letter to Thomas Wride, 'but are infinitely
over-balanced by the abuse of them; therefore, were it in my
power, I would banish them out of the world.'[17] It is doubtful
whether any 'Temperance tract' written subsequently was more
powerful than his *Word to a Drunkard*, which says bluntly and
convincingly: 'A drunkard is a public enemy. Above all, you
are an enemy to God. . . .'[18] Even the class-books of the period,
with their admissions and expulsions, show how general was the
evil. In the judgement of Wesley it was, in part, responsible for
the shortage of food and the high price of corn.[19] Because it was
a social and economic folly the first Methodists accepted the
'Rule', but the acceptance was decisive because it was realized
that drunkenness primarily outraged the love and purposes of
God. The ale which Wesley, like everyone else, drank as a
normal beverage varied in strength. He regretted the increased
proportion of hops used in its manufacture, and wrote an interesting article in the *Bristol Gazette*, which was quoted in Aris's
Birmingham Gazette, 28th September 1789, urging that ale should
be brewed without hops.[20] The taking of snuff and the use of
tobacco came in another category, though the Irish Conference
in 1765 forbade its preachers the use of snuff[21] and Wesley
condemned tobacco as uncleanly.[22]

It was generally understood that members of Society should
not take legal action against one another. Their differences

should be settled outside the courts of law. One of the members of Joseph Bowers' class in Bandon—Sally Brown—was apparently prosecuted by another member. As soon as Wesley heard of it he wrote to Samuel Bradburn: 'For God's sake, for the gospel's sake, and for my sake, put a full stop to this vile affair, the prosecution of poor Sally Brown. If it is not stopped, I shall be under a necessity of excluding from our Society not only Eliz. Sharp but Joseph Bowers also. She would not dare to proceed thus without his connivance, if not encouragement. He can stop her if he will. . . . But I insist upon this. All of them are or were members of our Society. Therefore they were not at liberty to go to law with each other, but are under an obligation to stand to the decision of me or the Assistant. . . . Put a full end to the business, that the scandal may be removed.'[23]

The strong hand of Wesley, the disciplinarian, had not weakened with the years, but generally speaking, his authority had been used wisely in maintaining the high standards of personal behaviour in the Societies. He ruled in such a realm, but this did not mean he trespassed on the privacy of spiritual experience. There were occasions when his control of conduct seems to us arbitrary and almost despotic, but it was always exercised with one end in view—the leading of the people into the service of their common Lord. The disciplinary machinery of Conference and the Societies was slowly emerging, but in this early stage, no one can reasonably question the value of his attitudes on most of the issues raised.

Some of the 'Rules' needed enforcement rather than interpretation. Amongst the most inhuman crimes were those committed by the wreckers, especially on the Cornish coast. Though the Methodists would 'have nothing to do with it'[24] they were less scrupulous, at first, in taking part in the smuggling which was almost a staple industry in the coastal districts! At Paul near Penzance, Richard Trewarvas on his mother's second marriage was 'taken off from school, and as his step-father was alternately engaged in fishing and smuggling, his stepson was for some time similarly occupied'. In almost every little fishing cove on the south coast of Cornwall contraband goods were landed regularly. Often an organized band of a hundred men or more would meet the ship running the cargo, unload her, and disperse the goods within a few hours. The preventive men did what they could to we are contented. If He give us anything we intend it for some laudable pious uses.' It was certainly a quaint theory of Providence which caused three men of such strict rectitude to take this action, and there seems to have been some misgiving, for the postscript adds: 'if you know of any sin in the offering to buy any part of a ticket or tickets, we are open to conviction. We are willing to decline the request and design. If there be no harm in it, as indeed we see none, we desire the favour of the purchase as above.'[33] Even John Wesley himself appears, for once, undecided. 'I never myself bought a lottery ticket; but I blame not those that do. . . .'[34] Whether the uncertainty arose, as in the case of Grimshaw, from his conception of the working of Providence it is impossible to say. It may have been that in his mind, there was some dim association of ideas, since he steadily maintained his agreement with the Moravians, in deciding great issues by the casting of lots. Whatever may have been the cause of what seems to have been a 'blind spot' there was obviously no intention of condoning gambling which he insisted was a cardinal sin.[35]

Uncharitable or unprofitable conversation was condemned and it will be seen later that Wesley himself approved the adoption of definite methods such as the use of Scripture cards, to help the people to overcome the temptation to idle gossip, when they met together.

The question of clothes would seem to be of secondary importance but it occupies quite a prominent place in the earlier pages of many of the personal diaries. The Rules forbade 'the putting on of gold or costly apparel' and the new outlook on life and its values gave the first Methodists furiously to think. Though it concerned the women more deeply, it affected the men also, for they were living in an age of colourful and expensive tastes. The question of how far the Christian should conform to fashion was, to them, a matter for serious consideration. Their reactions were not always the same. Some were inclined to go to foolish extremes, as though there were virtue in ugliness. Others took a more moderate view, holding that neatness and even beauty was not incompatible with true religion. The biographer of Lady Maxwell says: 'Her dress which was as much dictated by conscience as formed by taste, was very plain, being without ornament, or anything which could serve only for show; yet it was a plainness of her own, equally removed from the formal costume of the Quaker, and the frippery of fashion. . . . She did not degrade herself from her rank, nor detract from her personal appearance, by this plainness of apparel; but she found that she could relieve many a suffering creature, and give education to many an orphan child, with what numbers expend in useless decorations.'[36]

The determination to dress plainly was partly a matter of conscience, and partly due to the new appreciation of the importance of rightly using both money and time. When Mary Bosanquet made her great decision, she felt she must readjust much of her life. 'I prayed for direction,' she says, 'and saw clearly that plainness of dress and behaviour best became a Christian. As soon as I saw my way clearly I ventured to open my mind to my father concerning dress, as I had done before with regard to public places; entreating him to bear with me, while I endeavoured to show him my reasons for refusing to be conformed to the customs, fashions and maxims of this world.'[37]

The outward appearance of people who were contemptuously termed 'fanatics' and 'enthusiasts' mattered a great deal, and John Wesley, always a pattern of neatness, did his best to save them from extremes. The preachers were part of his problem! Almost incredible amounts were spent on barbers, hair-powder, and hair-dressing, and the high price of bread was partly attributed to the enormous amount of flour used in the 'dressing-shops'. One of the surprising items in the first Stewards' Books is the relatively large amounts paid out for wigs and shaving, for the travelling preachers. By contrast with the pitifully small allowances for other necessities of life, these payments seem abnormally large, but they must be measured against the current scale of prices. Generally speaking, there is no room to accuse these men of extravagance, for the first race of preachers lived Spartan lives. At the same time it is interesting to find the question being asked in Conference in 1782: 'Is it well for our preachers to powder their hair, or to wear artificial curls?' With considerable tact Wesley answered: 'To abstain from both is the more excellent way.'[38] On the general question he made his own view clear in his *Advice with regard to Dress*: 'Neither do I advise men to wear . . . gay, fashionable or expensive perukes.'[39]

Some of his directions are liable to give the impression that he was inclined to restrict the expression of personality to an unwarrantable degree: 'Should we insist everywhere on the rules of band? particularly that relating to ruffles?' The question was answered, obviously at the dictation of Wesley: 'By all means. This is no time to give any encouragement to superfluity of apparel. Therefore give no Band-tickets to any in England or Ireland, till they have left them off. In order to this, (1) Read in every society, the *Thoughts concerning Dress*. (2) In visiting the classes, be very mild, but very strict. (3) Allow no exempt case, not even of a married woman; better one suffer than many.'[40] Again he insists, 'Give no ticket to any that wear enormous bonnets'.[41] To Mrs. Madan, the wife of Colonel Madan, and one of Wesley's converts, he gives advice in answer to her request: 'All the time you *can* redeem from fashionable folly you *should* redeem. Consequently it is right to throw away as little as possible of that precious Talent, on dressing, visits of form, useless diversions, and trifling conversation.'[42]

Again and again restrictions seem to be imposed, and the casual reader is easily convinced that to be a Methodist, under the iron rules imposed by John Wesley must have been a depressing and deplorable experience. Then, suddenly, there comes some moment when we see the broader humanity peeping through the iron curtain! There was, for example, a memorable evening when he was staying at the house of Mr. and Mrs. Beard, at New Mills, Derbyshire. Someone present had made a caustic comment on their daughter's 'finery'. 'For my part,' said John Wesley, 'I do not wish to see young people dress like their grandmothers; and, I think, those who have the oversight of youth would do well to persuade them to get their hearts filled with the love of God, and then these outward things will adjust themselves.' The girl, who afterwards became Mrs. Holy was deeply impressed by 'the kind and gentlemanly behaviour of this great and good man that she ever after retained a vivid recollection of his features, gestures, and even the tones of his voice'.[43]

Many of the outstanding characters amongst the early Methodist women had the hardest of struggles to convince their families and friends that, in changing their mode of life, they must at once change their outward appearance by discarding anything that could be described as 'fine clothing'. The coming of a new spiritual experience was often prefaced by periods of

what amounted to real anguish. Their journals describe the
intensity of their own inner strife. How far the teaching of
Wesley himself was responsible and how far the less balanced
directions of some of his preachers, cannot be determined but
there are many things which point to Wesley's personal dislike of
mere asceticism.

The wife of Richard Trewarvas was eulogized by Richard
Treffry because 'the form and fashion of her dress underwent
little, if any alteration for the space of fifty years'.[44] In describing
his own mother, once the fashionable Jane Hawkey, he says:
'She assumed a dress that incurred but little expense, and
demanded but little care, the style of which underwent no alteration, through all the subsequent periods of her life.' In a footnote
he adds that he has examined his mother's accounts, since her
death, and finds that 'on her own apparel she expended some
fifty shillings a year, and in her charities six or seven times that
amount, on the average'.[45] The last part of the sentence forbids
any careless criticism of the first.

It is difficult to pass judgement on the general attitude as
shown in memoirs such as these, for once again the style in which
they are written prejudices the modern reader. At thirty-seven
years of age Frances Mortimer read William Law's *Serious Call to
a Devout and Holy Life*, and immediately writes in her diary:
'A Christian woman, employing herself in the embroidery of
dress, has the appearance of one who wishes to please the fashionable world, rather than Jesus Christ. Hence I entreated the Lord
to enable me to sacrifice every part of my dress, which might in
any wise contribute to flatter my vanity.' Later, on a morning
'ushered in with the most exquisite grief I ever remember to
have experienced . . . I resolved to love the cross, and be in
future negligent of dress'.[46] There is evidently nothing artificial
about the entry, for the struggle lasted for more than twelve
months. Nor must it be imagined that Miss Mortimer was a
neurotic, self-centred woman. She read, maintained her place in
a circle of cultured friends, rode regularly, but because of the
prominence given to dress amongst these friends with whom she
was popular, she tried hard to see things in their proper per-
spective. There is a poignancy in her note on 17th December
1774, which the style must not obscure: 'After many distressing
scruples about dress which had anew perplexed my mind,

o

I resolved to make to God the sacrifice I believed he required,
that no one might stumble at me. A superb spotted silk, the gift
of Mrs. Burton, I got the draper to exchange; and a quantity of
lace I gave to my sister to keep for my nieces. I wished to dress
in such a neat and easy way as might please the Lord, and in
such a way as would be the least noticed in the world either for
gaiety or negligence. But, ah! dress is nothing compared with
my wishes for a clearer evidence of justification, and the longing
of my heart after holiness.'⁴⁷ If Francis of Assisi had peeped
over her shoulder as she wrote, he would have understood her
tears, and gloried in the light which mastered them. Few women
of her day left such an environment as hers, to face life as the
wife of a travelling preacher, with greater courage or more conspicuous success. After her marriage to the Rev. John Pawson,
she worked in town and country with a zeal that never tired. When
the manse was a cellar under the chapel she conquered its gloom
by her spiritual radiance, and when fierce controversialists and
pamphleteers attacked her husband she stood by him bravely
and showed not only humility and common sense but an indomit-
able faith. 'The design is to hurt my husband's usefulness in
Wakefield,' she writes in 1805, 'but it will fail of effect. . . .
I wonder that this party should still fall upon us in old and feeble
age; but sometimes the tempest is permitted to rage till the ship
reaches port. Well, the will of the Lord be done.'⁴⁸ When she
came to the end of her long life, she asked that her class should
meet for tickets in her room, at three o'clock. At seven minutes
to three 'as they were assembling', she died, without doubt or
fear, having fulfilled a gracious ministry amongst rich and poor
wherever her husband had been stationed. Whatever judgement
might be passed on her action—or that of St. Francis—it is
evident that the day she parcelled up 'the superb spotted silk'
marked a crisis in her life, and the beginning of a victory which
endured.

Such personal decisions did not, by any means, imply narrowness of mind. The Pawsons were quite human in their outlook,
tolerant, and not without a sense of humour. In one of John
Pawson's letters to Charles Atmore, he says: 'The Scotch women
. . . one and all dress quite gay. Bro. Johnson's intended is what
we call an unkah duce Scotch lassie, but she dresses too: far
beyond the Band Rules. I intend to go to Edinboro' in about

G. R. THOMAS, JR.

three weeks when it is agreed I am to marry them.'[49] He performed the ceremony in due course, without any scruples. Evidently, 'Bro. Johnson's tolerably personable wife' was not expected to accept Frances Pawson's idea of dresses or dressmaking!

Old David Binns, of Bingley, was more rigid in his views, for when 'small clothes' were superseded by 'trousers' he refused to allow anyone wearing the new-fangled garments to enter his class.[50] (There is a legend that the Duke of Wellington was excluded from his club for the same reason, though the decision of the major-domo may have had no theological foundation.)

There is another aspect of the question which should not be overlooked. Some of the first Methodists were people of social standing and, in a day when class-distinctions were so marked, it was a notable event in town or village for 'the quality' to appear in a preaching-house with the ordinary people. However sincere the acceptance of spiritual kinship might have been, it would have appeared suspect had they arrived dressed in the extremes of fashion. True fellowship was hindered by such outward differences. The fashionable Elizabeth Flamank (afterwards Mrs. Shaw) confessed that her 'besetment was love of dress, not that she wore anything gay, such as bows of ribbon on her bonnet. . . . But she made it her study to get clothes of the finest and best materials, and to look "genteel" in a plain dress.'[51] It was, she says, due in part to the ministry of Dr. Coke, that she determined to 'lay aside the besetting sin'. Again it is easy to smile or sneer or pity, but there was a real cause for what to her was a sacrifice. The affectation of the lady of fashion of the period would have dismayed the little society of humble people at St. Austell. Perhaps some such considerations affected John Wesley and Thomas Coke when they were trying to weld together such diverse material. It was a spiritual unity at which they aimed, and it was not unnatural that they should do all they could to remove outward, if lesser, obstacles.

The result is seen in some of the portraits of the period in which a Quaker-like garb was adopted. Describing Mrs. Mary Lyth, her son John said: 'Her dress, the perfection of neatness, was modelled after the most approved style of the Society of Friends.'[52] It may have been, in this case, that the Quaker influence, so strong in York, predominated. In City Road, London, the custom was

general, and was, here, probably, due to the presence of John
Wesley, who had sometimes thought of suggesting a uniform
style for all the women of Methodism. In a record of Mrs. Sarah
Pearson, Stevenson wrote: 'She was a woman of a meek and
quiet spirit, a consistent member of the Society at City Road,
and dressed, as did all the older well-to-do Methodists, like a
Quakeress.'53 Though this may have been generally true of
York and London, it was neither the rule nor the custom everywhere. There were those who, like Lady Maxwell, tried to find
a happy mean in which, without ostentation, a woman could
be natural, and able to express her personality even in the lesser
things of her daily life.

In spite of their rigid Rules the Methodists were not so stereotyped as has often been supposed. Even the preachers 'rebelled'
against Wesley's desire that they should wear three-cornered
hats! He reproved them, and portraits of Adam Clarke and
George Holder, wearing this head-gear, were engraved to mark
his approval. Though the first did not appear in the *Arminian
Magazine* till 1796, they were reproduced elsewhere during
Wesley's lifetime.54 John Wesley, himself, was as neat in his
dress as he was tidy in his mind. He walked with firm step, and
even in old age his demeanour was marked by 'a cheerfulness
mingled with gravity; and a sprightliness which was the natural
result of an unusual flow of spirits, and yet was accompanied
with every mark of the most serene tranquillity. . . . In dress
he was a pattern of neatness and simplicity. A narrow plaited
stock, a coat with a small upright collar, no buckles at the knees,
no silk or velvet in any part of his apparel; and a head as white
as snow, gave an idea of something primitive and apostolic.'55
Comparing this description with the dress of the period, there is
nothing to suggest either eccentricity or sombre austerity. He
kept the Rules for which he was so largely responsible, but he
did not allow them to restrict his self-expression, and he allowed
some latitude to his followers.

If Jacob Jones, the eminent surgeon of Finsbury Square, decided
to wear a pig-tail, no one thought of excluding him from the
Society at City Road, of which he was a member for forty years.
When James Love, one of the first trustees of the New Chapel,
walked abroad wearing his full-dress wig, people remarked on
his likeness to William Pitt the Younger, but he remained a

respected member and official and an intimate friend of John
Wesley and George Wolff.[55]

The whole question of suitable 'apparel' is not to be dismissed
as superficial and unimportant for it offers a clue to the deeper
secrets of mind and heart. The educated and the illiterate found
occasion to discuss them. After the first severe interpretation of
the 'Rule' had been accepted, both men and women began to
moderate their views. In answering a question on the matter
Samuel Drew, the metaphysician, admitted a change in his own
attitude, and went so far as to criticize Quaker 'fashions' as
inconsistent. 'Philosophically', he said, 'I take plainness of dress
to be that which is such in relation to the ordinary costume of
individuals of the same age, rank and country; and scripturally,
that higher objects than the adorning of the body ought to
engage a Christian's attention.'[56]

When the dairyman's daughter went to church she saw only
her own simple problem: 'For a while regardless of the worship
of God, I looked around me, and was anxious to attract notice
myself. My dress, like that of too many gay, vain and silly
servant girls, was much above my station, and very different
from that which becomes a humble sinner who has a modest
sense of propriety and decency. The state of my mind was
visible enough from the foolish finery of my apparel. At length
the clergyman gave out his text: "Be ye clothed with humility."
He drew a comparison between the clothing of the body and
that of the soul. At a very early part of his discourse I began to
feel ashamed of my passion for fine dressing and apparel; but
when he came to describe the garment of salvation with which
a Christian is clothed, I felt a powerful discovery of the naked-
ness of my own soul. I saw that I had neither the humility
mentioned in the text, nor any part of the true Christian character.
I looked at my gay dress and blushed for shame on account of
my pride.'[58] It is a pathetic little record, and perhaps a later
generation of expositors might have allowed her a ribbon or two
without jeopardizing her soul, but Elizabeth Wallbridge was
groping for real values, and no one who knew her doubted that
she had found them.

In spite of these earlier austerities, in an age when social distinctions were still so tragically maintained, there is something
quite colourful and pleasing about the congregation as it gathers

on 'the morning for the travelling preacher'. If the critic complains that there is, even in the chapel at Swinefleet in 1775, some evidence of social status, let him compare the company at Drury Lane and the wretches who lurk in the shadows outside. Here in the little white-washed building he will find, not the contemptuous attitude of the quality at war with the inarticulate resentment of the desperately poor, but the germ of a new unity which was to develop eventually into a national consciousness of the worth of every individual, irrespective of wealth or rank. It is summer and the women are wearing print dresses, clean chocolate-coloured scarves over their shoulders, large checked aprons, and bonnets. They sit holding their red-backed hymn-books folded in their pocket-handkerchiefs, waiting for the coming of the preacher. The men, dressed in fustian or corduroy, or clean smocks, sit on the opposite side. Sturdy yeomen and their wives are in the pews, but the main body of the chapel is filled with labourers, tradesmen and farm servants. Presently the preacher enters the pulpit. Clean-shaven, with hair brushed down over his forehead, he wears a white scarf which is partly covered by the abnormally high collar of his black coat.[59] As he looks at his congregation they seem to be divided as to sex and status, but when he announces the number of the opening hymn and 'lines it out' for the benefit of those who cannot read, they begin to sing. The walls of partition are broken down, and they are one worshipping family, rejoicing in God.

> Christ, from whom all blessings flow,
> Perfecting the saints below,
> Hear us who Thy nature share,
> Who Thy mystic body are.
>
> . . . . .
>
> Love, like death, hath all destroyed,
> Rendered all distinctions void;
> Names, and sects, and parties fall:
> Thou, O Christ, art all in all.[60]

Another essential stressed in the Rules was the right use of time. This brought under review what were called the 'pleasures' of life, and included the attitude Christians, especially Methodists, should take towards the theatre. The popular impression seems to be that the early Methodists, and John Wesley in particular, frowned on all forms of amusement and forbade most of them. This view is justified by references in some of the personal diaries and by the journals of certain of the preachers, but it is not true of John Wesley himself. He censured the theatre of his day, with good reason, but he neither condemned plays nor the reading of them. People, in general, despised the strolling player, and the law was stringent against those who failed to get permission from the local magistrates to act in the town to which they came: 'All common players of interludes, and all persons who for hire or reward, act or cause to be acted, any interlude or entertainment of the stage or any part therein, not being authorized by law, shall be deemed rogues and vagabonds, and be punished accordingly.'[61]

In 1793, during a revival of religion in Halifax a company of players came to the town. On Monday, 4th November, this additional paragraph appeared on their playbill: 'To which will be added a favourite interlude, (never performed here) called the SECRET DISCLOSED; or the Itinerant Field Orator's Fanatical Gibberish, lately delivered in this town, accompanied by all their pious ejaculations, celestial groans, and angelic swoonings &c. &c.; to conclude with a heaven inspiring exit of young lambs. after their immaculate pastor. Orator—Mr. Grist. The flock— by a chosen set.'[62] A few hours after the play-bill was posted, a protest was printed on placards which were distributed through the town. The contents are worth reproducing in view of the sequel: 'Whereas it is Reported that the Stage Players in this town, are preparing an attempt to ridicule religion on the public theatre at the Shakespeare, this present evening, chiefly on account of the small phrenzy of a few ignorant and illiterate persons, who have lately discomposed the serious congregation at the Methodist meeting, near Shaw Syke. And whereas the idea of committing such blasphemy to be to the dishonour of God, and the disgrace of his sacred religion, has already much alarmed, and hurt many of the well-wishers of this town and neighbourhood; it is hoped, and earnestly requested, that the sensible and principal inhabitants will discountenance such pro- phane practices at all times, not only by refraining themselves, but also by restraining their servants and all those over whom they have any authority; to convince the world that this town is not so entirely devoted to that vice and wickedness, which are but too often found upon the stage in general. What judgements may this country expect to receive from the great and almighty supporter of the universe, when such insults are offered to his holy institutions?' The placard ended with the signature, in capital letters, NO METHODIST. Though the identity was hidden, the effect was immediate. The players put out a second bill in which, after protesting that they were grieved at the attack on their moral character, it was announced that Mr. Grist would deliver an address 'previous to the play, to satisfy the most scrupulous, of the purity of his intentions, and convince those who have any doubts, that an actor reverences and obeys the dictates of his Maker, as conscientiously as any other description of men'. But Halifax knew the players and had read the original play-bill, so Mr. Grist was not allowed either to deliver his address or stage the interlude.

The general public, in the previous fifty years, had had a surfeit of bawdy comedies, and coarse satires on religion.[63] Even the theatres at Drury Lane and Covent Garden had produced a sequence of vicious and licentious plays, and the Hay-Market had seen Samuel Foote in his play 'The Minor' which was an execrable caricature of George Whitefield and some of his followers. On 14th July 1760, *Lloyd's Evening Post* had not hesitated to comment: 'How educated and respectable people could listen to such ribald and blasphemous outpourings, it is difficult to imagine. The whole thing is so steeped in lewdness, that it would be criminal even to reproduce the plot.' Other plays, equally unpleasant, were produced, and it was only toward the end of the century that the quality improved.

It was this particularly coarse period in which the early Methodists formed their opinions. Though they never became as violent as George Whitefield in his sermons against the theatre, they could not consistently give their approval to the stage-plays of their day. The biography of John Dungett, at one time a successful amateur actor, states his opinion of the contemporary stage and 'the vile and blasphemous trash' which its writers were producing. In answer to the argument that in good plays, virtue was recommended and vice condemned, he said: 'the conduct of a bold, vicious rake always found more admirers, than the conduct of a steady and virtuous man found imitators'.[64]

During his early Oxford days John Wesley had gone to the

theatre in London, but his theatre-going ended very soon. This
does not mean that he ceased to read plays, for there are numerous
references to them in his *Journal*. He was a constant reader of
Shakespeare, and watched a performance of the *Adelphi* of Terence
by the scholars at Westminster, remarking in his *Journal* that it
was 'an entertainment not unworthy of a Christian'.[65] In his
invaluable study of the subject, Dr. T. B. Shepherd concludes
that 'the attitude of the Wesleys towards entertainments was that
they were not harmful, but that the usual type of play was
objectionable and the playhouse a centre of vice'.[66] This contention is borne out, in part, by a letter written by John Wesley, on
20th December 1764, to the Mayor and Corporation of Bristol.
In this he expresses his appreciation of their courtesy to his
brother and himself, and assures them that he is concerned for
their honour and 'the general good' of the City of Bristol. He
then continues: 'The endeavours lately used to procure subscriptions for building a new playhouse in Bristol have given us not
a little concern; and that on various accounts: not barely as most
of the present stage entertainments sap the foundation of all
religion, as they naturally tend to efface all traces of piety and
seriousness out of the minds of men; but as they are peculiarly
hurtful to a trading city, giving a wrong turn to youth especially,
gay, trifling, and directly opposite to the spirit of industry and
close application to business; and, as drinking and debauchery of
every kind are constant attendants on these entertainments, with
indolence, effeminacy, and idleness, which affect trade in an high
degree.'[67] The letter is a fair statement of his views against the
contemporary play-house and its plays, though it did not prevent
the erection, later, of the theatre in question.

The writings of William Law, and the fierce invectives in
Whitefield's sermons, had considerable influence on the interpretation of the 'Rule' by some of the first Methodists. For a
time the attacks made upon George Whitefield were applied to
Methodists in general, though Wesley was less often cited in the
controversies. To both Law and Whitefield 'the playhouse was
the house of the devil', and they would have been less inclined
to qualify their statement by reference to the contemporary state
of the stage than would John Wesley.

The distinction is seen in the attitude taken by Mr. Bosanquet
when his daughter, Mary, told him of her views and her decision.

In her diary she writes: 'I consulted some of my serious friends about the playhouse; but they said, "When you are older, we should know what to advise; but as you are but sixteen, if your parents insist on your going, we do not see how you can avoid it". The answer did not fully satisfy me; and I was much distressed both ways. I saw the duty I owed to an absolute command from my parents in a very strong light; and, on the other hand, I remembered that my obedience to them was to be "in the Lord"! I sought direction in prayer, and endeavoured to examine the question on both sides; but the more I searched, the clearer it appeared to me I must not comply. I laid open my whole heart to my father; apprising him I would not willingly be disobedient in anything, unless where conscience made it appear to be my duty. We conversed on the subject with great freedom; for my dear father was a man of deep reason, calmness, and condescension. He replied, "Child, your arguments prove too much, and therefore are not conclusive. If what you say be true, then all places of diversion, all dress and company, nay, all agreeable liveliness, and the whole of the spirit of the world is sinful." I embraced the opportunity, and said, "Sir, I see it as such, and therefore am determined no more to be conformed to its customs, fashions, or maxims." This was a season of great trial; but the Lord stood by me.'[68]

Once again there is a clash of loyalties and, if it was 'a season of great trial' for young Mary Bosanquet, it was not an easy experience for her father. She ceased to go with her family to such diversions. Who shall say that she was wrong? For her there was a clear path, and as she trod it she grew daily more useful to her generation.

The attitude of Charles Wesley to theatrical entertainments, and to the amusements in Ranelagh and Vauxhall Gardens was emphatically described in one of his hymns.[69] It was composed for a watchnight service, and drew a sharp contrast between the solemnity of such an assembly and what he felt to be 'vicious pleasures'. The fourth verse is, to say the least of it, quite definite:

> The civiller crowd
> In theatres proud,
> Acknowledges his power,
> And Satan, in nightly assemblies adore.

To the masque and the ball
They fly at his call;
Or in pleasures excel;
And chant in a grove to the harpers of hell.

The mention of a 'grove' is a reference to Ranelagh and Vauxhall, whose questionable amusements excited his particular anger.

It is ironical that it should be Charles Wesley who was accused of having allowed his two sons to give private concerts at his house on Sunday evenings. The 'slander' was supposed to have its origin in a statement by Lady Austen to William Cowper who, in his poem 'Progress of Error', reproves 'a fiddling Priest' whom he calls Occiduus. Some people, apparently, believed this referred to Charles Wesley and his musical evenings. The incident is important because it called forth an indignant protest from Agnes Bulmer. She refused to believe such a thing possible on the part of Charles Wesley because of his strong views on the theatre and the Sabbath. In his defence she quotes a letter from his daughter Sarah Wesley to Mrs. Elizabeth Mortimer, in which the following passage occurs: 'It is difficult to preserve young people from dissipation when they have fashionable connexions. . . . How much do I owe to my dear father for checking my theatrical taste when I was a child, and evincing to me his heart's sorrow, on seeing my desire to go to such exhibitions! This is the chief part of my youth which I recollect with delight; for I obeyed him, without conceiving the evils of a playhouse, and left my drama unfinished, which I began to write at eleven years of age.'[70]

Even music came under condemnation, from some of the extremists. There is a curious passage in a letter from Samuel, the son of Charles Wesley: 'We were kept closely at home that we might escape the corruptions of the world. Lord Mornington, who was a passionate lover of music, said, we had no occasion to go into the world, for the world would come to us.'[71]

It seems a far cry from the plays of Congreve or the Gardens at Vauxhall to the concerts in Charles Wesley's house or the performance of an oratorio. All came, however, under the condemnation of extremists, some of whom were devout and sincere. In his manuscript journal, John Valton wrote: '14 June, 1781. . . . I have heard that the present proprietor of the new Chapel at this town [Manchester] had consented to lend the Chapel for three days to have Oratorios performed in it for the valuable consideration of thirty guineas being paid for the use of the same. . . . The Oratorio is that of Sampson (*sic*). So Sampson will be called in to make them sport. I am afraid if it does not bring the house about their ears, it will, however, do much harm to the Society. The people murmur and my soul grieves.'[72]

The pendulum could not swing much farther, and the years have brought a reaction which moves perhaps too easily in the opposite direction.

The key to John Wesley's own idea of the Rule is contained in his letter to Mrs. Chapman: 'I am convinced, that true religion or holiness cannot be without cheerfulness . . . and that true religion has nothing sour, austere, unsociable, unfriendly in it. . . . Are you for having as much cheerfulness as you can? So am I. Do you endeavour to keep alive your taste for all the truly innocent pleasures of life? So do I likewise. Do you refuse no pleasure but what is an hindrance to some greater good or has a tendency to some evil? It is my very rule.'[73]

As the century drew towards its close a better type of play became popular, and the bitter attacks on the Methodists no longer held the stage in the more reputable theatres. Growing older, John Wesley travelled more often by chaise, and read on his journeys sometimes De Renty but sometimes Shakespeare! As he read, he made his marginal comments in pencil. Some of his preachers would not have understood such use of time. One of them discovering the annotated Shakespeare after his death, burnt it, thinking it of no account! Today, with the letter to Mrs. Chapman, it might have helped the modern Methodist to interpret the 'Rule'.

The attitude of early Methodism to card-playing has been completely misunderstood. Even H. W. V. Temperley in his fine survey of the 'Age of Walpole' makes a statement which requires qualification. Referring to John Wesley he says: 'His denunciations of harmless gaieties and of art show some inconsistency, exceptional narrowness, and a curious Puritanism. He advocated card-playing, but denounced dancing and ordinary pleasures. . . .'[74] The letter to Mrs. Chapman on 'the pleasures of life' has already been cited, and though it does not answer the charge of inconsistency, it reveals a broader and more natural outlook. The great concern was that time should be rightly used, but it was not yet clear to Wesley, or his people, that a right use of leisure might also be a right use of time. There is some faint suggestion of this possibility in the very matter of card-playing. It is almost certain that the cards he permitted, and even advocated, were not playing-cards at all. In a letter to James Barry in 1787 he is quite definite about his own attitude: 'I say . . . to one that asks, "Can't I be saved if I dance or play at cards?" I answer, "Possibly you may be saved though you dance and play at cards. But I could not." So far you may safely speak; but no further. So much and no more I advise our preachers to speak.'[75] On the other hand it is quite true that he advised the use of cards to prevent 'idle gossip'—but the reference is to Scripture cards or Draw-Cards as they were called.[76] There are many sets of these still in existence. They varied in size, the largest being $3\frac{3}{8}$ ins. by $2\frac{5}{16}$ ins. and the number in this pack was 52, but other patterns had from 30 to 100 in each pack. They had a text of Scripture on one side and a verse of a hymn on the other. A 'neat Black Case' contained them, and a set published by James Kenton in 1786, was to be obtained from 'Mr. Wesley's Booksellers in Town and Country'. This pack was described as 'Divine Amusement, in a Set of Scriptural Cards'. Though Charles Wesley contributed some of the verses, in packs that were actually described as 'Mr. Charles Wesley's Scripture Cards', the idea was not exclusively Methodist, and there is considerable evidence of such 'Draw Cards' having originated amongst the Moravians. The Baptists and Independents also used them, and a modern variant takes the form of a Promise-Box containing small scrolls of Scripture texts.

The more general use of the cards by Methodists was to start helpful conversation amongst little groups of friends. In a letter to Mr. Moseley, in 1890, Dr. George Osborn said: 'some of the old Methodists "played cards" frequently. With a packet like yours in their pockets they went to tea with their neighbours, and afterwards dealt out cards, read, conversed about them, sung and sometimes prayed over the verses, and so filled up a profitable hour or two, and excluded gossip. Perhaps one might copy them to advantage occasionally.'[77]

'We had a good time in drawing cards and in prayer,' wrote Hester Ann Rogers.[78] Unfortunately there was a danger of

attaching some Providential significance to the particular card
'turned up'. It was but a short step from this to their use in
what could approximate to fortune-telling. The difficulty was to
discountenance this and, at the same time, join with John Wesley
and the Moravians in defending the drawing of lots, or seeking
direction by 'opening the Bible'. On this point the criticism of
Dr. Adam Clarke is the most scathing. He condemns 'that dis-
graceful custom of dipping into the Bible'[79] and insists that the
great body of Methodists never used the cards, and the preachers,
in general, highly disapproved of them: 'Thank God! these have
never been very common among us; and are certainly not of
Methodist growth. In an evil hour they were first introduced
and have since been criminally tolerated. I have found them the
constant companions of religious gossips, and they have been
drawn for the purpose of showing the success of journeys, enterprises etc. . . . I do not find that Mr. Wesley ever made use or
approved of these things. . . .'[80] It would have been interesting
to be present with Dr. Clarke, Hester Ann Rogers and Charles
Wesley at a 'social gathering' where a pack of Scripture cards
was produced! There can be no disagreement with him in his
criticism of the semi-superstitious use to which they were sometimes put, but one is inclined to think that John Wesley would
not have permitted the advertisements in the magazine he so
carefully edited, if he had definitely disapproved of their use in
'permitting and guiding useful conversation'.

Whether any great number of Methodists used Scripture Cards
or not, it is certain that few of the earlier generation indulged in
card-playing in the ordinary sense of the term. Some seemed to
find evil in the cards themselves, but it is probable that the
majority, either consciously or unconsciously, were influenced by
the unpleasant associations of the card-table. The age was
notorious for its gaming, and people like Charles James Fox
played for stakes that rose to almost unbelievably high figures.
Fortunes and patrimonies were lost or won in a single night, and
the final tragedy of many a promising life ended as the candles
guttered in their silver sconces and the cards were scattered after
the last deal.

Writing to his son John, James Field cited the case of 'a godly
Minister' who 'being greatly solicited to play at cards, arose, and
uncovered his head. The company asked what he intended.

"To ask God's blessing," he replied. "O," they said, "we never ask blessings on such occasions." "Then," he rejoined, "I never engage in anything upon which I cannot ask the blessing of God." ' Later, in the same letter, he quoted a lady who had been influenced by the preaching of Mr. Romaine, but confessed to him that though she could accept his doctrine, she could not 'give up cards'. ' "You think you could not be happy without them?" he asked. "No, sir, I could not." "Then Madam, they are your god; they must save you." This honest reply issued in her conversion. I hope neither of my sons will ever be persuaded to handle these evil things. I had the temptation in my father's house, where it was a common practice; but I used to feel so disgusted, that I went out of the way. I hated cards, though I had none to tell me the evil of them. I never played one game in my life.'[81]

That is probably a fair description of the attitude of the average member of Society during the first fifty years. That such a view might be characterized as narrow is obvious, but it must be repeated that the associations of the gaming-table, like those of the contemporary theatre left the honest Methodist little choice in the matter. He set out determined to use his time in the service of God and his fellows, and neither he nor the people of the period had considered the psychological and indeed spiritual importance of mental and physical recreation or the right use of leisure.

Regrettable as was the development of 'Bibliomancy' it is difficult to see any difference between 'dipping into the Bible' and referring to a convenient selection of texts printed on cards or slips of paper. The wholesale condemnation of the simple faith which sought renewal in the constant remembrance of the divine promises is as unreasonable as the superstitious reliance on the turning of a card or a page as a guide in some detail of conduct. As the knowledge of the great principles of Scripture became better known and understood, the Scripture Cards were relinquished, and ideas of the value of recreation in maintaining physical, mental and spiritual health were developed.

It is not so easy to understand the sweeping condemnation of novel-reading. Many of the early Methodists had no opportunity of reading fiction. Their books were very few, and the Bible and Hymn-book with at most half a dozen religious or semi-religious classics completed their library. Some could not read at all. The remainder confined their attention to 'serious' books and considered fiction to be simply 'a waste of time'. In producing the 'Christian Library', a direct forerunner of the Everyman Library, John Wesley gave the people an opportunity of reading good literature, though his selection was certainly limited to books with a moral purpose.

Probably Frances Mortimer was one of the best educated of the early Methodist women. Her journals were beautifully written, many of them in excellent French. Her biographer, Joseph Sutcliffe, says: 'On leaving school, she took the route of the gay world, in what she called *innocent amusements*. Till about the age of thirty, she spent her time in dress, in reading novels, in receiving and returning visits.' When she first began to discover the reality of religion: 'She had to grope her way in the dark, and amidst a painful variety of opinions, and parties. As a previous step, she dismissed her novels,—books which powerfully beguile the fancy without improving the mind; and which, for the most part, are written by learned seducers and ruined women. This refined class of writers affect, indeed, to be masters of the human heart, while their own breast is polluted with the reveries of every vile affection.'[82] Whether Frances Mortimer felt as strongly as her biographer is doubtful, but she certainly gave up reading fiction and 'commenced a regular course of biblical reading' supplementing this with such other religious books as came her way.

In the vicarage at Macclesfield, little Hester Ann Roe was warned by her father, 'against reading novels and romances. . . . He said it was the ruin of youth to suppose they were only to spend their time in diversions'. Hard as the vicar's advice to his eight-year-old daughter seems to be, she assures us that she listened to it 'with great delight'. When she was seventeen she came to a decision as to her reading: 'About this time I grew tired of novels, and took great delight in reading history. I went through several English and Roman histories; Rollin's *Ancient History*, and Stackhouse's *History of the Bible*, intending to go through the *Universal History* also. And now I believed myself far wiser than any person of my age. Upon the whole, I believe I was at this time on the pinnacle of destruction!'[83] Perhaps a course of wholesome novel reading might have helped her to get a better sense of proportion, but with such a book-list, at seventeen, it is impossible to agree that she was wasting her time!

The rules which Mrs. Lyth of York, devised for the regulation of her own conduct contained one which guided her reading: 'Never let me trifle with a book with which I have no present concern; in applying myself to any book, let me endeavour to recollect what I may learn by it, and then beg suitable assistance from God.'[84] There is always the emphasis on what will be of direct help, and the poor novel-writer is rejected without any assessment of his indirect value in giving his readers a better understanding of human nature, to say nothing of affording them mental relaxation.

When someone asked Samuel Drew whether he thought all works of fiction were injurious, he answered: 'Too many, sir, certainly are; not because they are fictitious, but because their matter is such as creates a morbid appetite. Fiction has been, and may be made, the vehicle of most important instruction. Parable, which is one of its forms, was the favourite mode of teaching of Christ himself; and in fable we have transmitted to us the choice lessons of ancient wisdom. Well constructed tales are an illustration of moral precept,—they render that plain which many people scarcely know how to apply in practice. Unhappily, many of our modern works of fiction, by delineating passion rather than character, and giving distorted views of life, morals, and religion, are more likely to be injurious than beneficial. But to condemn the whole for the delinquency of a part is the blindness of fanaticism.'[85] This more mature judgement is symptomatic of the gradual development of a more liberal attitude in the last years of the eighteenth century and the first years of the nineteenth. On the evidence it is certain that the first two generations condemned novel-reading as a whole, but that their successors began to differentiate between the good novel and the bad, just as they began to apprise the real value of a play.

Dancing was another problem to be solved by the first members of Society, and John Wesley appears to have been more lenient on this issue than on some others. At least he did not condemn dancing in itself, though he had no sympathy with the 'routs' of his day.

A schoolmistress, Mrs. Haughton, in 1773, incurred the dis-

P

pleasure of some of her fellow-Methodists because she wore a very high and fashionable head-dress. Referring to this in a letter to James Barry, Assistant at Brecon, John Wesley included some words about dancing: 'Sister Haughton is an upright woman and desires to please God. I advise her rather to throw her high head into the fire than to pain one of the little ones. She will have no fewer scholars. God will make her amends. My mother never would suffer one of her children to "go to a dancing-school". But she had a dancing-master to come to her house who taught all of us what was sufficient *in her presence*. To this I have no objection. If I had convenience, I would be glad to have all our preachers taught, even by a dancing-master, to make a bow and to go in and out of a room.'[86] As he points out in another letter to James Barry, on 26th September 1787, he does not think it wise to condemn practices, such as dancing and card-playing, to 'an unawakened people. It will only anger, not convince them. It is beginning at the wrong end.' Here is an important point in the understanding of the 'Rules' as a whole. They were for 'awakened people' to whose responsive hearts and minds the personal application would, by the grace of God, be made clear. The letter continues: 'A plain preacher in London used to say, "If you take away his rattles from the child, he will be angry. . . . But give him something better first, and he will throw away the rattles of himself." '[87] This was the principle which Wesley and the best of his preachers remembered, believing that the 'converted' man or woman would of their own accord begin at once to readjust their conduct to their new profession and experience. To make the matter of the dancing and the card-playing quite clear to James Barry he says: 'You know that we do not suffer any that use them to continue in our Society.'

That great class-leader, James Field, wrote frequently to the members of his classes on their personal problems. To one who had failed to find the peace she sought, he said: 'Lately I was informed that you attend balls. At first I could not believe it, and argued warmly to the reverse; but, within these few days, I have had demonstrative proof that it is the case. I now no longer wonder that you do not experience the comforts of religion. While you act thus, you cannot *obtain* the Spirit of adoption; nor could you *retain* it if you had it.' In a long commentary on scriptural references to dancing, he builds up his argument and ends his letter with a strong appeal that Miss D—— will 'reject all invitations to balls, and accept *your Lord's invitation to heaven*'.[88] Of the early Irish Methodists few had a wider experience of life than this old soldier who took his sub-pastorate so seriously. Dancing, the theatre, horse-racing were all 'baneful' he felt, and he took care, from time to time, to read the Rules of Society to his four classes.

Hearing that the Curate at Macclesfield, a Methodist, preached against dancing, Hester Ann Roe decided she would find arguments to support her own view. Like James Field, she went first to her Bible, but unlike him, she wanted to find justification for her dancing. The result was unexpected: 'Nothing which I found in Scripture countenanced dancing in any measure. I then began to consider the objections urged against it.' One by one she examined them, admitted to herself that she found them convincing and then, very humanly, concluded: 'My conflict was great; yet I was resolved to run all hazards rather than give up this pleasure.'[89] When, later, there came to her a great spiritual experience, she abandoned the things for which she had fought so hard, because they no longer interested her. The child had thrown away the rattle, for this new and precious thing! It happened so in the lives of most of these first Methodists. The expulsive power of the new affection solved most of their problems of conduct. Whether the solution appeals to us or not, is of little consequence. For them there seemed to be no other way, and they accepted it, not as a penance, but a privilege.

The first section of the Rules may well seem to contain a mass of prohibitions, such as must end in narrowing the lives of those who tried to keep them. In point of fact this was not the case, for the simple reason that the new experience brought with it new interests and gave a new meaning to life itself. They had become subjects of a kingdom without frontiers. The world itself was their parish—but even the world was *only* a parish! The horizon of eternity was the sole boundary of their living, and what seem to a superficial critic unhappy surrenders were to them but the throwing away of the rattles they did not want any more.

There was, however, a positive side to the Rules, and it was this fact which put the prohibitions in their proper place. The members were not only to do no evil but they were to do all the good they could. It was a simple formula, but it led to immediate and far-reaching experiments.[90] The evangelization of England was extended to include the evangelization of the world. Social service took a hundred different forms, as they realized the needs and possibilities. Education and the development of Sunday Schools were their concern. They were the friends of Jesus, and so must befriend all mankind, including their nearest and more distant neighbours!

They made their experiments in practical Christianity in good faith and with good courage. Persecution did not lessen their zeal; it increased it.

In spite of the cynical contempt with which the world at large viewed their self-imposed restrictions, they went out into that same world and played their part as freemen of the spirit.

Physical courage was not wanting. When the *Anson*, frigate of forty-one guns, commanded by Captain Lydiard went ashore on Christmas Eve, off Looe, tremendous seas broke over her. Her mainmast snapped and some escaped to land on this precarious bridge. 'At a time when no one appeared on the ship's deck, and some supposed the work of death had ceased, a Methodist Preacher, venturing his life through the surf, got on board over the wreck of the main-mast to see if any more remained, and some brave hearts followed him. They found several persons still below who could not get up, among whom were two women and two children. The worthy preacher and his party saved the two women, but the children were lost. By three o'clock no appearance of the vessel remained. The body of Capt. Lydiard was picked up at sea on January 1st, 1808 and taken to Falmouth for interment.'[91] The unknown preacher may be caricatured because he lived by Rules and self-denying ordinances, but the Rules were positive enough to send him through the wildest seas, and the self-denying ordinance made him sure that his life might be well lost in saving life.

Moral courage was also a corollary of their faith. It was seen, not only in facing the fury of the mobs,[92] but also in overcoming the fear of ridicule and the contemptuous sneers of old companions. The daughter of Thomas Butts, Esq., of the county of Radnor, came to reside in Hereford in 1802. The Methodists met in a small house in a by-lane on the outskirts of the city. It was not easy for Frances Butts to make up her mind to join the little Society of humble people. 'The adversary did not fail

to render the meanness of the place, and the clamour of persecution, which often attacked the door and windows, a source
of powerful temptation to Miss Butts, who was led to reason
thus: "What led me to this despicable place? If I get out, I will
never be seen here again." But she soon discovered from whence
these reasonings came, took up her cross and went to it. . . .'[93]
Yet it would be so easy to miss that scene and be blind to that
moral victory. If Frances Butts had been only a cultured woman
finding a morbid satisfaction in self-martyrdom, as she put away
her silks and her satins the cynic might have justified his sneer,
but such people did not find their goal in mere negation. That
was why she stepped out boldly towards the preaching-house.
Past the great cathedral with its mellow stones and sacred
memories, through the quiet streets she goes to the little house in
the muddy lane. 'The place was often a Bethel to the souls of
preachers and people.' That was why she went. The caricaturists
did not portray that; they did not see it was there!

NOTES

1. *Memoir of Life and Labours of the Venerable Robert Peck*, J. Mills, p. 16. (Kent, London, 1856.)
2. *Experience of Mrs. Hester Ann Rogers*, pp. 6–8.
3. *John Wesley's Letters*, VII. 190.
4. *Wesley's Sermons*, II. 178. (Wesleyan Conference Office, 1865.)
5. *John Wesley's Letters*, V. 30.
6. *The Nineteenth Century* (April 1920). Quoted, *W.H.S.*, XII. 125.
7. *The Eighteenth-Century English Sunday*, W. B. Whitaker. (Epworth Press, London, 1940.)
8. *Methodism in Halifax*, p. 173.
9. *Methodism in Armley*, p. 40.
10. *Minutes of Conference*, 1782.
11. *Memoirs of Mrs. Mary Taft*, written by herself, pp. 45–6. (Stevens, London, 1827.)
12. *Wesleyan Methodist Magazine*, October 1839, pp. 788–9.
13. *Methodism in Lowestoft*, pp. 92–3.
14. Letter from Wilberforce to Wickham (12th September 1798). Quoted in full, *W.H.S.*, II. 9–10.
15. *John Wesley's Letters*, VII. 269.
16. *Cornish Cockney*, Sir Harold Bellman. (Hutchinson, London, 1947.)
17. *John Wesley's Letters*, VIII. 26.
18. 'Word to a Drunkard', *Wesley's Works*, XI. 169–71.
19. 'Thoughts on the Present Scarcity of Provisions, 1773', *Wesley's Works*, XI. 53–9.
20. *W.H.S.*, IV. 15.
21. *Methodism in Ireland*, I. 187.
22. *John Wesley's Letters*, V. 133.
23. ibid., VIII. 135.
24. *Journal of John Wesley*, VI. 123.
25. *Memoirs of Richard Trewarvas*, pp. 56–64.
26. *John Wesley's Journal*, IV. 220.
27. *Methodist Magazine*, 1837, p. 822.
28. *A Word to a Smuggler*, John Wesley, 1767. See *Works*, XI. 174–8.
29. *John Wesley's Letters*, VII. 214–15. *W.H.S.*, VIII. 163.
30. Journal of Richard Treffry, Senr. Quoted in *W.H.S.*, XVIII. 31.
31. 'A Word to a Freeholder', *Works of John Wesley*, XI. 196–8.
32. *John Wesley's Letters*, VII. 77.
33. Letter of William Grimshaw to Mrs. Gallatin. Quoted, *W.H.S.*, X. 167.
34. 'The Principles of a Methodist Farther Explained.' A Letter to Thomas Church. See *Letters of John Wesley*, II. 212ff.
35. ibid. See also 'A Word to a Gambler'.
36. *Life of Darcy, Lady Maxwell*, pp. 92–3.
37. *Holiness unto the Lord*, the Life of Miss Bosanquet, afterwards Mrs. Fletcher, pp. 26–7.
38. *Minutes of Conference*, 1782.
39. 'Advice with regard to Dress', *Wesley's Works*, XI. 466–80.
40. *Minutes of Several Conversations*, 1763, p. 6.
41. *Wesley's Works*, VIII. 307. See also Sermon 88 on 'Dress'.
42. John Wesley and the Madans, *W.H.S.*, V. 142.
43. Memoir of Mrs. Holy, *Wesleyan Magazine*, 1843, p. 90.
44. *Memoirs of Richard Trewarvas*, p. 122.
45. *Memoirs of Mrs. Jane Treffry*, Richard Treffry, Junr., p. 34. (Mason, London, 1830.)
46. *Experience of Mrs. Frances Pawson*, pp. 19, 21.

47. ibid., p. 43.
48. ibid., p. 137.
49. Letter from Glasgow, 30th March 1786, *W.H.S.*, XI. 113.
50. *Methodism in Bingley*, p. 89.
51. *Memorial of Mrs. E. Shaw*, p. 11.
52. *Memorial of Mrs. Mary Lyth*, p. 279.
53. *City Road Chapel*, p. 341.
54. *Arminian Magazine*, 1796 and 1797. *City Road Chapel*, p. 143.
55. *Methodism in Congleton*, pp. 107–8.
56. *City Road Chapel*, pp. 357, 533.
57. *Life of Samuel Drew*, p. 493.
58. *The Dairyman's Daughter*, pp. 90–1.
59. *Methodism in Marshland*, pp. 99–100.
60. Charles Wesley (*Methodist Hymn Book*, 720).
61. 17 George II, c. 5.
62. *Methodism in Halifax*, pp. 201–3.
63. *W.H.S.*, XX. 166–8, 181–5, and XXI. 3–7, 36–8 (a most careful study of
'Methodists and the Theatre of the Eighteenth Century', by T. B. Shepherd).
64. *Memoir of John Dungett*, p. 11.
65. *The Journal of John Wesley*, V. 294.
66. *W.H.S.*, XX. 183.
67. *Letters of John Wesley*, IV. 279.
68. *Holiness unto the Lord;* Life of Miss Bosanquet, pp. 23–4.
69. Charles Wesley, Hymn for a Watch-night.
70. *Memoir of Mrs. Elizabeth Mortimer*, pp. 201–6.
71. ibid., p. 206 (letter quoted, dated January 1797).
72. John Valton's MS. Journal (*W.H.S.*, VIII. 21).
73. *The Letters of John Wesley*, I. 219.
74. *Cambridge Modern History*, H. W. V. Temperley, M.A., VI. 88.
75. *The Letters of John Wesley*, VIII. 12.
76. *W.H.S.*, I. 15–25, IV. 6–8, 40–3. (These articles contain a detailed account
of collections in existence.)
77. *W.H.S.*, I. 22.
78. MS. Journal, Hester Ann Rogers (9th January 1783).
79. Letter of Adam Clarke. Quoted, *W.H.S.*, IV. 42.
80. ibid. Quoted *W.H.S.*, IV. 42.
81. *Memoirs of James Field*, pp. 160–1.
82. *Life of Frances Pawson*, pp. 11–12.
83. *An Account of Mrs. H. A. Rogers*, pp. 7, 19.
84. *Memorial of Mrs. Mary Lyth*, p. 30.
85. *Life of Samuel Drew*, pp. 493–4.
86. *Letters of John Wesley*, VI. 47; VII. 228.
87. ibid., VIII. 12.
88. *Memoirs of James Field*, pp. 161–4.
89. *Account of Mrs. H. A. Rogers*, pp. 17–19.
90. See Chapter III, also *More about the Early Methodist People*, Chapter I.
91. *Gentleman's Magazine*, 1808, pp. 77, 88.
92. *More about the Early Methodist People*, Chapter II.
93. Memoir of Frances Butts. Quoted, *W.H.S.*, XVII. 117–18.

CHAPTER VI

THEIR FAMILY LIFE AND THEIR CHILDREN

THE first Methodists were distinguished for many things, but nothing more became them than their 'sense of family', developed in their fellowship meetings but originated in their homes. It was something much deeper than native clannishness or community of opinions. Many of the early Societies grew rapidly because the living experience was communicated from father to son, from brother to sister, and so to the more distant kinsfolk. There was a homeliness about original Methodism which may have been due to its intimate sharing of thought and feeling, but was intensified by the fact that, like the primitive Christianity which was its pattern, it grew under persecution. The people who came down the Via Appia to the house of Hermes to worship together, though they risked death on every journey, were not so unlike the people in Wednesbury or Cornwall who faced the mobs without flinching, and prayed, though their homes were burned about them as they knelt. Children could not but admire such parents and seek to know the secret of their courage and their joy. Parents who had discovered so great a treasure could not but strive till their children found it too.

'For twenty years only six persons of our family were in connexion', said John Boothby of Kettleshulme. 'However I had confidence that the Lord would bring them all in; but "hope deferred maketh the heart sick". I began to be discouraged and almost left off praying for them. But my confidence again revived on hearing a discourse of Mr. Wesley's at Congleton, on raising the ruler's daughter, and which he applied to the conversion of our relations. . . . I bless God he has answered my prayers, and given me to see the desire of my soul, in the conversion of many of our family. My wife and seven children, and sixteen other near relatives are now in society; besides some who are gone to their everlasting rest.'[1] That is typical of the concern parents felt for their children, and all their kith and kin. How could it be otherwise since to them conversion had been, not an incident, but the supreme event?

It seems particularly tragic that John Wesley, who knew so

little of the joys of home life through all his long years, should have been the one most responsible for interpreting religion in terms of the closest human relationships. His *Journal* contains many little phrases which reveal his appreciation of family life. 'Thursday, July 25, 1771. I rode across the country to Whit-church, and spent an agreeable evening with that lovely family.'[2] Whether the family was named Brown or Parsons[3] does not matter greatly. He rode from Liverpool to Whitchurch for the joy of seeing them, and resting his body—perhaps his soul—in their home.

Though the Methodist was defined as a person who lived by rule, the rules which governed his family life must not be con-demned as harsh even though parental discipline was often severe or psychologically unsound. In Mr. Richard Crawley's home at Alpraham there was displayed a printed sheet on which appeared the following announcement for visitors to read:

'We and our House will serve the LORD: For God is Love: Therefore our Earnest Request is, THAT, every one who comes here will conform to our few RULES.

'I. We have no time given to throw away, but to improve for Eternity; therefore we can join in no Conversation that is unprofit-able, but in that only which is good to the use of edifying, ministering grace to the Hearers: Therefore

'II. We have nothing to say to the idle Gossip of the Town, and of the Business of others: But we desire to hear of things pertaining to the Kingdom of God.

'III. Neither have we anything to say to the misconduct of Others; therefore, let not the faults of an absent person be men-tioned, unless absolute necessity require it, and then let it be with Tenderness, without dwelling upon it. May GOD preserve us from a censorious and criticizing Spirit, so contrary to that of CHRIST.

'IV. We offer the right Hand of Fellowship to every one that cometh in the name of the LORD: But we receive not any to doubtful Disputation: but whosoever loveth the LORD JESUS in Sincerity, the same is our BROTHER, and SISTER, and MOTHER; for we cannot but remember that GOD IS LOVE.

'V. We neither receive nor pay formal Visits on the LORD's DAY, for we and our House desire particularly on that day to serve the LORD,

'VI. We do earnestly entreat every one to reprove us faithfully in affection, whenever we deviate from any of these Rules; so shall we be as Guardian Angels to each other, and as a holy mingled flame, ascend up before God.'[4]

The placard, introduced to Cheshire by Methodist preachers in 1749, must not be judged without allowances being made for the stilted phrasing of the eighteenth century. Though there is a suggestion of 'You have been warned' about its paragraphs, there is also evidence of sincerity and a genuine desire for friendship on the highest levels. Its essentials are implied in all Christian living of any age, though the printed proclamation may not appeal to every one today.

In many of the personal diaries there are indications of a deep affection, depending for its depth on conscious and direct relationship with God. Writing one Sunday evening as she sat alone in her house, the mother of George Osborn of Rochester pours out her soul: 'Now, in the evening, when all the family are gone to chapel, I desire to record in private what I could not proclaim in public, and say, Bless the Lord, O my soul, and forget not all His benefits. He has dealt very graciously with me this day, and all my past days. My whole life has been crowned with blessings; but this afternoon I felt almost overwhelmed with His goodness in giving me to see, on my right hand, my dear husband and two children, and on my left my aged mother and my sister, all uniting in the service of our glorious Redeemer. The scene has stirred me up to seek to serve the Lord more fully. May He give me the power and the strength so to do.'[5] As she sat in chapel, wearing her prim bonnet and quiet dress, few would have suspected the wealth of tenderness and love which swept over her when she unveiled her heart in the presence of God, in the solitude of the home she felt He had so richly blessed.

When Mrs. Jane Treffry, once the fashionable Miss Hawkey, took her boy to Kingswood, she returned home to write in her diary: 'This has been a day of great exercise. In the morning I went to Kingswood with my dear boy. He has been the child of many prayers. The Lord knows that I offered him up before he saw the light, and surely my God will hear me in his behalf. Preserve him from evil: nurse him up for Thyself: make him wise for present usefulness and for eternal salvation! In the evening I went to the hospital and spoke to a large company of sick and dying. . . .'[6] The next four weeks were busy with her classes and constant hospital visitation—then on 31st October she set out, walking eagerly from Bristol to Kingswood to see the lad, after that first month at school. (The sterner régime of the earliest Kingswood had evidently softened by this time into a more natural mode of life.) 'I felt my mind delightfully affected in looking round on so many dear children,' she writes, 'who are I trust trained up for usefulness here and glory hereafter. In this delightful place, you see nothing but good order, and though it is painful to part from my child, yet I am thankful that he is so well situated.'

There is the association of ideas, so common to these diarists—usefulness now, glory hereafter—but there is also the mother of little Treffry triumphing over the proverbial 'Mother in Israel' as her heart runs away with her pen 'though it is painful to part from my child, yet . . .' And young Richard watches from the gate, as his mother tramps back to the hospitals and the sick rooms and the thousand tasks that await a preacher's wife in Bristol.

Here is Frances Pawson, taking into her childless home her husband's niece, a very difficult girl, but writing, 'it was the best of deeds in my husband to take care of her. . . . We have put her to school, and discharge our duty to her as a daughter; yet from the peculiar obstinacy of her temper, I have discharged the duty as a cross, not as a delight. . . . This little task has been alleviated by the kindness of the best of husbands.'[7] It was a house where no childish laughter came, but, instead, a neurotic and melancholy girl. It would have been easy for Frances Pawson to refuse to take her, or to quarrel with her husband over her remaining after those first few weeks, but they persevered for many years, and their house became a happy home for the members of the Society.

When Mrs. Rogers decided to go to Conference with her husband, they travelled in the coach to Bristol with the Pawsons 'and as many more of the Preachers as the coach could contain'. They left at four o'clock in the morning and arrived at ten o'clock at night. It was a long journey, but what did it matter? Were they not going to Conference? Presumably, but Mrs. Rogers does not stress the point in her journal! There is a more important matter she has been thinking about while the crowded coach rumbled westward. 'We found our three sweet boys, thank God! all in health, and overjoyed in seeing us. Joseph is making swift progress in the printing business, and likely to make an excellent workman. Benjamin is approved by his master, beloved by his school-fellows, and above all, I trust he truly fears God. My James is very childish (he is but eight years old,) yet I think I see in him the dawnings of a noble spirit; which, if governed by grace, will one day give us comfort in him also, and make him a blessing to thousands.'[8]

Conferences and theological discussions, problems of administration and connexional finance—all very important, no doubt, Hester Ann, but in your heart you are thinking of Kingswood all the time! Who shall dare to condemn you as you continue writing: 'After different scenes, and manifold consolations during the time of Conference, on August 10th, we arose before three o'clock in the morning, and set off at four, on our journey home. Our friends were very affectionate, and our dear children also got up to see us off; and we left them all well, though sorrowful to part.' Huddled in the corner of the coach one seems to see her, thinking hard—but not of Conference or solemn assemblies. Oh, Joseph! O Benjamin! O little James! She smiles and, somehow, one knows she is proud—of those three boys, though half afraid they will too soon be men. 'I claimed my Lord's promise to preserve me in coming in as in going out; and I proved him faithful. . . . We arrived safe in our habitation by nine in the evening, and found the three children we had left all well. And though I felt inexpressibly weary, yet to be brought safe in so critical a situation, (not two months from the time of my expected confinement,) filled my soul with unspeakable gratitude.'[9] O happy home—even when the shadows fall, for perfect love casteth out fear!

An instinct for home-making developed in many of the early Methodists, even though some of them never had children of their own. In 1734 George Cussons was born at Ampleforth, Yorkshire, where his parents brought up a family of ten children 'with great care and circumspection'. When he was fifteen he was apprenticed to a joiner and cabinet-maker and, at eighteen, he was reading Bunyan's *Grace Abounding*, feeling anxious about his 'besetting sin'. After some contact with a Methodist family he became 'convinced that religion was an inward thing'. He was not morbid or unduly 'pious' but a strong youth, athletic in body and mind. As he strode along the road, his pack on his back, he resolved 'to give himself fully up to God' even though he was 'still a stranger to the grace of the gospel'. In Helmsley, he was greatly helped by the friendship and teaching of the evangelical Dr. Richard Conyers, and by reading sermons and books by John Wesley and William Law, and by the hymns of Charles Wesley.

'In September, 1760,' he records in his diary, 'I removed from Helmsley to Scarborough, where I immediately united myself to the Methodist society, which only amounted to thirty-six members: they were a despised people, but very circumspect in their conduct, and loving to each other.'[10] Though 'the preacher' visited Scarborough only once a fortnight George Cussons was guided by a regular correspondence with Dr. Conyers. 'I still continued to pray "Lord shew me the right way", and in the beginning of the following year 1761, the Lord began to shew me the plan of salvation more clearly.'

And, indeed, the plan developed into something more than the acceptance of a theological position. Soon he was appointed to lead a class, and though this brought him into a family circle, it did not satisfy him. 'About the same time [1761] I began to meet a little company of children every Sunday from one till two o'clock; we sang Dr. Watts' hymns for children; Mason's catechism they got by heart; I read to them short sermons adapted to their capacities, also Janeway's token for children &c., and have reason to believe my labour was not in vain.'[11]

He was not allowed to work peacefully for there were some in Scarborough who were determined to root out the Methodists, at all costs. They arranged that Cussons and three others should be seized by the press-gang, and this was effected, but before they were finally put aboard the man-of-war lying in the harbour, Dr. Conyers had intervened and they were released. Two years later George Cussons married Hannah Flintoft of Snailsworth, 'the daughter of parents who daily read the scriptures in the family. . . . According to their example, we regularly read portions of the Bible every day.' For six years they remained at Scarborough, and certainly had little leisure time! 'I arose in the morning a little after four o'clock, began my work at five, and left off at six o'clock in the evening: after this hour I usually attended preaching, when the chapel was open for that purpose, or public prayer meetings, or meetings for Christian communion; or if not engaged in any of these, then in reading and prayer. It was my desire to dedicate all my time to God.' In this strenuous programme he found room to continue his first creative adventure. The account is in the journal: 'I continued to meet the children once a week as beforementioned; some of them had been brought up in such ignorance, they did not know there was a God, or that they had a soul. After consulting with my wife, we agreed to put three of these children to a day school, which we thought we could afford to do, my wages being eleven shillings a week.'[12] So George and his wife had planned not only a wise economy of time but of money also—and, it would seem, they had agreed on a little conspiracy. Rather than pose as benefactors, the provision for the children's education was made in the name of Dr. Conyers! It was the grandmother of one of the children who, unconsciously, revealed the plot. She was 'employed to serve out the waters at the Spa, and seeing Dr. Conyers there, she thanked him for his kindness in putting her grandchild to school'. He was naturally astonished, but when George Cussons 'informed him how it was', he said 'let twenty more be put to school and I will pay for them'. Later, on his request, his brother-in-law, John Thornton, bought their books, gave two poor widows 'full employment in teaching, and an unknown number of children , . . a plain and useful education'. As Hannah and George sat together at the end of the day, there were no children in the house, but they were very happy for there were children in their hearts, and who dare call them childless? Certainly not the old grandmother at the Spa, nor the learned Dr. Conyers, nor the bairns who went each day to school!

The years were passing and Cussons was so good a workman that his friends thought he should launch out into business on his own account. 'I felt no desire to be rich. I was already worth near forty pounds, beside my furniture, and never thought of adding ten pounds more to my stock.' Forty pounds—eleven shillings a week—the children's school-fees! One begins to suspect that Hannah Cussons was a good manager, and that the benevolent scheming of George was a family affair!

At last he was persuaded, by Dr. Conyers and his wife, to go to London for a few months to get experience, so that he might

become independent. In September 1769, he began his journey
on foot, in company with a young man who was also a carpenter.
It took them a week to walk, but they arrived safely 'without
weariness or pain, except being a little footsore'.[13] London
appealed to him. He sent for Hannah after six months, and,
greatly daring, they took a house in Wardour Street. Though
John Thornton offered to lend them three hundred pounds,
George would accept only fifty and, with this sum and their little
capital, they challenged London! It was perhaps one of the
strangest challenges the great city had ever known, for they did
not seek riches but a home, and that, not for themselves but for
any who might need its shelter. 'Now I found, indeed, my dear
Hannah, to be a help-meet for me,—in prayer, in industry, and
in carefulness. Our business was but small; but we were indus-
trious and did our utmost to be punctual, and laid all our concerns
daily before the Lord.'[14] So the new home was shaped—partly
on the pattern of the one in Helmsley, where Dr. Conyers now
sat alone, for Jane was dead.

In Wardour Street, amongst the growing library of books,
George placed a Bible which had come to him from Helmsley.
On its first page there was this inscription: 'This Book was
the property of the late Mrs. Jane Conyers, and given to
George Cussons by Dr. Conyers *her* affectionate husband and *his*
sincere friend.' It was symbolic of the love on which the home
in Helmsley had been built, and by which the grim house in
Wardour Street would be transformed. The business prospered,
though its profits went to help the apprentices, or the members
of the class George led, or the Naval and Military Bible Society
he helped to found. What a family this childless couple had.
How often their home robbed London of its loneliness for the
stranger who came shrinking and afraid.

In 1800, when he was sixty-six, George Cussons and his wife
took a holiday! It was a memorable three months spent in
Yorkshire. They visited their kinsfolk in Little Edstone and
Helmsley, in Hawnby and Hamilton, Kilburn and Sproxton,
Kirby and Whitby, and came at last to Scarborough where their
home-making had begun. No 'Grand Tour' was ever so great
a delight as was this simple 'visitation', and they returned to
London to continue their life together—a life which had in it the
qualities that are eternal. Hannah lived to be sixty-seven, and

George eighty-two, but in death they were not divided. All
through the years they had 'breathed the spirit of thankfulness
and praise', which is the atmosphere in which homes are made,
and from which love does not pass away.

The eighteenth-century marriage was treated cynically by the
dramatists, and the early novelists often smothered it with senti-
mentality or wrecked it in a shameless transaction in the money
market. Some of the Methodists took a solemn or pompous
attitude, but others mixed sentiment with common sense. The
opinions of Samuel Drew are always worth considering as a
guide to contemporary opinion at its best. He was disgusted by
any attempt 'of people in middle life, to bring up their daughters
as fine ladies, neglecting useful knowledge for showy accomplish-
ments. The notion which they acquire of their own importance
is in an inverse ratio to the true value.'—'What are they fit for?'
he asks. 'Nothing that I know, but to be kept like wax figures
in a glass case. Woe to the man that is linked to one of them.
If half the time and money wasted on their music, dancing, and
embroidery, were employed in teaching them the useful arts of
making shirts and mending stockings, their present qualifications,
as wives and mothers, would be increased fourfold.'[15] Though
the philosopher of St. Austell was rather hard on the fine arts,
the country girl aping the fine lady was even worse than the
model she copied, with her vapourings and artificiality.

Honest Henry Longden, of Sheffield, had little use for such
nonsense, but he was quick to discern domestic tragedy, and
sympathetic in his handling of such problems. Travelling far
and wide as a local preacher, he became a pioneer of Marriage
Guidance Council work. On one occasion he arrived at a house
where he had often been entertained. Outwardly all was as
usual, but he realized a tension between his host and hostess,
which their warm greeting could not hide. When he had sat
awhile, he said, 'I cannot stay here! O how miserable I am!
God used to dwell in this house, but He is now departed. I cannot
stay. . . .' His friends protested, begging him to remain, and
presently told him their pitiful little story—so trivial in its beginning, so tragic in its swift climax. He listened with patience and
understanding, giving them a new sense of proportion and bringing them both to their knees. 'The snare was broken; they
joined in prayer and intercession to God, and He graciously

healed them. Their habitation was again the house of God'[16]—
which is Henry Longden's way of spelling 'home'.

The idea of John Wesley giving advice on 'marriage' is grimly
humorous, but he never hesitated. To Thomas Mason, a shopkeeper at Limerick, he wrote: 'A conversation I had yesterday
with C. Proctor determined me to write immediately. The
person at Birr will not do: not only as she is far too young; little
more than a child; but as she has only little, if any, Christian
experience. You want a woman of middle age, well tried, of
good sense and of deep experience. Such an one in every respect
is Molly Pennington; but whether she is willing to marry or no,
I cannot tell. If she is, I hardly know her fellow in the kingdom.
If I meet with any I will send you word.'[17] It is an extraordinary
letter from a still more extraordinary man! The fact that Thomas
Mason did not marry Molly Pennington is proof of his independence, or hers; but it did not damp John Wesley's ardour in giving
advice, even on the subject for which, above all others, he
was unqualified.

There were those, however, besides Wesley, who had their
own ideas about the suitability of wives—especially for the
travelling preachers. From Grimsby, in 1788, William C. Fish,
an older minister, wrote to young Alexander Kilham, then on
probation: 'I will now draw you a picture of a preacher's wife:—
1. She should be a woman of solid piety; or she will be a burden
to her husband, and a stumbling block to others. 2. She must
be well established in the Methodist Doctrine, and zealous for
our discipline; else there will be danger of her doing harm
among the people. 3. She should be a woman of gifts as well as
grace, able to preach by the fireside and in the class, or by a sick
bed, as her husband is in the pulpit. 4. She should have a good
natural disposition; else should she fall from grace, she will be
a very devil. 5. She must be of a free open spirit; if not, the
people will dislike her, and perhaps her husband too for her
sake; yet she must be able to keep a secret, and not show too
great freedom with the other sex. 6. She must be of a meek
spirit, to bear contradictions, which she must expect to meet
with. 7. Of a humble spirit; or she will take too much on herself.
8. Possessed of Christian fortitude; or she will sink under trials.
9. Zealous and active, that she may be useful wherever she goes.
10. Generous without prodigality. 11. Notable and frugal, with-

Q

out covetousness. 12. Cleanly, both in her house and apparel. 13. Exceedingly exemplary in her dress, not using gaudy nor costly apparel; if she does, her husband need never say a word against dress, as it will be all lost labour. 14. Fully reconciled to a travelling life; or she will be perpetually teasing her husband to settle, and never let him rest till he yields to her intreaties. 15. It would be well if she had a good constitution, that her husband may not be hindered in the business of the Circuit by nursing his sick wife. 16. If to all these good properties, she have as much fortune as will maintain herself, her husband and her children, if need be, she will be no worse but better.'[18] It must certainly be called a reasoned statement and, at least, the writer, unlike Wesley, did not suggest the name of any such paragon of excellence! How sorely she would need a good constitution— and a good temper! Whether the letter was responsible or not, Alexander Kilham married a woman of remarkable personality. Little enough she knew of home life in those six years of religious conflict which she shared with her husband before he died. Yet in her lonely widowhood she braved the hardships of pioneer work in Africa alone and, judged even by the severities of William Fish, she passed muster.[19]

There is a naïveté about the descriptions of these marriages which is not to be mistaken for smug self-satisfaction. That John and Frances Pawson were very happily married is amply proved by their journals. The letter John wrote to Charles Atmore, in 1785, describes the wedding: 'I was married at York the 12th. of last month. We had a Christian wedding, and all dined at Mr. Fitter's, whose great kindness I shall not soon forget. All sides seemed perfectly satisfied, my own relations being very much pleased. As to myself, I do from the ground of my heart, praise the Lord, who has, I am well satisfied, pointed out my way, and I have good reason to believe, has given me a help-meet, a truly pious, sensible, good natured woman who, I really believe, will be made a blessing to me. To say all in one word, I am perfectly satisfied.'[20] The operative word, to use the modern jargon, seems to be 'satisfied' but John Pawson was a better judge of a wife than he was of a manuscript, and their married life was more than 'satisfactory'.[21]

The early Methodists placed high value on the marriage ceremony and on the suitability of the person who performed it.

Because George Osborn had been deeply impressed by the writings of the Rev. John Newton he came from Chatham to St. Mary Woolnoth in London to ask the rector if he would officiate at his wedding. Though it was impossible to fix a convenient date Newton said: 'If you think an old man's blessing of any value, and will bring your good wife and take tea with me on Tuesday next, I shall be very glad to see you.' The invitation was accepted, and the young couple arrived at Coleman-street-buildings, to find a large party assembled. They were introduced as Mr. Newton's 'Wesleyan friends from Chatham'. After tea the old rector read and expounded the fourth chapter of Philippians, dwelling particularly on the nineteenth verse. 'But my God shall supply all your need according to his riches in glory by Christ Jesus.' This beautiful promise he wished his newly married friends to consider as especially addressed to them, showing how many occasions would arrive when its suitableness would be felt; and having concluded his exposition, he commended them to God in earnest prayer.'[22] It was a memorable hour, and its influence remained with George Osborn and his wife to the end of their days. To them it was a benediction which rested on the new home, and did not depart when the family grew up and left the parents, wistful but rich in their children's affection. There are some things a registrar's office, though it be bright with flowers, cannot give, and George Osborn and his like counted such things as precious.

To advise a son about his marriage is no easy task, but these first Methodists did not shrink from duty because it was difficult. Sometimes their counsel seems ponderous, and dogmatic, but, at least, it was sincere. When James Field was invalided, after the battle of Corunna, he came to Chatham, feeling anxiety about his sons. He wrote to them 'strongly and yet scripturally' on the subject of unequal marriages. To his letter he added 'the resolutions of Bishop Beveridge'. The passage leaves one in no doubt as to James Field's own views: 'I shall endeavour to make choice of such a woman for my spouse, as hath made choice of Christ for her Spouse; that none may be one flesh with me, who is not one spirit with the Lord. . . . And as love is the great duty, so it is the great happiness of the married state: I do not mean hers, but my own love; for if I have not that cordial esteem and affection for her, what happiness will it be to me to be beloved by her? If I should marry for riches, my love and happiness may take wings, and flee away with them; if for beauty, I shall love no longer than it continues, which is only till age and sickness blast it,—and then farewell both duty and delight.'[23] 'These my dear children,' added James Field by way of postscript, 'are the resolutions of that learned and holy man. . . . I was surprised to find his sentiments so exactly my own.'

It was natural enough that these people should take the 'long view' even of their marriage problems. Their restricted lives had been suddenly extended beyond the limits of time and space. As the individual looked over the temporal boundaries, and believed they were no longer final, he sought a partner whose life, like his, was beyond the clutching years. It was small wonder that he shrank from an 'unequal marriage'.

There was more buoyancy and happiness in their married life, than some of the memoirs suggest. Of Elizabeth Flamank's marriage to the young minister at St. Austell in 1797, her biographer writes: 'To her husband she gave a true wifely love; and during the little time they were permitted to live together, they were helpers of each other's joy.'

When Mary Burdsall married John Lyth, a young farmer living near York, she wrote in her journal: 'Memorable day! I gave my hand to John Lyth at Hymen's sacred altar. I endeavoured to do it by faith, as well as I could. . . .' Who would suspect that the occasion was radiantly happy, yet that was certainly the case. The wedding took place in the parish church of Holy Trinity, York, and her biographer's account, written from first sources,[24] says that it was solemnized 'so far as the principal parties were concerned with intensely religious feelings. Indeed Mr. Burdsall's loud and hearty responses to the prayers superseded the functions of the clerk, and somewhat astonished the officiating minister. The wedding dinner was spiced with the presence of the Rev. Samuel Bardsley, whose portly person, and beautiful simplicity contributed not a little to the amusement of the younger guests: and the same evening, the good old man preached an appropriate sermon, selecting for his subject, the marriage feast in Cana of Galilee.' Poor little Mary Lyth! Not even the buoyancy of her father and the good nature of 'Sammy' Bardsley could save her from those phrases in her diary. Yet it was not a dull affair, and in her heart there was a joy her pen never knew.

The account of Mary Bosanquet's marriage to John Fletcher of Madeley was written by Elizabeth Ritchie and would astonish the chatty columnists of today. The wedding took place from Cross Hall, where the bridegroom 'dressed in his canonicals' announced one of Charles Wesley's marriage hymns and then took family prayers. On the way to the church at Batley, he spoke to them all of the 'mystery couched under marriage, namely, the union between Christ and the Church'. After the wedding the little party returned and spent a considerable time in prayer and singing. 'The time after dinner (which was a spiritual meal, as well as a natural one) was chiefly spent in prayer and conversation. Mr. Valton preached in the evening.' —Times have changed and, for most people, such a day would seem incongruous, yet there is more behind it all than even Elizabeth Ritchie can convey. Twenty-five years before, John Fletcher had seen Mary Bosanquet and fallen deeply in love. He did not use those words when he recalled the memory a few days after his marriage. 'Five-and-twenty years ago, when I first saw my dear wife, I thought if ever I married, she would be the person of my choice, but her large fortune was in the way, she was too rich for me, and I therefore strove to banish every thought of the kind.'[25] A quarter of a century had passed since then, and Mary was in debt! She had spent her fortune on the orphans of Leytonstone and the West Riding. She was poor enough now—or was it that she was rich enough—to marry, even that saint of God, John Fletcher? In the church at Batley that November day, in 1781, one sees them as two lovers, a man and woman who have found each other at last, and are pledging their troth in a great happiness that not even the 'canonicals' or the poke bonnet can hide.

None of the early Methodists had a richer conception of home life than had Dr. Adam Clarke and Mary, his wife. The anniversary of their wedding-day was always kept with great joy. In 1799, the eleventh of such anniversaries, Adam gave Mary a gold watch and with it a letter:

Bristol, April 17, 1799.

My very dear Mary,—This gold watch,—the beautiful dial of which is an emblem of thy face, the delicate pointers of thy hands, the scapement of thy temples, the balance of thy conduct in thy

family, the gold case of thy body, and the cap of thy prudence,—
thy affectionate husband presenteth to thee on this eleventh
anniversary of our wedding day.

Adam Clarke.[26]

In the watch he found a parable, but in the woman he found
a wife who made a home.

It is generally agreed that John Wesley and the first Methodists
failed to understand the outlook of the child. This blindness was
common to the eighteenth century as a whole, and Wesley did
not differ in this respect from his contemporaries, except, as Dr.
Workman says, 'in his clearness of expression. Among the
unrealized dreams of history, we may wonder at the difference
that would have been made in the welfare of our own country if
Wesley had understood children, and, with a heart as tender as
St. Anselm's or St. Francis, had tried to meet their needs.'[27]
That he loved them is beyond dispute but, only occasionally
does he comprehend. Then, for a moment, he seems to be a little
child, himself, again. It would be absurd to try to defend the
severity of the discipline he imposed on the first scholars at
Kingswood or his insistence on the doctrine of 'total depravity'
applied to little children.

On the other hand, there are some things which the wisest of
critics may easily overlook. The reaction of children to John
Wesley was often remarkable, and his own close contacts with
them revealed, sometimes, a tenderness which seems to challenge
the Kingswood rules and the theological condemnation. The
man the children saw and remembered through the years was
a man they seemed, instinctively, to have loved. The children
he saw, and so imperfectly understood, were laid on his mind
and heart more tenderly than is often realized. If one is to
examine the unnaturally hard discipline, and to attempt an
analysis of the religious precocity of some of the children, it will
be wise first to make sure of this background.

Here then are two simple questions: How did the children see
Wesley and how did he look at them?

On 3rd June 1780 he preached at Northallerton in a yard
belonging to Jacky Wren, a weaver. A little girl, six years of age,
sat on her mother's knee and listened. Eighty years after she
said she could still remember the sun shining on his face, nor

did she ever forget his text: 'If the salt have lost its savour, where-
with shall it be salted?' Afterwards she remembered walking by
his side, clinging to the hem of his clerical gown. Children do
not walk so intimately with people they dislike, nor with those
who do not care. When Mrs. Shepherd, widow of the Governor
of York Castle, looked back over the years and remembered, she
was not bemused by age, for her childish memory is confirmed
by John Wesley's *Journal*: 'At noon I preached to a large congregation at Northallerton. The sun shone full on my face when
I began.'[28] But there was something more than the sunlight
which lingered for eighty years!

The visits of Wesley, in later years, became occasions which, in
themselves, left an impression, but the memory of the day
seldom left out the picture of the man. As late as 1863 old
Nanny Wood of Bingley, recalled 'Wesley Fair', as the event
had been named, but she said she remembered as a girl, about
twelve years of age, following the crowds to see him 'in his
gown and bands' walking to the steps from which he preached.
Even Wesley had been surprised at the great number of children
who came to his Friday morning service.[29]

If children were present in his congregation, he did not treat
them with indifference, nor did his words, spoken directly to
them, make them afraid. However lamentable his ignorance of
child psychology, there was evidently something which made the
children realize he was 'on their side'. In carefully sorting out
his early memories James Everett selected one vivid impression
of the coming of Wesley to Alnwick, when he was an old man,
and Everett only six: 'After we as scholars had received proper
instruction on the subject of good behaviour, we were taught to
expect the presence of a great and good man. . . . We were
summoned from our seats, and arranged in the front of the
communion rails, forming two-thirds of a tolerable circle. The
pulpit surmounted a small passage leading from a back door
into the chapel, boxed off to the floor, a door right and left
leading to the pews on each side of the ground floor, and a pair
of folding doors opening into the communion immediately
beneath the pulpit.' The boy of six watched eagerly as he saw
the old man enter. He noticed his 'flowing, curled wig' and
was surprised that so old a man walked with such a springy
step. 'He addressed us, as we stood before him, briefly but

affectionately.' There is no fear in the recollection—only the memory of an old man who said he loved them.[30]

Quite a different emphasis is given in a letter by General Perronet Thompson in 1865: 'I distinctly remember Mr. Wesley preaching on the grass plot of Mr. Terry's house at Newland. . . . I was so young that I remember I was allowed to wander away from the preaching, and botanise in the environs. I suppose I was about ten years old. . . . Of the personal appearance of the preacher I have a considerably strong impression, but not of the matter. His manner, I recollect, was calm.'

The children, who have been quoted, begin to create not only a picture but an atmosphere—the man with the light shining on his face, so kindly a face that little hands stretch out to clutch his gown; the man of many years, yet with springy step and loving words for a boy of six; and, again, the man who seems so calm, even to the boy who plays at the edge of the garden.

When Elizabeth Flamank was a little girl she travelled with John Wesley in his chaise, on a journey to West Cornwall. Total depravity or no total depravity—he played bo-peep with her and she never forgot it. In 1786 he took 'little Betsey' into the Conference Chapel at Bristol, 'that she might see the preachers assembled there'—the only recorded instance of 'bo-peep' at Conference![31]

Another little girl, Jane Hawkey, remembered his coming, an old man, to stay at her mother's house. The climax of his visit, for her, was the moment when he 'dandled her on his knee'. Though Mrs. Jane Treffry and Mrs. Elizabeth Shaw wrote journals, grave enough and solemn, they were the little children, once, with whom John Wesley played and they did not forget.[32]

How could Mary Burdsall be afraid of the man who, after he had preached, came down from the pulpit and seeing the little child, 'placed his hand upon her head, and gave her his blessing'? It was his last service in York, and 'the word was as fire, and all that heard it seemed to feel the power thereof' but the preacher did not miss the child, nor his opportunity, and the child remembered.[33]

Little George Gainer, in Clonmain, when twelve years old, went with his grandfather to hear John Wesley preach. When he climbed on the table and began to speak the boy was deeply impressed. Remembering the occasion, years afterwards, he says,

'I looked on him no longer as an earthly man, but as one that was heavenly and divine'. As he listened, understanding little of what it all meant, his Celtic imagination was stirred: 'I thought the gods were come down to us', he said.

Such were the memories of some of the children, who looked on him and formed their own opinions, more accurate, perhaps, than the judgement of older and more prejudiced critics. But how did *he* look at the children?

'For nothing was he so remarkable than his love to children', said Thomas Jackson. 'Often did he lay his hands upon them and bless them in the name of his great Master. He was in the habit of selecting small silver coins of peculiar freshness, and of presenting them to the children of his friends, as memories of his affection.'³⁴ There is something convincing about that phrase 'of peculiar freshness'. A ruler may fling largesse to the crowd, a father chooses clean and shining coins one by one and gives them to his children.

The problem of Wesley's attitude is complex but, perhaps, the secret of the seeming failure to understand is to be found in his own childlessness. If only—but he had to content himself with brief contacts on his ceaseless rounds. He had no child of his own!

At Bolton he was thrilled by the singing of the children, from the new Sunday schools. 'About a hundred of them (part boys and part girls) are taught to sing; and they sang so true that, all singing together, there seemed to be but one voice.' Nothing would do but they must sing to him again. In the evening, seeing they were 'hovering about the house' he asked them to come in and sing 'Vital spark of heavenly flame'. It was a strange choice and he noticed how some were 'not able to sing for tears, yet the harmony was such as I believe could not be equalled in the King's Chapel'. Nine months later, on 19th April 1788, he came to Bolton again, and declared there was not such a set of singers in any of the Methodist congregations in the three kingdoms. On what does he base his statement? 'There cannot be,' he says, 'for we have near a hundred such trebles, boys and girls, selected out of our Sunday schools, and accurately taught, as are not to be found together in any chapel, cathedral, or music-room within the four seas. Besides, the spirit with which they all sing, and the beauty of many of them, so suits the melody, that I defy any to exceed it; except the singing of angels in our Father's house.'

Next day he met nearly a thousand children belonging to the Sunday schools, and noticed their clean clothes and their good behaviour. 'Many, both boys and girls, had as beautiful faces as, I believe, England or Europe can afford. When they all sung together, and none of them out of true, the melody was beyond that of any theatre; and what is best of all, many of them truly fear God, and some rejoice in his salvation.'[35] Good voices, beautiful faces, spiritual experience—at least it is the commentary of one who is not merely interested but concerned about the child.

It was at Bolton that he preached his famous Children's Sermon in 'a simple, plain familiar style' in which he used no words of more than two syllables.[36]

At Whitehaven he established a Junior Society Class[37] and six years later, in 1772, evidently met them again, himself: 'The same power was present at the meeting of the children.'[38]

In his heart there was always a blending of deep human affection and spiritual concern. When the two young sons of Richard Holden, of Coldwell, Haslingden, came to the Sacrament of the Lord's Supper he welcomed them. He paused before the younger boy, Robert, and could not resist laying his hand on his head, and saying 'Suffer the little children to come unto Me, for of such is the Kingdom of Heaven'. The boys did not forget that hour, and, growing up they both became local preachers, who served faithfully for fifty years.[39]

In his later years Wesley rode, rather reluctantly, in a chaise. It impressed the children, and 'Dave' Hirst, of Morley, Leeds, remembered holding the horses, the chaise all painted yellow, but most of all the kindly man who sat within.[40]

The same old chaise calls up a more tender memory. Old Mrs. Hughes of Bath recalled that John Wesley used to order his carriage half an hour before he wanted it himself, so that the children might have a few minutes' ride, 'as many at a time as the coach would hold'.[41]

Tenderness, shrewd observation, ghostly counsel and common-sense advice—all these elements had a place in his attitude to the child, an attitude which was never blurred by sickly sentiment. At a missionary meeting in Coleraine, Sir Edward Nicholls, a distinguished soldier, recalled seeing him when, as a youth, he, himself, was about to enter the army: 'He laid his hand on my

head, and said: "Never turn your back on a friend or a foe."
. . . I have never forgotten this advice. My wounds prove that
I always faced the foe; and my presence here shows that I have
not turned my back on my friends.'[42]

Whatever may be said about his psychological mistakes, and
said justly, all the evidence available tends to prove that his
influence on children was wholesome and abiding. They did not
shrink from him in fear, and they remembered him, in love,
long after he had passed on his way.

Unfortunately there is another factor which cannot be ignored.
Whilst Wesley was struggling to express his natural, paternal
instincts, in spite of their tragic frustration, he was also living in
an age which was quite ignorant of the processes of the mind and
spirit of a little child. Either, on the one hand children were
treated with indifference or, on the other, regarded as adults.

The early Methodists, like their leader, were desperately anxious
about the 'spiritual condition' of everyone, irrespective of age.
Unwilling to leave the child out of account, they imposed a discipline that was harsh and unnatural. It is difficult to reconcile
the attitude which arranged that the old yellow chaise should be
available to give the children rides half an hour before its owner
started on a journey, with that which led the same John Wesley
to refuse either games or holidays to the boys at Kingswood,
stating plainly 'he who will play as a boy, will play as a man'.
There is something in the fact that age mellowed him a little,
but even this fails to explain the situation completely.

The parental discipline which Henry Longden exercises is
repugnant to the modern mind. 'He viewed children as fallen
creatures, who have before them an eternal existence, which
must be an everlasting curse or blessing.' Remembering his own
childhood, he resolved that his children should be first taught
obedience, and the lessons began as soon as they were twelve
months old. They were taught 'implicit obedience to their
parents, without reference to reward' and next came instruction
'in the nature of filial obligation and gratitude'. At five years of
age things began to move rapidly! The omnipresence, the
omniscience and the omnipotence of 'God, the Creator, Preserver
and Governor of the world' were explained to them. After a two
years' course, the little seven-year-old was 'taught the nature of
moral obligation with regard to God . . . our great Parent and

Benefactor' and then 'with regard to our fellow-creatures, and as consisting of subjection and respect to our superiors, condescension to our inferiors, and civility to all; an abhorrence of falsehood, and constant adherence to truth. . . . After laying this foundation he would explain the nature of our moral depravity; our total helplessness, and insufficiency to save ourselves; and the everlasting punishment which is prepared for the wicked. He would then unfold the plan of our recovery and salvation by Jesus Christ. . . . These instructions were accompanied with fervent prayer.' It was all desperately sincere and well-meaning, but at first so pitifully blind. 'He was truly circumspect in his deportment, before his children; there was no lightness or jesting on the one hand, nor sullenness or moroseness on the other. His conversation tended to edifying.' Just when they wanted to play 'bo-peep'!

At the same time, 'that they might respect the people of God, he was careful not to mention in their hearing the occasional inconsistencies of professors; that they might love religion, they beheld him happy in the experience and enjoyment of it'. Before he 'corrected' his children he knelt in prayer, asking God's blessing on the correction. It is understandable against the background of the period, but it was none the less deplorable from the standpoint of the little child. As he grew older, Henry Longden mellowed, and his disciplinary methods were evidently moderated. He became 'more lenient, though equally firm; and when his children arrived at a proper age, he made himself familiar with them.'[43] What tragic blindness—a proper age!

It is a welcome relief to turn from this 'planned discipline' and discover the simpler methods of James Bowmaker, master-bricklayer and builder of Alnwick. He was a quiet man, not given to anger, but he had an effective method of dealing with family upheavals. 'It was his custom, when the children quarrelled, to put one out at the back door, and another at the front, until peace was restored.'[44] It was not a difficult operation, and avoided theological complications, or questions of total depravity!

The original curriculum at Kingswood and the long hours at the Charity Schools are justly condemned, but the attempt to provide education and the discipline which was intended to develop character were, at least, significant of an interest in childhood which was so often entirely lacking elsewhere. Any critical survey of the contribution made to education, in general, lies outside the scope of this book, and the subject has been admirably treated in two recent theses.[45] There is, however, another aspect of child-life which should be considered, particularly as it affects the children of the first Methodists. The journals reveal a religious precocity which is almost incredible.

In an age of illiteracy the child of Jane Treffry had 'read the greater part of the Bible before he was four years old'. His mother was being taught 'the doctrine of man's depravity, the atonement and justification by faith' when she was quite a little girl, yet she was by no means an objectionable child. Rather surprisingly she grew up a witty tomboy, riding difficult horses, climbing high trees, and helping her brothers with their Latin, so that they could go out to play![46]

By the time he was eight years of age Thomas Wright had read through the Old and New Testaments and 'was well acquainted with every remarkable story to be found there, and in the Apocrypha'.[47]

In Derby, Joseph Pearson, a pioneer of Sunday-school work, attended when young, a weekly meeting for children, conducted by Mrs. Dobinson, on Sunday afternoons. He says in his journal: 'Our lessons and tasks were taken out of "Janeway's Tokens for Children". She gave us religious instruction before Sunday schools were established. . . . At the races, she invited us to her house, and gave us some fruit to prevent us from having anything to do with them.' The 'alarming sermons' which he heard caused him to become so 'intent' that as a small boy he listened to 'one hundred and forty-nine sermons in a year'.

When he was fourteen years old he took his part in the celebrations of the centenary of the Revolution of 1688. His journal gives us some insight into this 'holiday': 'Nov. 5th, 1788. The Revolution of 1688, was commemorated in Derby, by roasting an ox in the market-place, and several sheep in different parts of the town, which caused great rejoicing among the people. . . . After this, I went into the vault of All-Saint's Church, to see the coffins of the Devonshire family. I saw the coffin of the long-armed Duke, that took part in the Revolution of 1688. It brought my mind into a state of sober reflection. This is the house appointed for all living, and yet how few lay these things to heart.' Whether this entry is an echo of words he had heard his elders use, or whether it was made later when he was more mature, is an open question. It is not difficult to imagine it was his attitude at fourteen! When he gave his rabbits a little extra clover on Sunday, he was not at all surprised to find they were dead on Monday morning. He 'felt the admonition in his conscience; he had done wrong, and reaped his reward'.[48] In his later years he became a sensible and successful business man, and took a leading part in establishing Sunday schools in Somerset, in spite of his warped childhood, with its unnatural fears and its astonishing solemnity.

It is not always possible to discriminate between the forced or conventional expressions of piety so often used in the religious memoirs of the period, and the actual experience, hidden behind a phrase. Looking back on her childhood Mary Lyth wrote: 'The Spirit of God strove with me when but a little child. One time, I remember, while repeating my prayers to my aunt, the grace of God shone so sweetly upon me, I was melted down into tenderness before the Lord; and it seemed as if the glory of the Lord shone round about me, while I repeated the well-known hymn: "Glory to Thee, my God, this night". . . . Thus the Lord brooded upon my infant mind.' Did little Mary Burdsall say her prayers in the midst of such glory, or was Mary Lyth idealizing a childish memory? He would be a bold man who would utterly deny the happening for, so doing, he would deny the same glory to certain poor shepherds who were, themselves, but children in the dark.[49]

'When I was between seven and eight years old, musing one day on that thought, "What can it be to know my sins forgiven and to have faith in Jesus?" I felt my heart rise against God,' says Mary Bosanquet, 'for having appointed a way of salvation so hard to be understood; and with anguish of soul, I said, "If I were to die a martyr, I could do it; or, to give away all I have; or, when grown up, to become a servant, that would be easy; but I shall never know how to believe." ' Poor little bairn— her mind vexed with a problem that would have taxed Luther or the Council of Trent, and she but rising eight!

'When I was about thirteen,' she continues, 'the things of God began to return with more power on my mind.'[50] Was it that such children were precocious, or that their elders had forced their spiritual perception and produced an unhealthy fear, or is there a further possibility—that they, like their parents, were in a strange age of sudden awakening and rubbed their little eyes, half-blinded by the light? Again and again, as one tries to answer, with fierce denunciation, there comes the reminder that many of these children grew up mighty in faith and under-standing. Has not Mary Bosanquet an honoured place in the history of the Church? Perhaps it was in spite of those early days and not because of them, and yet——!

The examples that have been cited are not exceptional cases. The memoirs and journals have almost invariably such passages. The childish experiences of Hannah Ball or Mary Tatham are as detailed as those of Jane Treffry or Mary Bosanquet. Nor are they confined entirely to Methodists, for Silas Told and Hester Ann Roe knew a 'covenanting childhood' as severe and unnatural to the people of today, as they were customary to the devout evangelical of the eighteenth century, whether he were Anglican, Methodist, or Dissenter.

That there was an unhealthy element of fear must be at once admitted. That there was an appalling ignorance as to the working of a child's mind is equally apparent. On the other side it is clear that the motive which urged the Wesleys and the early Methodists as a whole, was a deep-seated love of the child himself. To suggest that they were unsympathetic or indifferent is ridiculous and, in the light of the evidence, untrue. Nor must the issue be decided, without reference to the ultimate result.

Anyone who reads the journal of John Nelson must shrink from the story of the Sunday night, when, a boy of nine, he 'sat on the ground, by his grandfather's chair as he read the twentieth chapter of the Revelations', and saw the apocalyptic vision till 'the flesh crept on his bones'. Yet John Nelson grew up to preach a gospel of hope and not of fear.

Little Henry Taylor wandered in the Somerset fields and sometimes knelt down 'to pray that God would make him good'. There was nothing morbid about it all, for coming to London as a youth he became a sturdy citizen, for fifty years a voluntary but regular visitor of the Benevolent Society, a class-leader and a local preacher.[51]

The children of the first Methodists were often admitted as members of Society at the age of nine or ten,[52] and before one passes a final criticism on such admissions, the alternatives offered to the child of the period should be considered. Had the eighteenth century, with its appalling dearth of anything like popular education or even physical recreation, provided much in the way of character training or youth movements? What value did the state or the populace place on child life, that it should cheerfully acquiesce in the employment of children, five years of age, in mines, or as chimney sweeps crawling slowly to their death in a world of darkness? What was the worth of the charity child, cowering in the wagon that took him from the indifferent city to die quickly in the northern mills?

They made their mistakes—these early Methodists—and they would have done more with their children if they had understood them better, but they loved greatly and, in the end, love does not fail. And there *were* moments when John Wesley forgot to teach them the doctrine of total depravity and took them in his arms and blessed them—which, after all, is what his Master did. Behind the idea of original sin there lay the idea of original righteousness, and all the straining after the salvation of the child was based on the splendid possibility of his becoming what God meant him to be, a partner in His creative activity.

Though charity schools and Sunday schools were not originated by the Methodists, they were developed by them, and long before Robert Raikes began his work at Gloucester, schools and classes for children were established, independently, in many of the Methodist Societies. The high value placed on education and mental discipline by John Wesley was gradually appreciated by his people, and they joined him in a vigorous attempt to provide schools for the less privileged children. When he opened the 'enlarged' school at Kingswood, on 24th June 1748, he preached on the text: 'Train up a child in the way he should go', and he took care to sign-post the way with the rules and curriculum which have been so severely criticized ever since. The Conference, earlier in June, had approved the arrangements,[53] and boys from six to twelve years of age faced a syllabus of religious and classical subjects which might have dismayed a classics master—and probably did! The standards of Wesley were high, for he said, confidently, that an average boy could learn 'more here in three years than the generality of students at Oxford or Cambridge do in seven'.

So they took out the books he had himself edited or revised,—

Kennet's *Antiquities of Rome*, Potter's *Greek Antiquities*, Lewis's *Hebrew Antiquities*, Dr. Cave's *Primitive Christianity*, English, French, Hebrew, Latin, and Greek grammars, books on logic and history, and set to work. Poor little souls of six and seven, many of them the children of travelling preachers, wondered why the birds and the beasts were so free, and they so bound by rules which governed the long hours of a summer day.—'Never let the children work but in the presence of a master.'—Nor could they eat unless under supervision, and as play was forbidden, they knew no freedom save in their dreams!

It was a grim, bleak sort of life, in those early years, and the shadow of the schoolroom in the Epworth Rectory seemed to have stretched to Kingswood.[54] There perhaps lies the secret of what seems unpardonable severity. The discipline was not some private invention of John Wesley; it was symptomatic of the age. Even the proverb 'He that plays when he is a child will play when he is a man', was of German origin. The great distinction between Wesley and so many of his contemporaries is that he, like Susanna his mother, had a bright vision of the child becoming a man—after God's own heart. At school the boy was on his way to his high destiny, but the road might have been less steep, and the hedges not so high, for even the son of a travelling preacher would work better for a scramble over the hills, or an hour hiding in the woodland glades as Robin Hood! Even before Wesley's death the rules and general conditions became less Spartan, and the school began to justify its foundation in the success of its first 'old boys'.

In Lambeth Mrs. Edwards taught a hundred children, including twelve daughters of travelling preachers. She maintained and educated these children at her own expense.[55]

Two of the earliest Methodist 'charity schools' were established in Bristol and London. Little is known of the Bristol venture, though it was evidently a development of the school founded by the Nicholas Street Society in 1739. When it was transferred and became 'The New School-house in the Horsefair' Wesley appointed four masters and a mistress on the staff, though two of the masters were soon discharged as superfluous.[56]

The children in the London streets were a source of anxiety to Wesley, and the Society at the Foundery agreed readily to his proposal to open a school. It was quite distinctive in its arrange-

R

ments, for he had in mind not only those who, because of the poverty of their parents, were running wild without any kind of education, but also those who were at schools with no religious background, and, whilst learning to read and write, 'learned all kinds of vice at the same time. . . . At length,' he says, 'I determined to have them taught in my own house, that they might have an opportunity of learning to read, write, and cast accounts (if no more), without being under almost a necessity of learning Heathenism at the same time. . . .'[57] So two masters were found, 'men of honesty and of sufficient knowledge . . . with their hearts in the work'. One of these was Silas Told, who gave up a relatively good position as a clerk to teach the children at a salary of ten shillings a week. Many of them were in rags and the little Society decided to clothe them and to pay most of the expenses by voluntary contributions. In a few weeks Silas had 'collected threescore boys and six girls'. Having the children under his care 'from five in the morning till five in the evening, both winter and summer, sparing no pains' and aided, only, by an usher and four monitors, he soon 'brought near forty of them into writing and arithmetic'. At the end of seven years he had 'discharged two hundred and seventy-five boys, most of whom were fit for any trade'.[58] It was a good piece of work, and the Society recognizing its demands, boarded and clothed his daughter, in an attempt to augment his inadequate salary.

In his preface to the autobiography of Silas Told, John Wesley describes him as 'a man of good understanding, although not much indebted to education'. It was fortunate that he was not expected to undertake a Kingswood curriculum! Remembering the shrewdness of the London street urchin, compelled to live 'on his wits' it is probable that Silas found the Foundery School more exacting than the slave-ships. The verdict of many a parent must have been like that of an old Launceston Methodist who said, concerning his son's education: 'The maister cud'en taich un any more. 'Ee was larned out.'[59]

The rules of the school, which continued till 1772, were strenuous. Children were admitted at six years of age, and were expected to be present at morning service at five a.m. Their school hours were from six to twelve and from one to five. They had no 'play-days'—nor apparently much in the way of play-hours, and two days absence without leave in one week, meant dismissal. Was there a way of escape by taking *one* day without permission? If so, the little Londoners would surely have discovered it, and small blame to them!

The Society, as a whole, was keenly interested. Two stewards were appointed to look after the finance, to talk with the masters regularly, to pray with the children and consider their conduct and progress. Every Wednesday morning they met the parents and 'exhorted them to train the children at home in the ways of God'. These arrangements were dependent on the members of the Society at the Foundery, and they seem, like the masters, to have done their work well. Compared with the amenities of today, the prospect of schooling at the Foundery seems grim and unattractive, but a new world was opened to the children who had lived in squalor and complete ignorance of the meaning of life. Their rags were taken away and the women at the Foundery, sewing in their scanty leisure hours, clothed them warmly and decently. 'They learned reading, writing, and arithmetic swiftly' and were soon 'fit for any trade'. It was a successful and praise-worthy experiment, and John Wesley's verdict was sufficient to justify it: 'A happy change was soon observed in the children, both with regard to their tempers and their behaviour.'

Soon after the opening of City Road Chapel, a house was taken near by, and another charity school opened in succession to the Foundery School. On the recommendation of Dr. Adam Clarke, Arthur Jarrett was appointed master, and for twenty years he held the post with great credit.[60] The school was conducted on similar lines to its predecessor, and in 1786 Wesley described it modestly as 'our little charity-school where forty boys and twenty girls are trained up both for this world and the world to come'.[61] It was undoubtedly as G. J. Stevenson says, 'a great blessing to many of the poor members of Society who had large families, or where there were fatherless and orphan children.'[62]

In 1808 what was described as the 'Methodist Charity School, belonging to the New Chapel, City Road', seems to have been an institution especially for girls. At number 27 Providence Row, Moorfields, the children were apparently taught needle-work in addition to the regular subjects, for a circular was issued containing a price-list for fifty-six different articles. Amongst the items are—a frilled shirt 2s., a plain shirt 1s., a pair of sheets

4*d.* to 10*d.*, nightcaps 3*d.* to 6*d.* each, frilled night caps 8*d.*, ladies' pockets 4*d.* and 6*d.* per pair.[63] Whether the Rules were extended to permit *frilled* night caps remains a mystery!

In the West Street Chapel another London charity-school owed its origin to Margaret Stile, a servant-girl, who made herself responsible for an orphan boy, giving sixpence each week out of her own wages, and collecting another eightpence in half-pennies from the members of her class. This developed into a school with a hundred and forty scholars, and was eventually moved to the Great Queen Street Chapel. One of the happy features about this work was that, in 1802–4, the members of the Church of St. Mary's-le-Strand, made regular collections towards its maintenance.[64]

Amongst other schools of this kind, was one in Edinburgh, established by Lady Maxwell in 1770. The children were taught, free of cost, for three years, and during the course she helped in their religious instruction and character-training, presenting each with a Bible when their training was over. During her life-time eight hundred scholars passed through the school, and when she died she left it permanently endowed.[65]

In examining even these few examples it is evident that the spiritual experience of the first Methodists, so far from being self-centred, was constantly expressing itself in practical forms, not the least of which were these attempts to give poor children an opportunity to become intelligent citizens. The training they received was modest enough in its range, but, at least, it gave them self-respect and taught them to earn an honest livelihood. In many recorded cases it resulted in the development of strong personalities and the achievement of intellectual distinction. Best of all, it helped them towards a consciousness of the divine purpose, in what had been their neglected and often lonely lives.

The attempt to combine secular and religious teaching resulted inevitably, under the conditions of eighteenth-century life, in the establishment of Sunday schools. The unfortunate thing was that, in their earliest stages, they were not realized as part of the living organism—the Christian Church. As Dr. Workman puts it: 'They were generally regarded as outside the Church, at the best its flying buttresses, never as an integral, necessary part of the adaptation of the Gospel to varying conditions.'[66] The actual Sunday-school movement did not begin till John Wesley

was an old man, but he saw farther than most of his contemporaries when he said: 'I find these schools springing up
wherever I go. Perhaps God may have some deeper end than
men are aware of. Who knows but some of these may become
nurseries for Christians.'[67] This judgement was passed as early
as 18th July 1784, when the Sunday school, as such, was only
a year old.

There was no doubt as to his sympathetic support of the new
movement, for he inserted 'An Account of the Sunday Charity
Schools, lately begun in various parts of England' in the *Arminian
Magazine* in 1788 and the article was written by Robert Raikes
himself. In a letter of appreciation, written to Richard Rodda
who extended and reorganized the work in Chester, he said:
'I am glad you have taken in hand that blessed work of setting
up Sunday schools in Chester. It seems that these will be one
great means of reviving religion throughout the nation.'[68]

The history of the Sunday-school movement has been written
in detail, but some aspects of the work serve to build up the
picture of the early Methodists. There has been some suggestion
that they anticipated the work of Robert Raikes many years
before he established his school in Gloucester. This is a purely
academic question and it might be argued that all such work
was but a development of the catechetical schools of primitive
Christianity. On the other hand the many independent ventures
made by members of the first Methodist Societies, has its own
value, in showing their attempts at self-expression, and their real
concern for the children. It is said that Sophia Cooke, a young
Methodist of Gloucester, marched with Robert Raikes, the editor
of the *Gloucester Journal*, when, in 1780, he led his troop of ragged
urchins to the first Sunday school. Whether she suggested the
idea to Raikes or not, she certainly gathered some of the children
employed in her uncle's pin factory, and after teaching them,
took them to the service, conducted by the Rev. Thomas Stock,
headmaster of the cathedral school.

Many independent schools were already in existence which,
though they met on Sundays, were not specifically called Sunday
schools. They were the response of individual Methodists to the
inarticulate appeal of children, particularly poor children, who
were unable to read or write, and for whom no one seemed to
feel any responsibility.

In 1768 John Valton 'met and catechised the children on the Lord's day morning, and procured them necessary books'.[69] His wife, previously a widow named Purnell, living at Brean, near Bristol in 1780, 'was much grieved to see the profligacy of the poor children in the village, who were running about and making an uproar in the street on the Lord's day. She laid this deeply to heart, and confiding in the grace of God invited them to her house; and began, I believe,' says John Valton, 'the first Sunday School in England'.[70]

One of the most interesting of these early experiments was begun by James Heys, of Little Lever, Lancashire, in 1775. He was better known as 'Old Jammy o' th' Hey' and was a poor man, who earned a meagre living by winding bobbins for the weavers. Out of the goodness of his heart he began to teach the 'draw boys', weavers' assistants, to read. Some of the young women then asked him to teach them also, but he could not find sufficient leisure. Nothing daunted, he offered to give them lessons while he went on with his work at the wheel. For this they paid him three half-pence a week. The children next asked if they could come to him on Sundays, and a neighbour offered the front room in her cottage. They were so eager to attend that the crowd became unmanageable. He decided to be remorseless about the time of admission, and since he had no bell to ring, he used an old brass mortar and pestle. As soon as he sounded it the scholars, a happy and eager little crowd, came trooping in from the lane where they were always waiting long before the time to start.[71] Primitive as it was, it compares well with the reception given a few years later to charity children from London on their way to 'the dark, satanic mills' where they found neither instruction nor release, dying without even the recording of their names.

The work of Hannah Ball, who established a school in High Wycombe in 1769 is better known. She met the children on Sunday and again on Monday, 'earnestly desiring', as she said to John Wesley, 'to promote the interest of the church of Christ'. In her journal for 3rd June 1770, she states her purpose, quite simply, for her own private satisfaction: 'I desire to spend the remaining part of my life in a closer walking with God, and in labours of love to my fellow creatures,—feeding the hungry, clothing the naked, instructing a few of the rising generation in the principles of religion, and in every possible way I am capable, ministering to them that shall be heirs of salvation.'[72]

In Scotland Lady Maxwell followed up the work of her charity school by opening a 'Sabbath-school' in 1787. There were thirty-one scholars present and she immediately took steps to open another 'twenty-five miles south of Edinburgh'. In 1795 she rejoiced because the numbers in Edinburgh were 'sixty young men remarkably alive to God, and many young women truly desirous to flee from the wrath to come'. It seems that the school was intended for youth, and that the children continued to attend her charity-school.[73]

In Ireland as early as 1769 Samuel Bates was a pioneer who gathered the children of Charlemont together every Sunday 'for regular instruction'. In 1778 the Rev. Dr. Kennedy, vicar of Bright, transformed a singing class into a Sunday school to which children of all denominations came with such Bibles and Testaments as they possessed. Eight years later it was reorganized on the English model, with a staff of teachers, but it remains an early example of a united school.[74]

The growth of Sunday schools in Ireland was rapid, and the Irish Methodist Conference, in 1794, issued a definite direction: 'Let Sunday Schools be established, as far as possible, in all the towns in this kingdom where we have Societies.'[75] In Bluestone Joseph Malcomson, largely by the work of the Sunday school he founded in 1789, transformed a notorious neighbourhood, and in Derryscollop in Armagh, Thomas Taylor raised the whole tone of a degenerate village by the school he established. In a barn at Donaghadee, Mary Carey gathered a few poor children, every Sunday, and 'taught them the Scriptures'.[76]

In most of these early ventures the school seemed to be intended for the children who were neglected or even outcast. It was some time before it took its place in England or Ireland as part of the normal Church life. Though it was forty years before the English Conference took action as positive as that taken in Ireland,[77] the schools grew rapidly in numbers and efficiency.

One of the difficulties was that in most cases a great deal of time had to be spent in teaching the children to read and write. In Radcliffe there were a few night schools where youths were taught reading and writing for fourpence a week, but arithmetic was extra! The Methodists in their little white-washed room in

Sugar Lane, with its 'forms and chairs and boxes, a table or two covered with primitive gingham and one or two texts and coloured Scriptural scenes on the walls' provided secular and religious education for a clamorous crowd.[78]

In Rochdale the first Sunday school was opened by James Hamilton in a room 'down the White Bear Yard'. Its plan was simple—to teach the children to read and write and, as often as possible, take them to some place of worship. There was no available Methodist chapel in 1784 and James marched his twenty-three scholars to the Parish Church to the consternation of the beadle who, resplendent in his official red-collared coat, with his silver-headed black staff, refused them admission. The protests of James Hamilton were in vain and, after a fearsome display of handcuffs, the beadle locked the door and went off to report to the vicar, the elderly Dr. Wray. Hearing that two men had brought a lot of dirty children to church, 'calling them a Sunday school' the vicar answered: 'Put them in some corner out of sight.' For this, he is no more to be blamed than were the majority of Christians who seemed incapable, at first, of realizing that the Sunday school was not an outside institution, nor even an auxiliary, but actually part of the Church itself.

The heart of John Wesley was rejoiced when he visited Bingley and preached in the Parish Church on 18th July 1784. 'Before service I stepped into the Sunday school, which contains two hundred and forty children, taught every Sunday by several masters, and superintended by the curate. So many children in one parish are restrained from open sin, and taught a little good manners, at least, as well as to read the Bible.'[79] It was this united school which made him see that here was 'a nursery for Christians'.

At Upper Steps Mill, Honley, the Independents, Anglicans and Methodists joined in opening a school in 1790. Teachers and scholars came from all the villages in the neighbourhood. Writing was one of the subjects on the simple curriculum, and the materials were certainly not elaborate. 'Each scholar was provided with a box of Calais sand for copybook, and a pointed piece of wire for pen. The writing was easily erased by running the hand over the sand.' The united school continued until, in 1814, the Methodist scholars were able to remove to their new Chapel at Green Cliff, and leave room for the increasing number of children

who wished to attend.[80] In Chester three schools were started in
1782, but organized Sunday schools were largely the creation of
Richard Rodda and the Methodist Societies four years later.[81]

Towards the end of the century a definite pattern evolved, and
the organization of the work made for efficiency, though some
features appear grotesque today. In Bristol William Smith, 'a
servant in a respectable Linen Warehouse', was the founder of
the first Methodist Sunday school. Whilst visiting for the
Strangers' Friend Society, he had been deeply moved by the
plight of the poorer children, during a fever epidemic. He urged
the ministers, James Buckley and John Pawson, to help him to
purchase some of Dr. Watts's *Hymns for the Children*, and a few
spelling-books that he might gather the children together and
form a school. A beginning was made in 1804 at George Street
Chapel, and about fifty children were present. They were ragged
and dirty, and Mr. Stock, the barber, was sent post-haste to the
chapel to cut their hair. This elementary hygiene accomplished,
the school settled down to regular Sunday sessions, modelling its
rules on those in use at Stourport. Visitors were appointed to
see that books were available and discipline observed. The hours
were from ten to twelve in the morning, and two till half-past
four in the afternoon. An elaborate system of fines was in operation to ensure the punctuality and regular attendance of visitors,
members of the committee, teachers and the superintendent!
From eleven o'clock to twelve reading and spelling were taught
and a form of prayer 'selected from the Morning Service in the
Liturgy of the Church of England' was regularly used. The
Committee subscribed as much as they were able towards the cost
of books, lighting, and heating and the upkeep of the rooms and
then, very wisely, sent out an appeal to the public to accept their
responsibility and privilege in helping the work to develop. 'The
inhabitants of Bristol are known over the kingdom, by their
benevolency, humanity and philanthropy. Surely they will not
come behind in this gift. No; you will feel for those children
whose parents cannot spare them to attend week-day schools,
nor afford to pay for their instruction at evening schools; but
who may be taught in the Sunday school free of expense, and
without loss of time. In contributing to this you will not only
relieve the minds of the parents who ardently desire their children
to be taught, but you will help to prevent pilfering, stealing and

depredation, the common faults of ignorance and idleness: you will assist in training up children to industry, cleanliness, sobriety, honesty and virtue.'[82] Such was the gist of the appeal, and it represents the general principles on which the little band of Methodist teachers were working. The later developments are indicative of their progressive spirit. Promotion-tickets were awarded to satisfactory scholars. Canes were forbidden, and the teachers agreed to talk to the children in simple language but 'in an affectionate manner, endeavouring to make them sensible that we love them'.

Eventually, in 1812, the Bristol Adult Society was formed by the Methodists. 'All parties were invited to participate' and, as a result, hundreds of adults were taught to read, and to understand their Bibles.

In the children's Sunday school there was a carefully designed system of awards, which took the form of money, books or clothing according to necessity. There were 'Classes of Disgrace' and 'Classes of Merit'. Methodist libraries were established, and the children, as a whole, responded eagerly.

Though these developments did not take place till the first years of the nineteenth century, they are important to an understanding of the earlier period. The lines they took indicate what was in the mind of those who struggled through the initial difficulties.

One can imagine them looking wistfully to the slum area in Mount Pleasant. The district known as Cock Road was notorious for its wickedness and was described as 'emphatically a den of thieves'. As soon as they had consolidated the work at George Street and a few other centres, the little band of enthusiasts turned, eagerly, to Cock Road, and on 26th July 1812, seventy-five boys and girls, fifty-eight of whom did not know the alphabet, presented themselves at the new Sunday school. A contemporary record describes the situation: 'Many of those, whose fathers are now in prison, are entirely dependent on a system of robbery and plunder for their support.'

As the work progressed, with increasing success, it was found that, on the average, seventy-five per cent. of the children were completely illiterate. They were soon taught to read—for such children are shrewd and quick to learn—and the gratitude of the parents astonished the teachers. It was not merely a triumph over general ignorance; it became a signal victory for the Christian faith. Nothing could be more unreasonable than to sit in scornful judgement of methods, in face of this revolution in morals, and the establishment of spiritual values amongst a people who had been social outcasts and a menace to the community.[83]

Similar work was done in Bath by Joseph Pearson, the Methodist secretary of the Bath School Union for thirty-two years.[84] In most parts of the country, indeed, the Methodist Societies accepted the idea of the Sunday school with enthusiasm. In some places they adopted the 'Rules' as drawn up by Robert Raikes and his associates, and in others they devised their own. The school at Haslingden issued a document, in 1790, with the formidable title 'Articles to be observed by the masters and scholars of the Methodist Sunday School in Haslingden'.[85]

One of the important facts to be noticed is that the Methodist schools almost immediately adopted the principle of voluntary teaching, though for a long time in the majority of other schools the staff was paid.[86] It was, no doubt, with some justifiable pride, that John Wesley wrote, on 27th July 1787: 'Thence we went to Bolton. Here are eight hundred poor children taught in our Sunday Schools by about eighty masters, who receive no pay but what they are to receive from their Great Master.'[87] Again in 1790 he comments on the same fact, when he visited the Sunday school at Newcastle where 'six or seven hundred were present. None of our masters or mistresses teach for pay. They seek a reward that man cannot give.'[88]

Advice was given to the preachers in 1784 when they were urged to meet the children, and to 'give them suitable exhortations and explain to them in an easy familiar manner the Instructions for Children, and the Tokens for Children',[89] but it was obviously impossible and unwise for the preachers to attempt the tremendous task. A 'Plan for Sunday Schools' was issued in 1798 though many schools followed the directions of the Sunday School Union, using *The Union Hymn Book for Scholars*, their specially produced spelling books, and Bibles 'bound up in a very coarse cloth or harden'.[90]

Though he never seems to have had any doubts about the value of Sunday schools, John Wesley was quick to notice results. A local preacher named Michael Longridge gathered a school together in 1786 in Monkwearmouth. It was undenominational, but the workers were almost all Methodists. When Wesley visited the town in 1790 he showed his appreciation of the work, in his record for Sunday, 13th June: 'In the morning I preached a charity sermon in Monkwearmouth church, for the Sunday school, which has already cleared the streets of all the children that used to play there on a Sunday from morning to evening.' One seems to detect, in this and many similar comments in other sources, a particular gratitude for something which would help to keep the Sabbath holy. In so far as the Sunday schools gave the children education and religious instruction and, at the same time, prevented noisy and disorderly conduct on the Sabbath they were doubly blessed.[91]

The first consideration, however, continued to be the saving of the children and, if this sometimes had a narrow interpretation in contemporary records it may be broadly interpreted by the facts, for the scholars were certainly improved in body and mind as well as in spirit.

The work grew rapidly, in spite of many difficulties, for the people who were inspired to undertake it were strong characters. 'We were pleased to find that very great good continued to be done by means of the Bolton Sunday School,' says Mrs. Elizabeth Rhodes in her journal for 1794. 'The number of scholars had increased to about eleven hundred. The masters abode in their stations as men of God who laboured to do all the good they could. The Lord has owned them, and greatly blessed their labours. . . .'[92]

The difficulties, many of them matters of accommodation, were overcome, even though it meant improvisation which involved no little hardship. When the Methodists established a Sunday school at Gillow Heath, they met in a room in a house, but it was soon too small for the crowd of eager children. An old, disused pottery was 'fitted up' and the school was held there, until 'the mining operations which were carried on underneath it so shook the walls, as to render it dangerous and unfit for use'. Eventually the gallant little company set to work and built a chapel.[93]

There is something quaintly fascinating about the first attempts to celebrate the Sunday-school anniversaries. Singing and the reciting of verses which were certainly original and confident were important items from the earliest days. The inhabitants of

Frome were, doubtless, entertained by a duologue, which ran to forty-nine lines. Four of these were recited by the boy, and then, by way of antiphon, the girl replied, fortunately at half the length, for it was certainly hard going:

> *Boy:* Devoid of sweet instruction's light,
> And wrapt in darkest shades of night,
> No friendly hand to mark the way
> Up to the realms of endless day.

> *Girl:* When lo! our mental gloom to cheer,
> We sought and found reception here.

So it worked up gradually to a climax, which was more severely practical!

> *Boy:* Britons, we ask,—nor ask in vain,
> Assur'd we shall your aid obtain;
> 'Tis England's glory, England's pride,
> Her sons are found on virtue's side.

At this psychological moment, one imagines, the girl pointed with dramatic suddenness to the scholars, standing in stiff rows and declaimed:

> See there that youthful train, and say
> Can you withhold your help today?[94]

It is amusing in its naïve appeal, and yet it is not to be judged harshly. The children of Frome, like the children of Bristol and Bolton and Donaghadee had entered into a rich inheritance of love. Crude though some of the methods may have been, they were perhaps no more so than our own will appear in a hundred and fifty years. It would be folly to view the first Sunday schools as permanent patterns and refuse to see their faults. It is at least as foolish to sneer at the crudities, and remain content with a school of gymnastics or a social club as a substitute for the threefold purpose which led our forefathers to high endeavour, and changed the den of thieves in Cock Road into a company of grateful people, lifted from their outlawry and hopeless poverty into a rich fellowship and a purposeful, self-respecting life.

.   .   .   .   .   .

The creation of home-life, and the realization of the child as the most important member of the community was a discovery which the first Methodists helped to make. In themselves they had achieved 'a sense of family' rarely seen in the history of human kind.

When Wesley preached his farewell sermon in Ireland the great congregation was deeply moved. He announced his closing hymn, 'Come let us join our friends above . . .' It seemed to him that brother Charles was very near. Many hundred came to kneel at the Table of the Lord. He broke the bread to them. 'Take and eat. Feed on Him in your hearts, by faith with thanksgiving.' The crowd moved silently away. In Richard D'Olier's house he knelt and prayed for the little family in whose midst he had been so happy. On the quayside a multitude was waiting—part of that greater family in heaven and on earth. At the gangway he paused before going aboard the ship. The crowd sang a hymn. He knelt and prayed—for them, their families, the Church and Ireland. A great wave of emotion swept over the people as they bowed their heads. When they looked up he had climbed aboard the ship. Her moorings were cast off and she moved out to sea. They watched him as he stood there, but his hands were raised in prayer—for them and all the family of God.

NOTES

1. *Methodism in the Congleton Circuit*, p. 89.
2. *Journal of John Wesley*, V. 424.
3. *W.H.S.*, XX. 116.
4. *Wesleyan Methodist Magazine*, October 1912; *Methodist New Connexion Magazine*, 1839; *W.H.S.*, VIII. 173-4.
5. *A Family Memorial, Memoir of George Osborn*, p. 59. (Privately printed, London, 1877.)
6. *Memoirs of Mrs. Jane Treffry*, pp. 94-6.
7. *Experience of Mrs. Frances Pawson*, pp. 118, 132.
8. *Life of Mrs. Rogers*, pp. 200-1.
9. ibid., p. 201.
10. *Memoirs of Mr. George Cussons*, p. 29. (Gill, Easingwold, 1845.)
11. ibid., p. 37.
12. ibid., pp. 50, 53.
13. ibid., pp. 54, 61-2.
14. ibid., p. 67.
15. *Samuel Drew*, J. H. Drew, p. 499. (London, 1834.)
16. *Life of Henry Longden*, p. 69.
17. *Letters of John Wesley*, V. 254.
18. *W.H.S.*, XXI. 32-3.
19. *Memoir of Hannah Kilham*, Sarah Biller. (Darton and Harvey, London, 1837.)
20. *W.H.S.*, X. 192.
21. Pawson burnt Wesley's annotated Shakespeare, thinking it was of 'no importance'.
22. *A Family Memorial, Memoir of George Osborn*, pp. 9-10.
23. *Memoirs of James Field*, pp. 157-9.
24. *Memorials of Mrs. Eliz. Shaw*, p. 33.
25. *Memoirs of Mrs. Mortimer*, pp. 95-6.
26. *Life of Mrs. Adam Clarke*, p. 115.
27. *Methodism*, H. B. Workman, p. 55.
28. *Methodism in Thirsk Circuit*, John Ward; *W.H.S.*, VII. 31-2; *Journal of John Wesley*, VI. 282.
29. *Methodism in Bingley*, pp. 41, 44.
30. *W.H.S.*, VIII. 94-5.
31. *Memorials of Mrs. Eliz. Shaw*, pp. 3, 9.
32. *Memoirs of Mrs. Jane Treffry*, p. 4.
33. *Memorial of Mrs. Mary Lyth*, p. 14.
34. *Centenary of Wesleyan Methodism*, p. 215.
35. *Journal of John Wesley*, VII. 306, 377-8.
36. *W.H.S.*, IV. 119.
37. *Journal of John Wesley*, V. 172.
38. ibid., V. 453.
39. *Methodism in Rossendale*, pp. 119-20.
40. *History and Antiquities of Morley*, Smith, p. 86.
41. *Southey's Commonplace Book*, 4th series, p. 672; *W.H.S.*, IV. 181.
42. *Methodism in Ireland*, II. 80-1.
43. *Life of Henry Longden*, pp. 152-5.
44. *W.H.S.*, VII. 66.
45. *The Contribution of Methodism to Popular Education*, H. F. Mathews; *The Methodist Contribution to the Nineteenth-Century Secondary Education*, F. C. Pritchard.
46. *Memoirs of Mrs. Jane Treffry*, pp. 5-8, 139.
47. *Autobiography of Thomas Wright*, p. 24.
48. *Memoirs of Joseph Pawson*, pp. 1-17; *Methodist Magazine*, 1803, p. 557.
49. *Memorial of Mrs. Mary Lyth*, p. 13-14.

50. *Life of Miss Bosanquet*, pp. 12–20 (abridged edition, 1876).
51. *Methodism in Halifax*, pp. 9–10.
52. *City Road Chapel*, p. 362.
53. *Bennet's Minutes*, 54–7.
54. *Son to Susanna*, G. Elsie Harrison.
55. *Journal of John Wesley*, VI. 218; VII. 344.
56. ibid., II. 458.
57. *Life of Silas Told*.
58. *Life of Silas Told*, written by himself, p. 126. (London, 1789.)
59. *Truly Rural*, p. 88.
60. *Methodist Magazine*, 1826, pp. 430, 520.
61. *Journal of John Wesley*, VII. 222.
62. *City Road Chapel*, p. 88.
63. ibid., p. 42.
64. *Wesleyan Methodist Magazine*, 1829, pp. 153–4; *Two West-End Chapels*, J. Telford, pp. 73–4. (Wesleyan Methodist Bookroom, 1886.)
65. *Life of Lady Maxwell*, pp. 43–4.
66. *Methodism*, H. B. Workman, p. 57.
67. *Journal of John Wesley*, VII. 3.
68. *Letters of John Wesley*, VII. 364.
69. *Arminian Magazine*, 1784, pp. 73, 130; 1794, pp. 142–3.
70. *Memoirs of Joseph Pearson*, p. 242, footnote.
71. *Wesleyan Methodist Magazine*, 1836, p. 285.
72. *Memoirs of Miss Hannah Ball*, Joseph Cole and John Parker, pp. ix, 71–2. (London, 1839.)
73. *Life of Lady Maxwell*, pp. 220, 260.
74. *Methodism in Ireland*, I. 230, 302.
75. Irish *Minutes*, 1794, p. 9.
76. *Methodism in Ireland*, II. 10–11, 47.
77. *Minutes of Conference*, 1827, 1837.
78. *Radcliffe Methodism*, p. 26.
79. *Journal of John Wesley*, VII. 1.
80. *Methodism in Huddersfield*, pp. 27–8.
81. *Wesleyan Methodist Magazine*, 1846, pp. 562–3.
82. *A History of the Origin and Progress of the Sunday Schools in the City of Bristol and Its Vicinity*, John S. Broad, pp. 44–5. (1816.)
83. ibid., pp. 109–10.
84. *Memoirs of Joseph Pearson*, Henry Fish. (London, 1849.)
85. *Methodism in Rossendale*, p. 150, footnote.
86. *Wesleyan Methodist Magazine*, 1846, p. 564, footnote; *Education in Great Britain*, Horace Mann. (Official Report, Census of Great Britain, 1851, London, 1854.)
87. *Journal of John Wesley*, VII. 305–6.
88. ibid., VIII. 70.
89. Myles' *Chronological History*, p. 86.
90. *Methodism in Marshland*, pp. 75–6.
91. *Wesleyan Methodist Magazine*, 1910, p. 170; *Journal of John Wesley*, VIII. 71.
92. *Memoir of Mrs. Elizabeth Rhodes*, p. 137.
93. *Methodism in Congleton*, p. 117.
94. *Methodism in Frome*, pp. 63–5.

EPILOGUE AND SUMMARY

In the preceding chapters two main facts emerge: The ordinary Methodist people entered into an extraordinary spiritual experience, and, having been led by John Wesley to its threshold, they accepted him as interpreter and guide. He combined the functions of the pedagogue who led them to Christ, and of the tutor, who, afterwards, gave personal and loving oversight to their progress and conduct, in the Christian Way.

The ideal he continually set before them in speech, in the written word, and, above all, in his life, influenced their development, especially in its early stages. Later, they began to make their own decisions and shape their several courses. At their best they realized they were not slaves of a system, but new-born freemen of the spirit.

The little Societies grew naturally, and houses were built, which became spiritual homes founded on a kinship of souls.

To these small groups each individual came with a personal experience, not stereotyped, but distinctively his own. It began in the consciousness of his relationship to God, made possible by the forgiveness of those sins which had caused a gulf between himself and his Maker and the love of Christ which bridged over the gulf. By faith he crossed the bridge.

In the deepening intimacies of fellowship, the experience developed. The timid approach of the penitent, became the confidence of the child to the Father, and presently the growth in grace which would not cease until it became perfect love. Even then, as they discovered in the close contacts of the class-meetings and the bands, it had no finality, but went on from grace to grace. As, together, they realized what might be, so, individually, they saw the imperfection of what, so far, had been their progress.

All this experience had to be translated in terms of conduct. At times their reactions were clumsy and resulted in narrowness. They seemed, at first, to rob themselves of something of the fullness of life which God offered them, but they no longer lived selfishly, and they cheerfully abandoned whatever they thought would make them unfit to serve God and their fellows.

Their personal conduct affected their home life, and it would be true to say that, in the second half of the eighteenth century, there were no happier homes in England, than those of the first Methodists. Though they shared, to some degree, the ignorance of the child-mind, which was common to the world in which they lived, they began to make valiant efforts to give their children, and all children, their rightful heritage. In Charity schools and in Sunday schools the child was recognized and taught. The appalling rate of child mortality was no longer a reason for negligence on the ground that the birth-rate was high and that there were always other children to take the place of those who fell in a massacre of innocents. Instead, it became an incentive to care for the child in body, mind, and spirit, so that every babe who was born had the best chance of survival they could give. Again, it must be acknowledged that the first efforts seem to us crude and often mistaken in method. One can only pause, in that easy criticism, and ask oneself how our modern education may appear to the critics a century and a half after we have gone.

There is a famous instance cited by Baron von Hügel, and first used by Dr. James Martineau, which might serve as a corrective to incautious criticism. A young American, intelligent and wealthy, came to Europe to seek guidance. He believed that religion was an illusion, but was uneasy in his negative belief. Coming to Dr. Martineau for advice he was told to make an experiment: 'Live for the first six months among simple, slow-minded, narrow, even superstitious peasants, brought up in and practising a rigid traditional faith. Share their lives as intimately as you can. And then go for the second six months to alert, cultured, modern intellectuals, who have given up and despise all Church and religion. And then ask yourself: which of these two groups of people—if either—has got the mysterious thing, a hold on the secret of life? Which knows better how to meet the deepest, most crucial realities of life—birth—suffering —joy—passion—sin—failure—loneliness—death?'[1] The American agreed and spent the first six months in Germany with a Westphalian peasant family, narrow and prejudiced, often offending his sense of good taste, but faithful and devout. The second six months he lived amongst students in Berlin. They were, in some ways, charming people, keenly intelligent, but completely without moral or religious prejudices. When Martineau asked him how each group faced 'the dread and unescapable realities of life' he said of the first little family they *knew* because their lives were penetrated and possessed by something greater than themselves. Of the intelligentsia of Berlin, he said 'They were helpless' or as a colloquialism of today would put it 'They were without a clue'. In referring to the same incident Evelyn Underhill says that they had 'no inwardness'.

If one made the same experiment in imagination, with one of the early Methodist Societies, and a group of 'the quality' in Bath or Tunbridge Wells or London, say in 1775, would not the results be similar? If the deaths of William Carvosso and Beau Nash be compared the answer would be the same. However over-stressed such last scenes may appear to be in the private journals, no one could deny the happy triumph of the one or be anything but depressed by the squalid tragedy of the other. Like the early Christians in Rome, the first Methodists out-died their opponents because they out-lived them, and the reason they faced the deepest, most tremendous crises in life with courage and with joy, was because of their conscious relationship with God, and their vision of His far-off purpose.

Some of their characteristics have thus been considered. Others will be examined in a later volume. The way in which they faced persecution and triumphed, the 'local' preaching of their men and women, their first attempts at social service focused gradually on the evils of the day, their varied daily occupations, their educational standards, and, not the least important, their modes of public and private worship—have still to be investigated from the records they have left.[2]

In the conclusions so far reached, the influence of John Wesley and his immediate circle must not be forgotten. He gave the Societies an ideal which they tried to realize in their daily lives. Without 'the common people' it would have survived as an interesting specimen in the generally unattractive museums of eighteenth-century divinity. It would have had little more than an academic value today. Instead, it was translated into life— by the men and women whose records remain not only in the pages of their journals, but in the Church of which they helped to lay the foundations.

As he came to the end of his life, John Wesley was venerated both in Britain and America. At his death the chapels were hung with black cloth. At Halifax, the large east window, behind the pulpit, was covered, and on the sable drapery a full-length portrait of Mr. Wesley had beneath it the words 'am not I a brand snatched from the eternal burning?'[3] The local historian remarks 'The whole presented an appearance not easily described', and wins a deeper approval from us than he could have expected! And yet—if this had been only hero-worship or idolatry, how different would have been the superscription! In that sorrowful hour, with all its grotesque trappings, it was not Wesley but his Saviour of whom they finally thought.

Less than a fortnight before he died, he had written to Miss Susanna Knapp of Worcester, telling her that he was too ill to plan his future journeys.[4] On hearing of his death she came to London to attend the funeral. As he lay in state in City Road Chapel, great crowds gathered to pay their silent tribute. At seven o'clock in the morning Susanna arrived: 'We had but a transient view of our dear and reverend father,' she says, 'being obliged to pass by so quick, by reason of the vast number of people before and behind us, but it was the most affecting sight my eyes ever saw. The number of people was incredible. I heard that there was one day supposed to be ten thousand.'[5] The crowds, indeed, were so great that it was decided to arrange the funeral itself at five a.m., and so, by the light of torches and lanterns, his body was laid to rest. That night Susanna Knapp finished a sampler she had lately begun. The words on the canvas were a panegyric on John Wesley, and the little lady from Worcester worked it with her own hair.[6]

It was a strange but personal memorial—and it was typical of similar happenings all over the country. People who had only heard him on a single occasion, as they stood amongst the crowd, and some who had never seen him at all were conscious of a sense of loss so deep, and so intimate that words could not express it. The explanation does not lie in the fact of his dominating personality, but in the more important fact that he had led them to God. They sought eagerly to express themselves in what was to them a dark hour. They draped themselves and their buildings in black—but they arranged that the black cloth should be of good quality that it might be given later to the poor widows for dresses. In that very fact lay a hint of the continuing Church.

Their father in God had passed on his triumphant way. They must now turn their private grief into public service.

So the people called Methodists gave thanks, took courage, and went on with their work, commissioned not by man, but by God.

The blacksmith of Aberford, speaking in his own tongue, said: 'I bless the Lord that ivver I saw that man o' God. . . . Bless the Lord that ivver he teld me o' me sinful state. I thowt I wur a dacent man befoare; but he browt th' great hammer o' th' law, and slew me altogether. But he did not leave me there: He set Christ befoare me as a willing and compleat Saviour, and that wur good news to a poare lost sinner. Glory be to God.'[7]

The patrician, Lady Maxwell, wrote to her friend Mrs. Johnson: 'And so that great and good man is gone . . . after a long life of unwearied diligence, and unexampled activity, in the service of his God, and the general interests of mankind. . . . May the Lord still be the head of the large body of Christians he has left behind. O that one soul may animate the whole.'[8]

The witnesses agree! They are followers not of a great man, but of the Lord and Master of them all. Far from being either ideal Methodists, still less ideal Christians, they were pressing on toward the goal, and the rank and file of these early Methodists were as essential as the preachers assembled in Conference for the evangelization of England and the world.

Methodism has grown beyond the boundaries of London, Bristol, and Newcastle. It has spread over lonely countrysides, it has crossed the borders into Scotland and Wales, and crossed the narrow seas to Ireland, the Isle of Man and the Norman Isles. It has gone westward to the Americas and the Indies, and eastward to India and Ceylon. Soldiers and sailors, planters and merchants have carried its message to the four quarters of the globe—ordinary folk transfigured as they became messengers of God.

NOTES

1. *Essays and Addresses*, Baron von Hügel, Series II, p. 126.
2. *The Early Methodist People*, L. F. Church, Vol. II. (Epworth Press, London, 1949.
3. *Methodism in Halifax*, p. 182.
4. *Letters of John Wesley*, VIII. 263.
5. *Life of Susanna Knapp*, E. Rowley-Hamilton, p. 10. (Adams, London, 1866.)
6. *W.H.S.*, III. 20.
7. *Memoirs of Samuel Hide*, p. 7.
8. *Life of Darcy, Lady Maxwell*, p. 242 (letter to Mrs. Johnson, 14th March 1791).

BIBLIOGRAPHY

MANUSCRIPT SOURCES

Letters of Charles Wesley.
Early Miscellaneous Letters (in the custody of the Methodist Publishing House).
Class-Book (and Journal) of Thomas Goulding, of Upwell (property of the Rev. Dr. B. S. Bonsall).
Local Minute-books.
History of Methodism in Leeds (Thos. Wray) in MS.
Fleet Prison Commitment Book (Public Record Office).

CONTEMPORARY PRINTED PERIODICALS, ETC.

Arminian Magazine, 1778–97.
Methodist Magazine, 1798–1835.
Gentleman's Magazine, 1738–1810, etc.
(Many contemporary Minutes and Journals have been reprinted, as a whole or in part, by the Wesley Historical Society. They have been published in the Society's *Proceedings*.)
Minutes of Conference from 1744.

STANDARD WORKS OF REFERENCE

Journal of John Wesley. (Standard Edition in 8 vols. edited by Nehemiah Curnock. Kelly, London, 1909.)
Letters of John Wesley. (Standard Edition in 8 vols. edited by John Telford. Epworth Press, London, 1931.)
Sermons of John Wesley. (Standard Edition in 2 vols. edited by E. H. Sugden. Epworth Press, London, 1921.)
Works of John Wesley. (3rd edition in 14 vols. edited by Thos. Jackson. Mason, London, 1829–31.)
Lives of Early Methodist Preachers. (3rd edition in 6 vols. Wesleyan Conference Office, London, 1865. Other editions, including one under title *Wesley's Veterans*.)

MEMOIRS, JOURNALS, AND DIARIES

(The names of the subjects of the memoirs are printed first, since these volumes are chiefly private journals, edited. The names of the editors or compilers follow the titles.)

BALL, HANNAH.
  Memoir of Miss Hannah Ball of High Wycombe. John Parker. (Mason, London, 1839.)
BARRITT, MARY (MRS. TAFT).
  Memoirs of Mary Taft, formerly Miss Barritt. By herself. (Stevens, London, 1827.)
BEDE.
  Seth Bede, written by himself. (Tallant, London, 1859.)
BENNET, GRACE.
  Memoirs of Mrs. Grace Bennet, of Chinley. Wm. Bennet. (Bayley, Macclesfield, 1803.)
BENTLEY, SARAH.
  The Living Sacrifice, Biography of Sarah Bentley of York. John Lyth. (Mason, London, 1859.)
BOSANQUET, MARY (MRS. FLETCHER).
  Holiness unto the Lord, Character of Miss Bosanquet of Leytonstone. Stephen Cox. (W.M. Conf. Office, London, 1876.)
  Life of Mrs. Mary Fletcher. Henry Moore. (Mason, London, 11th edn., 1844.)
BRACKENBURY, ROBT. CARR.
  Raithby Hall, Memorial Sketches of R. C. Brackenbury, Esq. Mrs. Richd. Smith. (Wertheim, London, 1859.)

BROOKE, HENRY.
    Memoirs of Mr. Henry Brooke. Isaac D'Olier. (Napper, Dublin, 1816.)
BURDSALL, MARY (MRS. LYTH).
    Blessedness of Religion in Earnest, Memorial of Mrs. Mary Lyth, of York. John Lyth. (Book Society, London, 1861.)
BUSH, THOMAS.
    Memorial of Thos. Bush, of Lamborne. Editor unnamed. (Mason, London, 1849.)
CARVOSSO, WILLIAM.
    Memoir of Mr. William Carvosso of Mousehole. By himself. (Mason, London, 1860.)
CLARKE, MRS. ADAM.
    Life and Correspondence of Mrs. Adam Clarke. Anonymous. (Partridge and Oakey, London, 1851.)
CUSSONS, GEORGE.
    Memoirs of Mr. George Cussons (with Diary and Letters). (Whittaker, London, 1845.)
DREW, SAMUEL.
    Life, Character and Literary Labours of Samuel Drew, A.M., of St. Austell. J. H. Drew. (Longman, London, 1834.)
DUNGETT, JOHN.
    Memoir of Mr. John Dungett of Newcastle-on-Tyne. J. Heaton. (Mason, London, 1833.)
FIELD, JAMES.
    Memoirs of Mr. James Field, of Cork. Robt. Huston. (Mason, London, 1851.)
GATE, ROBERT.
    Life of Mr. Robert Gate, of Penrith. G. G. S. Thomas. (Elliot Stock, London, 1869.)
HAMPTON, RICHARD.
    'Foolish' Dick, the Pilgrim Preacher. S. W. Christophers. (Haughton, London, 1873.)
HICK, SAMUEL.
    Memoirs of Samuel Hick, in His Own Dialect. By himself. (Nicholson, Halifax, 1858.)
    The Village Blacksmith, Memoir of Samuel Hick. Jas. Everett. (Newton, London, 18th edn., 1879.)
HUMPHREYS, W. H.
    Memorial of Capt. W. H. Humphreys. R. Newstead. (Mason, London, 1840.)
HUNTINGDON, SELINA, COUNTESS OF.
    Countess of Huntingdon and her Circle. Sarah Tytler. (Pitman, London, 1907.)
JENKINS, SARAH.
    Memoirs of Miss Sarah Jenkins. Mary Tooth. (Mason, London, 1829.)
KILHAM, HANNAH.
    Memoir of Hannah Kilham. Sarah Biller. (Darton and Harvey, London, 1837.)
KNAPP, SUSANNA.
    Life of Susanna Knapp. E. Rowley. (Hamilton, Adams, London, 1866.)
LOMAS, MRS. MARY KNOWLES.
    Memorials of Mrs. Mary Knowles Lomas, of Manchester. A. Bell. (Mason, London, 1844.)
LOMAS, REBECCA.
    Memoir of Miss Rebecca Lomas. J. Renshaw. (Barnett, Nottingham, 1811.)
LONGDEN, HENRY.
    Life of Henry Longden, of Sheffield, from his Memoirs and Diary. By himself. (Mason, London, 1846.)
MAXWELL, DARCY, LADY.
    Life of Darcy, Lady Maxwell. W. Atherton. (Mason, London, 1863.)
    Correspondence of Lady Maxwell. J. G. Wilson. (Mason, London, 1863.)
MORE, HANNAH.
    Memoirs of Hannah More. W. Roberts. (Seeley, London, 1838.)
MORTIMER, FRANCES (MRS. PAWSON).
    Experience of Mrs. Frances Pawson. Jos. Sutcliffe. (Mason, London, 1834.)
NEWTON, ELIZABETH.
    Memorials of Elizabeth Newton of Roxby. By her daughter. (W.M. Conf. Office, London, 1868.)

OSBORN, GEORGE.
A Family Memorial, Memoir of George Osborn of Rochester. Dr. George Osborn for Mrs. Ballard. (Privately printed, London, 1877.)

PEARSON, JOSEPH.
Memoirs of Joseph Pearson. Henry Fish. (S.S.U., London, 1849.)

PECK, ROBERT.
Memoir of the 'Venerable' Robert Peck of Loughborough. J. Mills. (Kent, London, 1856.)

PICKFORD, ELIZABETH.
Life and Diary of Mrs. Eliz. Pickford of Salisbury. Peter M'Owan. (Hamilton, Adams, London, 1858.)

REEVES, WILLIAM.
Father Reeves, the Methodist Class-leader of Lambeth. E. Corderoy. (Woolmer, London, 1882.)

RHODES, MRS. ELIZABETH.
Memoir of Mrs. Elizabeth Rhodes. By herself. (Mason, London, 1829.)

RICHARDSON, CHARLES.
The Peasant Preacher, Memorials of Mr. Chas. Richardson. J. E. Coulson. (Hamilton, Adams, London, 1867.)

RITCHIE, ELIZABETH (MRS. MORTIMER).
Memoirs of Mrs. Eliz. Mortimer. Agnes Bulmer. (Mason, London, 1859.)

ROE, HESTER ANN (MRS. ROGERS).
Experience and Spiritual Letters of Mrs. Hester Ann Rogers. By herself, her husband and Dr. Coke. (Mason, London, 1840.)

RUSTON, RICHARD.
Memoir of Richard Ruston of Chatteris. A. S. Ruston. (Riley, London, 1864.)

SHAW, ELIZABETH.
Memorials of Mrs. Elizth Shaw. R. C. Barratt. (W.M. Conf. Office, London, 1875.)

SPENCE, ROBERT.
Memoir of Robert Spence, of York. Richd. Burdekin. (Burdekin, York, 1840.)

SUGDEN, JONAS.
Memorials of Jonas Sugden, of Oakworth House. R. S. Hardy. (Hamilton, Adams, London, 1858.)

SUTCLIFFE, WILLIAM.
The Closer Walk, Memoir of Wm. Sutcliffe, of Bacup. W. L. Watkinson. (W.M. Conf. Office, London, 1876.)

TATHAM, MARY.
Memoirs of Mrs. Mary Tatham of Nottingham. Joseph Beaumont. (Simpkin, Marshall, London, 1838.)

TATHAM, THOMAS.
Memoirs of Mr. Thomas Tatham of Nottingham. Samuel Dunn. (Tegg, London, 1847.)

THORNEYCROFT, G. B.
Memoir of G. B. Thorneycroft. J. B. Owen. (Hamilton, Adams, London, 1856.)

TITHERINGTON, MARY.
Account of Mary Titherington of Liverpool. Henry Moore. (Richardson, York, 1819.)

TOLD, SILAS.
Life of Mr. Silas Told. By himself. (W.M. Conf. Office, London, 1789, etc.)

TREFFRY, JANE.
Memoirs of Mrs. Jane Treffry. Richd. Treffry, Junr. (Mason, London, 1830.)

TREWAVAS, RICHARD.
Memoirs of Mr. Richard Trewavas, Senr., of Mousehole. Richd. Treffry. (Mason, London, 1839.)

VERRAN, MICHAEL.
Michael Verran and Thomas Carlyle. Isaac Foot. (Epworth Press, London, 1946.)

WALLBRIDGE, ELIZABETH.
The Dairyman's Daughter. Legh Richmond. (Warne, London; many editions.)

WORTH, ANNE.
Account and Poems of Mrs. Anne Worth. By her husband. (Baynes, London, 1813.)

WRIGHT, THOMAS.
Autobiography of Thomas Wright, of Birkenshaw. Ed. by grandson. (Smith, London, 1864.)

SHORT BIOGRAPHIES BASED ON PERSONAL MEMOIRS

CROOKSHANK, C. H.
  Memorable Women of Irish Methodism. (W.M. Book-Room, London, 1882.)
KEELING, ANNIE E.
  Eminent Methodist Women. (Kelly, London, 1889.)
LAWSON, W. D.
  Wesleyan Local Preachers. (Lawson, Newcastle-on-Tyne, 1874.)
STEVENS, ABEL.
  The Women of Methodism. (Tegg, London, 1876.)
TAFT, ZECHARIAH.
  Sketches of Holy Women. (2 vols. Kershaw, London, 1825, 1828.)

LOCAL HISTORIES

(This selection includes the more important volumes, dealing with the beginnings of Methodism in the eighteenth century. The place-names are arranged alphabetically.)

ALMONDBURY.
  History of Methodism in Almondbury. Richd. Roberts. (Tressider, London, 1864.)
AMBLESIDE.
  Faith Triumphant: Memoir of Mrs. Barnett (Fanny Holmes). To which is added a History of Methodism in Ambleside. Myles Holmes. (Crossley, Farnworth, 1873.)
ARMLEY.
  Methodism in Armley: With Stray Notes on Methodism in Leeds. T. Hardcastle. (Walker, Leeds, 1871.)
BATH.
  An Interesting Historical Sketch of the Rise and Progress of the Wesleyan Society in Bath. John Rigg. (Vivian, Bath, 1848.)
BELFAST.
  Belfast Methodism, 1756–1893. J. W. Jones. (Adams, Belfast, 1893.)
BELPER.
  Records of Wesleyan Methodism in the Belper Circuit, 1760–1903. G. A. Fletcher. (Privately printed.)
BINGLEY.
  Historical Sketches of the Rise and Progress of Methodism in Bingley, with brief Notices of other places in the Circuit. John Ward. (Harrison, Bingley, 1863.)
BIRMINGHAM.
  Early Methodism in Birmingham. W. C. Sheldon. (1903.)
  Protestant Nonconformity: A Sketch of its general History, with an Account of the Rise and present State of its Various Denominations in the Town of Birmingham. J. Angell James. (Hamilton, Adams, London, 1849.)
BISHOP AUCKLAND.
  History of Methodism in Bishop Auckland Circuit. M. Braithwaite. (Braithwaite, Bp. Auckland, 1885.)
BLACKBURN.
  Rise and Progress of Wesleyan Methodism in Blackburn and the Neighbourhood. John Ward. (Barton, Blackburn, 1871.)
BOLTON.
  Records of Early Methodism in Bolton. W. Walker. (Cunliffe, Bolton, 1863.)
  Origin of Methodism in Bolton. J. Musgrave. (Bradbury, Bolton, 1865.)
BRADFORD.
  Historical Notices of Wesleyan Methodism in Bradford and its Vicinity. W. W. Stamp. (Mason, London, 1841.)
BRECON.
  Wesleyan Methodism in the Brecon Circuit, and Introduction of English and Welsh Methodism into the Principality. T. Wynne Jones. (Poole, Brecon, 1888.)

BRISTOL.
Bristol Methodism in John Wesley's Day. John S. Pawlyn. (Hemmons, Bristol, 1877.)
A History of the Origin and Progress of the Sunday Schools in the City of Bristol. John S.
Broad. (Bristol, 1816.)
Centenary History of Ebenezer Chapel, King St., Bristol. R. Burroughs. (Hemmons,
Bristol, 1895.)

BURNLEY.
History of Wesleyan Methodism in Burnley and East Lancashire. B. Moore. (Burnley,
1899.)

BURY.
A Century of Methodism in Bury. Anon. (*Bury Guardian*, 13th November 1886.)

CHANNEL ISLANDS.
Historie du Methodisme Wesleyen dans les Isles de la Manche. François Guiton. (London,
1846.)

CHESTER.
*Some Account of the introduction of Methodism into the City and some parts of the County of
Chester.* W. Janion, Senr. (Evans, Chester, 1833.)
Early Methodism in and around Chester, 1749–1812. F. F. Bretherton. (Philipson and
Golder, Chester, 1903.)

CONGLETON.
History of Wesleyan Methodism in the Congleton Circuit. J. B. Dyson. (Mason, London,
1856.)

CORNWALL.
Truly Rural: History of North Hill Circuit. H. Bolitho. (Whitehead, Leeds, 1947.)
Notices of Twenty Parishes in East Cornwall. J. Venning. (Latimer, Plymouth, 1934,
4th edition.)

CREWE.
History of Wesleyan Methodism in the Crewe Circuit. C. Caine. (Hinchcliff, Crewe,
1883.)

DERBY.
One Hundred Years Ago: Wesleyan Methodism in Derby. J. Jones. (Carter, Derby, 1883.)

DEVON.
History of Methodism in North Devon. J. G. Hayman. (Conf. Office, London,
1871.)

DEWSBURY.
Notes on Early Methodism in Dewsbury, Birstal, and Neighbourhood. J. R. Robinson.
(Fearnsides, Batley, 1900.)

DORSET.
Methodism in Dorset. John S. Simon. (Sherren, Weymouth, 1870.)

EASINGWOLD.
Memoirs of Early Methodism in Easingwold Circuit. J. Rockledge. (Hayman, 1872.)

EXETER.
History of Methodism in Exeter and the Neighbourhood from the year 1739 until 1907.
E. Chick. (Drayton, Exeter, 1907.)

FROME.
Wesleyan Methodism in Frome. Stephen Tuck. (John Tuck, Frome, 1814.)

FYLDE.
The Apostles of Fylde Methodism. John Taylor. (Conf. Office, London, 1885.)

GLOUCESTER.
*A Brief Account of the Occasion, Process and Issue of a late Trial at the Assize, held at
Gloucester, the third of March, 1743.* John Wesley, from Letter of George Whitefield.
(Farley, Bristol, 1748.)

GRANTHAM.
History of Wesleyan Methodism in Grantham and its Vicinity, etc. Thomas Cocking.
(Bushby, Grantham, 1836.)

GRIMSBY.
*Brief History of Wesleyan Methodism in the Grimsby Circuit; including references to Horncastle,
Boston, etc.* Joshua Hocken. (Mason, London, 1839.)
Grimsby Methodism (1743–1889). Geo. Lester. (Conf. Office, London, 1890.)

HALIFAX.
History of Methodism in Halifax and its Vicinity, from its commencement in 1741 to 1824. W. Hatton. (Walker, Halifax, 1824.)
History of Wesleyan Methodism in Halifax and its Vicinity, from its commencement to the present period. J. V. Walker. (Walker, Halifax, 1836.)

HASLINGDEN.
Notices of Methodism in Haslingden. John Stott. (Privately printed, 1898.)

HUDDERSFIELD.
History of Methodism in Huddersfield, Holmfirth, etc. Joel Mallinson. (Kelly, London, 1898.)
Story of Lindley Zion Methodist Church. J. R. Firth. (Woffenden, Huddersfield, 1947.)

HULL.
Remarks on Revivals of Religion; with Brief Notices of the recent prosperity of work of God in Hull. Richd. Treffry. (Hull, 1827.)
Early Chapters in Hull Methodism, 1746–1800. W. H. Thompson. (Fretwell, Hull, 1895.)

IRELAND.
A Consecutive History of Rise, Progress and Present State of Wesleyan Methodism in Ireland. W. Smith. (Doolittle, Dublin, 1830.)
History of Methodism in Ireland. C. H. Crookshank. (3 vols. Belfast and London, 1885, 1886, 1888.)

ISLE OF MAN.
History of Wesleyan Methodism in the Isle of Man. James Rosser. (Quiggin, Douglas, 1849.)

ISLE OF WIGHT.
Methodism in the Isle of Wight. J. B. Dyson. (Burt, Ventnor, 1865.)

LEEK.
Brief History of Rise and Progress of Wesleyan Methodism in the Leek Circuit. J. B. Dyson. (Hallowes, Leek, 1853.)

LEYTON.
Brief Chronicle of Wesleyan Methodism in Leyton, Essex, 1750–1895. C. Caine. (Hubbard, Leyton, 1896.)

LINCOLN.
History of Methodism in Neighbourhood and City of Lincoln. A. Watmough. (Mason, London, 1829.)

LONDON.
City Road Chapel, London. Geo. J. Stevenson. (Stevenson, London, 1872.)
Two West-End Chapels: or a Sketch of London Methodism, 1740–1886. John Telford. (Book-Room, London, 1886.)
John Wesley's London Chapels (W.H.S. Lecture No. 12). J. H. Martin. (Epworth Press, London, 1946.)

LOWESTOFT.
History of Wesleyan Methodism in Town of Lowestoft, Suffolk. Author of *Little Welborne.* (Barber, Yarmouth, 1843.)

MACCLESFIELD.
Methodism in Macclesfield. B. Smith. (Conf. Office, London, 1875.)

MANCHESTER.
Wesleyan Methodism in Manchester. Jas. Everett. (Russell, Manchester, 1827.)

MARSHLAND (YORKSHIRE).
Methodism in Marshland. Geo. West. (Gardiner, Goole, 1896.)

MASHAM.
Notices of Wesleyan Methodism in Masham, 1796–1896. W. W. Morrell. (Mood, Masham, 1896.)

MELTON MOWBRAY.
Sketches of Wesleyan Methodism in Melton Mowbray. J. Ward. (Toune, Melton Mowbray, 1874.)

MOUSEHOLE.
Appendix to Memoirs of Mr. R. Trewavas, Senr. Rich. Treffry. (Mason, London, 1839.)

NEWCASTLE.
  The Orphan House of Wesley, with Notices of Early Methodism in Newcastle-upon-Tyne.
  W. W. Stamp. (Mason, London, 1863.)
NORWICH.
  A Concise History of the First Establishment of Wesleyan Methodism in the City of Norwich,
  in the year 1754. W. Larkin. (Matchett, Norwich, 1825.)
NOTTINGHAM.
  Memoirs of Mr. Thomas Tatham and of Wesleyan Methodism in Nottingham. S. Dunn.
  (Tegg, London, 1847.)
  History of Wesleyan Methodism in Nottingham and its Vicinity. G. H. Harwood. (Ellis,
  Nottingham, 1872.)
OLDHAM.
  A Centenary Memorial: or Brief Records of the Origin and Progress of Wesleyan Sunday
  Schools in Oldham and Neighbourhood. J. Marrat. (Halbert, Oldham, 1885.)
PENRITH.
  The Christian Patriarch: Life of Mr. R. Gate, with some Notices of early Methodism in
  Penrith. G. S. Thomas. (Stock, London, 1869.)
PORTSMOUTH.
  Wesleyan Methodism in Portsmouth. H. Smith. (Portsmouth, 1895.)
PRESTON.
  History of Methodism in Preston. R. Allen. (Toulmin, Preston, 1866.)
RADCLIFFE BRIDGE.
  Survey of Religious Methodism at Radcliffe Bridge. F. Merriday. (Hayhurst, Radcliffe,
  1895.)
REDDITCH.
  Sketch of Wesleyan Methodism in Redditch, 1752–1892. A. Tucker. (Redditch, 1892.)
ROSSENDALE.
  Account of Methodism in Rossendale, etc. W. Jessop. (Tubbs, Manchester, 1880.)
ST. JUST.
  Memoirs of Mr. J. E. Trezise of St. Just: with some Account of Methodism in St. Just.
  Rich. Treffry, Junr. (London, 1837.)
SALISBURY.
  The Biographical Record: or Sketches of Lives of Members of the Wesleyan Society in Salisbury.
  J. Dredge. (Salisbury, 1833.)
SCOTLAND.
  Methodism in Scotland. T. L. Parker. (Hepworth, Knottingley, 1867.)
  Methodism in Scotland: A Brief Sketch of its rise, Progress and present Position in that
  Country. D. Wilson. (Ogilvie, Aberdeen, 1850.)
  Methodism in Scotland (W.H.S. Lecture No. 13). Wesley F. Swift. (Epworth Press,
  London, 1947.)
SELBY.
  Notices of Wesleyan Methodism in Selby, 1744–1892. W. W. Morrell. (Bellerby, Selby,
  1892.)
SHEFFIELD.
  History of Norfolk Street Chapel and Wesleyan Methodism in Sheffield. T. A. Seed.
  (Jarrold, London, 1907.)
SHROPSHIRE.
  Early Methodism in Shropshire. W. Phillips. (Napier, Shrewsbury, 1896.)
SOMERSET.
  Early Methodism in West Somerset. W. Symons. (Kelly, London, 1898.)
SOUTHERN COUNTIES.
  Sketch of the History of Wesleyan Methodism in some of the Southern Counties of England.
  W. W. Pocock. (W.M. Book-Room, London, 1885.)
STOURPORT.
  History of Methodism in Stourport from 1781 to 1899. J. F. Wedley. (Stourport, 1899.)
SWALEDALE.
  Methodism in Swaledale and the Neighbourhood. J. Ward. (Harrison, Bingley, 1865.)
THIRSK.
  Methodism in the Thirsk Circuit. J. Ward. (Peet, Thirsk, 1860.)

TROWBRIDGE.
   Wesleyan Methodism in Trowbridge. E. Dyer. (Collins, Trowbridge, 1862 and 1877.)

WALES.
   Origin and History of Methodism in Wales and the Borders. D. Young. (Kelly, London, 1893.)

WEDNESBURY.
   Some Papers giving an Account of the Rise and Progress of Methodism at Wednesbury in Staffordshire, etc. Anon. (Roberts, London, 1744.)

WENSLEYDALE.
   Recollections of the Rise and Progress of Methodism in Wensleydale. E. Peacock. (Penney, Darlington, 1872.)

WEST BROMWICH.
   Methodism in West Bromwich from 1742 to 1885. J. Hall. (1886.)

WHITBY.
   Short History of the introduction and rise of Wesleyan Methodism in Whitby Circuit for 100 years. G. Vasey. (Horne, Whitby, 1861.)
   The Rise of (Whitby) Methodism. R. T. Gaskin. (Whittaker, London, 1863.)

YARMOUTH.
   History of Methodism in the Town and Neighbourhood of Great Yarmouth, etc. A. Watmough. (Kershaw, London, 1828.)

YORK.
   Memorials of Mr. Robt. Spence: with notices of the early introduction of Methodism into York. R. Burdekin. (Burdekin, York, 1840.)
   Glimpses of Early Methodism in York, etc. J. Lyth. (Sessions, York, 1885.)

YORKSHIRE.
   Synopsis of Wesleyan Methodism in Yorkshire, etc. W. B. Haigh. (Spink, Leeds, 1830.)

GENERAL

ANONYMOUS.
   The Centenary of Methodism. (Dublin, 1839.)

BARR, J. H.
   Early Methodists under Persecution. (Meth. Book Concern, New York, 1916.)

BETT, HENRY.
   The Spirit of Methodism. (Epworth Press, London, 1937.)

BOND, JOHN.
   Golden Candlesticks. (Elliot Stock, London, 1873.)

BRASH, W. B.
   Methodism. (Methuen, London.)

BREADY, J. W.
   England Before and After Wesley. (Hodder and Stoughton, 1938.)

CANNON, W. R.
   The Theology of John Wesley. (Abingdon-Cokesbury Press, New York, 1946.)

CARTER, H.
   The Methodist. (Epworth Press, London, 1937.)

CHURCH, L. F.
   Oglethorpe: A Study of Philanthropy in England and Georgia. (Epworth Press, London, 1932.)

CROOKSHANK, C. H.
   History of Methodism in Ireland. (3 vols. Allen, Belfast, 1885.)

DIMOND, S. G.
   The Psychology of the Methodist Revival. (Oxford Univ. Press, 1930.)

EDWARDS, MALDWYN.
   John Wesley and the Eighteenth Century. (Epworth Press, London, 1939.)

FITCHETT, W. H.
   Wesley and His Century. (Smith, Elder, London, 1906.)

FLEW, R. N.
   The Idea of Perfection in Christian Theology. (Oxford Univ. Press, 1932.)

GRIFFITHS, A.
   Chronicles of Newgate. (2 vols. London, 1884.)

HAMMOND, J. L. AND B.
The Town Labourer, 1760–1832. (Longmans, 1938.)
HARRISON, A. H.
The Beginnings of Arminianism to the Synod of Dort. (Duckworth, 1937.)
HARRISON, G. ELSIE.
Methodist Good Companions. (Epworth Press, London.)
HARWOOD, G. H.
History of Wesleyan Methodism. (Whittaker, London, 1854.)
JACKSON, THOS.
Centenary of Wesleyan Methodism. (Mason, London, 1839.)
LAVINGTON, BP. G.
Enthusiasm of Methodists and Papists Compared. (Knapton, London, 1752.)
MCCONNELL, F. J.
John Wesley. (Epworth Press, London, 1939.)
NORTH, E. M.
Early Methodist Philanthropy. (Meth. Book Concern, New York, 1914.)
OVERTON, J. H.
John Wesley. (Methuen, London, 1891.)
PIETTE, MAXIMIN.
John Wesley in the Evolution of Protestantism. (Sheed and Ward, 1937.)
RATTENBURY, J. E.
The Conversion of the Wesleys. (Epworth Press, London, 1938.)
SANGSTER, W. E.
The Path to Perfection. (Hodder and Stoughton, London, 1945.)
SHEPHERD, T. B.
Methodism and the Literature of the Eighteenth Century. (Epworth Press, London, 1940.)
SIMON, JOHN S.
John Wesley and the Religious Societies. (Epworth Press, London, 1921.)
John Wesley and the Methodist Societies. (Epworth Press, London, 1923.)
John Wesley and the Advance of Methodism. (Epworth Press, London, 1925.)
John Wesley, the Master-Builder. (Epworth Press, London, 1927.)
John Wesley: The Last Phase. (Epworth Press, London, 1934.)
SMITH, C. RYDER.
The Bible Doctrine of Salvation. (Epworth Press, London, 1941.)
TEMPERLEY, H. W. V.
Camb. Mod. Hist., Vol. VI, Chap. 2. (Camb. Univ. Press, 1909.)
TYERMAN, LUKE.
Life and Times of John Wesley. (3 vols. Hodder and Stoughton, London, 1890, 6th edn.)
URWIN, E. C., and WOLLEN, D.
John Wesley, Christian Citizen. (Epworth Press, London, 1937.)
WATERHOUSE, E. S.
The Philosophy of Religious Experience. (Epworth Press, London, 1923.)
WATKIN-JONES, H.
The Holy Spirit from Arminius to Wesley. (Epworth Press, London, 1929.)
WEARMOUTH, R. F.
Methodism and the Common People of the Eighteenth Century. (Epworth Press, London, 1945.)
WHITELEY, J. H.
Wesley's England. (Epworth Press, London, 1938.)
WHITTAKER, W. B.
The Eighteenth-Century Sunday. (Epworth Press, London, 1940.)
WORKMAN, H. B.
Methodism. (Camb. Univ. Press, 1912.)

INDEX

Printed in Great Britain by
The Camelot Press Ltd., London and Southampton

Date Due
